Burma is one of the world's long forgotten tragedies. Its ruler, Than Shwe, has presided over a regime guilty of crimes against humanity. Benedict Rogers' book helps us understand how Than Shwe rose to power, how he operates, and what he thinks. It is a valuable resource for anyone who wants to understand Burma.
—YOZO YOKOTA, former UN Special Rapporteur for Human Rights in Burma

Benedict Rogers vividly describes the rise to power of a ruthless and mysterious man, and the impact of his rule on a country already ravaged by civil war and economic mismanagement. His book—written with passion and balance—also provides a valuable treatise on Burma's contemporary history that is fascinating and compelling in its own right.
—PASCAL KHOO THWE, author of *From the Land of Green Ghosts*

Benedict Rogers has to be commended for exploring a subject that has to date proved a black hole—Burma's leader Senior General Than Shwe. Although in power for nearly two decades, not a single book has surfaced about the reclusive junta chief, until Benedict Rogers came along. This is not, as the author acknowledges, the definitive work because many gaps still need filling, but for now it's indispensable not for just students of Burma, but anyone interested in the workings of authoritarian leaders.
—DENIS GRAY, Bangkok Bureau Chief, Associated Press

Finally we have the first "unauthorized" biography of the enigmatic General Than Shwe. This is an important work that will be useful to anyone who is interested in contemporary Burmese politics or is concerned about its future.
—SURAPONG JAYANAMA, former Director-General, Thai Ministry of Foreign Affairs

Impressively researched and compellingly written, this book tells the story of a modern dictator. Few people have traveled in Burma as extensively as Benedict Rogers, and his unique experiences and grasp of detail have given him unrivalled insights into the country, its people, and its military regime. This is essential reading for anyone wanting to understand Burma, and a harrowing set of charges against a war criminal.
—LORD ALTON OF LIVERPOOL, former Member of Parliament, UK

To understand the dictator "extraordinaire" of Southeast Asia, read this book.
—KAVI CHONGKITTAVORN, Assistant Group Editor, *The Nation*

Burma's dictator Than Shwe is a reclusive person, surrounded by rumor, some of which is true and some not. Benedict Rogers has produced a book full of facts and interesting stories, which will be a useful resource for researchers, scholars, democracy activists, and policymakers. The international community and the Burmese people need to kn~~~ ~ ~~~~~~~~~~~~~ grateful to Benedict Rogers for his contribution to the
—SOE MYINT, Editor, *Mizzima News*

This book provides a vivid, first-hand account of the crimes against humanity perpetrated by one of the world's most brutal dictators, and a fascinating insight into one of the world's least-known tyrants. It tells the story of modern-day Burma through the life of its ruler, describing his rise to power and the cruel oppression inflicted on those he rules.
—BARONESS CAROLINE COX, former Deputy Speaker, British House of Lords

A fascinating read, showing how a man from such an ordinary background can go on to become one of the world's most brutal dictators. I have been on the receiving end of Than Shwe's brutal rule, forced to flee my country. This book helped me understand more about the man responsible for years of attacks and abuses against my people.
—ZOYA PHAN, author of *Little Daughter*

The atrocities Than Shwe and his military junta have inflicted on the world's poorest people reverberate well beyond the country's borders. Burmese refugees are present in every capital and major city in the region. Most of us in the Asian human rights movement have been pressuring the Indian government to listen to its conscience and to the cry of the oppressed. Mr. Rogers' meticulously and passionately written book will help us press our case with Parliament and the human rights fraternity in India, as well as the rest of the world.
—JOHN DAYAL, Member, National Integration Council, Government of India

Than Shwe: Unmasking Burma's Tyrant provides very useful insights into the rise of one of the world's most brutal dictators and the military regime that rules Burma today. It also builds a strong case for the UN Security Council to investigate crimes against humanity committed by Than Shwe and all his subordinates.
—YUKI AKIMOTO, BurmaInfo

Few people have spent a longer time in Burma, have studied the country in more detail, or have a more instinctive affinity with the plight of the people of that country than Ben Rogers. His biography sheds much needed light on the oft-neglected situation in Burma and sets it in its historical context. Ben's book is a hugely important study of a man who has perpetrated many crimes against humanity. It is a book as enlightening as it is chilling.
—JOHN BERCOW, MP, Speaker of the House of Commons

THAN SHWE
UNMASKING BURMA'S TYRANT

BENEDICT ROGERS

SILKWORM BOOKS

For the people of Burma,
who have suffered too much for too long,
with too little attention from the international community

Published in 2010 by

Silkworm Books
6 Sukkasem Road, T. Suthep
Chiang Mai 50200 Thailand
info@silkwormbooks.com
http://www.silkwormbooks.com

ISBN: 978-974-9511-91-6

Typeset by Silk Type in Minion Pro 10 pt.
Printed in Thailand by O. S. Printing House, Bangkok

10   9   8   7   6   5   4   3   2   1

FOREWORD

by

VÁCLAV HAVEL

Former President of the Czech Republic

IN DEALING WITH oppressive regimes, we need to try to understand them. That is why books such as this are important. But while reading about dictators responsible for the suffering of millions of people, we should not focus just on their personal characteristics and their actions. It is even more important to keep in mind the circumstances, the reasons why all of this happened and why they could do what they did. That is what this book does, combining the character of Than Shwe with the history and context that explain his rise and his rule.

For forty years, my country was under Communist rule. When we were in need, we were helped by people in the free world who spoke out for us. Now that we are free, we have to help those who do not live in freedom.

CONTENTS

Acknowledgments   *ix*
Author's note   *xi*
Abbreviations   *xiii*

Introduction   *1*

1. From Postman to Tyrant   *9*

2. The Land of Green and Orange   *45*

3. The Democratic Challenge   *79*

4. Than Shwe's Crimes against Humanity   *95*

5. The New Emperor   *115*

6. The Seat of Kings   *163*

7. The Monks and the Storm   *175*

8. The Rivals, the Heirs, the Cronies, and the Future   *189*

Notes   *217*
Bibliography   *239*
Index   *251*

ACKNOWLEDGMENTS

MANY OF THE people who provided considerable assistance to me in the course of my research cannot be named, either for their own security, in the case of Burmese citizens, or because they continue to travel to Burma or retain the hope of doing so. I have received invaluable help from them in terms of the information they provided, often at risk and with great courage, and also with regard to the translation of Burmese language materials. To those who have helped me, but who must remain anonymous, I am enormously grateful.

Burmese defectors and former military officials who assisted me greatly and are willing to be named include Aung Lynn Htut, Ronny Nyein, Khin Maung Nyunt, Thant Zin Myaing, and Bo Htet Min. To them I express my sincere appreciation. I am also grateful to other dissident Burmese, including Aung Saw Oo, Min Zin, Win Min, Aung Din, Steve Dun, and Soe Aung.

Former UN Special Envoy Razali Ismail, former UN Special Rapporteur for Human Rights in Burma Yozo Yokota, and former ambassadors and diplomats from a variety of countries, including the United States, the United Kingdom, Australia, Japan, and Thailand have all been generous in providing time and comment. Mark Canning, the British ambassador to Burma from 2006 to 2009, was exceptionally helpful, as was the US ambassador to Burma from 1987 to 1990, Burton Levin.

Bertil Lintner has provided unique information, and has been unfailingly helpful in correspondence. I am also grateful to other authors who assisted me either in person or through their own published work: Mary Callahan, Andrew Selth, Maung Aung Myoe, Josef Silverstein, Martin Smith, and Christina Fink, in particular. Additionally, I acknowledge the intrepid reporting of *The Irrawaddy* magazine and online news service,

Mizzima News, and the Democratic Voice of Burma, three of the most important sources of information on modern day Burma.

Several friends read the manuscript and provided vital amendments and additions, and to them I am extremely grateful. They include Bertil Lintner, Christina Fink, Win Min, David Eubank, Martin Morland, Robert Gordon, Dr. John Dale, Dr. Sean Turnell, Dr. Martin Panter, Mark Farmaner, Amy Alexander, Christine Gettings, Victor Biak Lian, Julia Evans, Matthew Jones, Marie-Laure Verdier, and Juliet Rogers.

Marie-Laure Verdier spent many torturous hours painstakingly transcribing hours of almost indecipherable recorded interviews and deserves considerable appreciation.

Friends who have generously provided beautiful places of peace and quiet in which to write have my eternal gratitude: the Trinity Forum Academy in Maryland, as well as Ann and Simon Morgan in Cumbria's Lake District, and Parry and Juliet Rogers in the rolling English countryside of Dorset.

My employer, Christian Solidarity Worldwide (csw), has been exceptionally generous in giving me time and space to research and write this book. csw made it possible to carry out all the travel involved in researching the book, and provided many working hours and several complete weeks in which to write.

I owe a particular debt of gratitude to my good friend Jeremy Woodrum, co-founder and former director of the U.S. Campaign for Burma, who inspired this project and provided invaluable and extensive research, including conducting several interviews. Jeremy also spent many hours reviewing the manuscript and provided detailed suggestions for improvement.

Finally, I am grateful to Trasvin Jittidecharak and her team at Silkworm Books for taking on this project, and for all their support at every stage of the process.

AUTHOR'S NOTE

AT ITS FORTIETH press conference on May 26, 1989, the military regime in Burma changed the name of the country to "Myanmar." The democracy movement and the leaders of the ethnic resistance organizations, however, continue to refer to the country as "Burma." They have urged the international community to do the same, arguing that the regime had no mandate to change the name of the country. In this book "Burma" is therefore used instead of "Myanmar," except in direct quotations from other sources.

The regime also changed the names of various cities and divisions: Rangoon became "Yangon," the Irrawaddy Division became "Ayeyarwady," and Maymyo became "Pyin Oo Lwin." Karen State is called "Kayin," while Karenni is referred to as "Kayah." I have generally used the older names—Rangoon instead of Yangon, Irrawaddy instead of Ayeyarwady, and Karen rather than Kayin, because they are more easily recognizable for international readers.

The Burma Army is commonly known as the *tatmadaw*, and I use this throughout the book.

All references to sources are cited in the endnotes. Any unsourced material should usually be understood to have come from direct interviews I conducted with sources, whether named or unnamed. Some notes include information to clarify or explain particular points.

ABBREVIATIONS

BDA	Burma Defense Army
BIA	Burma Independence Army
BNA	Burma National Army
BSPP	Burma Socialist Program Party
CPB	Communist Party of Burma
DKBA	Democratic Karen Buddhist Army
DSA	Defense Services Academy
DVB	Democratic Voice of Burma
KIO	Kachin Independence Organization
KMT	Kuomintang
KHRG	Karen Human Rights Group
KNDO	Karen National Defense Organization
KNU	Karen National Union
LID	Light Infantry Division
NDD	Network for Democracy and Development
NLD	National League for Democracy
NUP	National Unity Party
OTS	Officer Training School
SLORC	State Law and Order Restoration Council
SPDC	State Peace and Development Council
USDA	Union Solidarity Development Association
UWSA	United Wa State Army

FIG. 1. *The Shwedagon Pagoda in Rangoon is one of Burma's most sacred Buddhist temples and the site where Aung San Suu Kyi delivered her first public speech to tens of thousands of supporters in 1988. In 2007, monks from Shwedagon joined the Saffron Revolution in protest against Burma's military dictatorship, and demanded that General Than Shwe and his regime enter into meaningful dialogue with the country's democracy movement. Photo by Benedict Rogers.*

INTRODUCTION

TYPING THE WORDS "books about dictators" into the Google search engine elicits an impressive array of documentation about authoritarians, despots, oppressors, strongmen, evildoers, and autocrats. Barnes and Noble, the ubiquitous American bookstore chain, even maintains on its website a "dictators and fascists" section, detailing biographies of the world's most ignominious rulers, including Heraldo Muñoz's revealing tome *The Dictator's Shadow: Life Under Augusto Pinochet*, Adam LeBor's comprehensive work *Milosevic: A Biography*, Joachim Fest's 800-page history *Hitler*, and Robert Service's authoritative *Stalin*.[1] The prolific sports writer, journalist, and encyclopedia author David Wallechinsky has summarized the cruelties of select leaders in *Tyrants: The World's 20 Worst Living Dictators*, including the human flesh-eating "Butcher of Uganda" Idi Amin as well as Sudan's Omar al-Bashir, a man accused of genocide by both the United States and the prosecutor at the International Criminal Court.

As a result of scholarship, investigations, and the resourcefulness of authors, journalists, and not least, defectors and dissidents, the world has come to understand the severity of the atrocities committed by these dictators. Their crimes against humanity are written into the pantheon of collective world memory and the ubiquitous phrase *"never again."* In some cases their work has even helped spur the creation of institutions and has provided levers designed to prevent future atrocities.

Yet despite the plethora of information about previous dictators, one modern, living man has escaped almost all international scrutiny for his crimes. He is Than Shwe—the ruler of the Southeast Asian country of Burma. There are no books about Than Shwe, no movies, few web pages, and only a handful of report references. Even though Than Shwe has destroyed as many villages as al-Bashir, carried out a rape campaign similar to the crimes of Serbia's Milosevic, and recruited possibly more child soldiers than any other country in the world (shattering misplaced perceptions of child soldiers as an "African" problem), he is virtually unknown to the outside world.[2]

Burma is ranked along with Sudan as one of the top two "Red Alert" countries at the highest risk of genocide in the Genocide Risk indices,[3] and has been on the UN's monitoring list for genocide since 2006. The Minority Rights Group claims Burma is in the top five countries whose ethnic minorities are "under threat," and in the "Failed States Index" Burma is ranked number thirteen just below Pakistan and Haiti and only one notch higher than North Korea.[4] The Heritage Foundation's Index of Economic Freedom lists Burma among the five most repressive economies in the world, while the U.S. State Department cites Burma as one of the worst violators of religious freedom.[5] Reporters Without Borders puts Burma at 171 out of 175 countries in their Press Freedom Index, only trailing Iran, Turkmenistan, North Korea, and Eritrea,[6] while the Committee to Protect Journalists ranks Burma as the worst country in the world for Internet bloggers, and the world's third worst jailer of journalists.[7] Virtually every survey on freedom or human rights issues finds Burma among the worst violators.

For those loosely familiar with Burma, its government is often referred to as a "military regime" or "military junta." Yet as sources for this book contend, the regime in Burma probably no longer functions as a collective decision-making body. Than Shwe consolidated power in 1993 and has since become the sole authority as the dictator of Burma—other members of the junta are almost completely subservient to his power.

Inside Burma, the name "Than Shwe" inspires fear, loathing, and ridicule in equal measure. He is a man who has presided over a regime guilty of every possible violation of human rights, including war crimes, crimes against humanity, and, arguably, attempted genocide. He is a man who has suppressed dissent, and equally ruthlessly maneuvered and manipulated his rivals within the regime. He is a man who changed the capital of his country, and built a new one in a remote jungle location at vast expense, calling it the "Seat of Kings."[8] He is a man known to consult soothsayers and astrologers, although there is little evidence to suggest that he makes key decisions based on their advice. He is a man who sat and watched as

Cyclone Nargis wrought devastation upon his people, including ethnic minorities. Despite having received numerous warnings from India of the impending natural disaster, he did nothing to help people prepare for it.[9] According to the *Bangkok Post*, air force jets were moved out of the storm's path, as were commercial airplanes belonging to an airline that the *Washington Post* reports may be a joint venture between Than Shwe's family and one of the regime's top business cronies, Tay Za.[10] Than Shwe is also a man who not only failed to help when natural disaster struck, but initially refused and actively restricted efforts by the international community to deliver aid to the victims. He is a man whose cronies in the business world allegedly spent up to us$50 million in gifts for his daughter's opulent wedding,[11] while his regime spends less than one dollar per person per year on health and education combined.[12] The list of charges does not end here.

There are parallels with other dictators but Than Shwe outstrips a good many of them. Like North Korea's Kim Jong-il, Than Shwe is reclusive. Like Zimbabwe's Robert Mugabe, he has publicly expressed little sympathy at the scale of his people's sufferings. Tanzania's former ruler Julius Nyerere once dubbed Zimbabwe "the jewel of Africa," and at one time the country was known as the "bread basket" of Africa. Burma was similarly once known as "the rice bowl of Asia," rich in natural resources and a major exporter of rice. Both countries have been ruined economically by their rulers, and both have ended up among the poorest in the world. Lee Kuan Yew, architect of Singapore's extraordinary economic success, said that the Burmese junta is led by "rather dumb generals when it comes to the economy," and concluded that the regime had pushed a "hungry and impoverished people to revolt."[13]

Writing a book about one of the world's least-studied dictators is no easy task. Than Shwe is probably one of the most inaccessible biographical subjects among living people. I wrote to him to request an interview, but no response was forthcoming. I also wrote to the Burmese ambassadors in London and in Washington DC to invite them for an interview. Again, not a word came in response. They were given a chance to explain Than Shwe's side of the story, but they did not take it.

The availability of people who have known Than Shwe personally, and are willing and able to talk, is scarce. I was able to find several defectors

and former officials from the Burmese military and intelligence apparatus that claimed to have known Than Shwe at different stages of his career,
and they provided vital information. I have also been able to interview
former foreign ambassadors and diplomats to Burma that have met Than
Shwe on several occasions. To those who have shared their insights, I am
extremely grateful.

A further complication in writing this biography is the fact that it is
impossible to approach the subject from a position of true impartiality.
When faced with evidence of the crimes over which Than Shwe has presided, one cannot remain completely dispassionate. Inevitably as a human
rights activist I am biased, in favor of ending mass atrocities and supporting the principles of democracy, freedom, rule of law, and human rights.
Nevertheless, I have attempted to approach the subject matter as objec-
tively as possible. I have sought to interview and consult the writings of a
wide range of people, including some whose perspectives on Burma and
views on appropriate policies and solutions I may not always share.

I have also sought to obtain as much information as possible about
Than Shwe's early career as well as his political rise. In trying to paint a
picture of life in Burma today, I have attempted to capture a sense of how
Than Shwe himself has evolved. Like Hitler, Stalin, Pinochet, and Mugabe,
Than Shwe was not always a monster, and it would be sensationalist if
he were portrayed as such. Extravagant enrichment was not always an
aspect of his life. According to some who knew him almost thirty years
ago when he was a middle-ranking military commander, he was known
in his personal life for his simple lifestyle and quietness.

Mugabe had similar characteristics. Denis Norman, who worked with
Mugabe during his early years as president, described him as "a very disciplined man" who treated people with respect, was unfailingly polite,
and "wasn't lavish in his lifestyle." While there are many crucial differences between Than Shwe and Mugabe, Denis Norman's description of
Mugabe's personality can be applied almost word for word to Than Shwe.
"Mugabe isn't a flashy man driven by wealth but he does enjoy power,"
he argues. "That's always been his motivation."[14] Another of Mugabe's
acquaintances provides further details that equally apply to Than Shwe:
"If you look at Mugabe's entire political career, what is always missing is
the essence of the person. He is a shrewd politician, a great survivor, but

very, very ruthless. ... He is mean-spirited even towards his own people. He is not moved by the plight of Zimbabweans, by people suffering and dying. He's immune to such calls on his feelings; he doesn't respond to pity."[15] Moreover, he thrives on "the tension of disputes and conspiracies among enemies," claims Heidi Holland in her book *Dinner with Mugabe*— a characteristic that can be seen in Than Shwe too. Mugabe, says a close acquaintance, "is always trying to behave like a medieval king."[16]

Holland describes Mugabe as behaving in ways "typical of a spoilt child when told he cannot do as he pleases," and again, Than Shwe is quite similar. Their common attitude is to wave their fist at the world and vow "I'll do what I want and you see if you can stop me. I want it my way and if you won't give it to me, I'll show you! You'll see what I can do!" The casualties of both men's narcissism include not only human lives destroyed and misery wrought upon an entire nation, but the destruction of the understanding of right and wrong, truth and lies. Right and wrong are so confused, Holland writes, that the listener "cannot identify the moral line any longer."[17] And yet to the observer, while Aleksandr Solzhenitsyn was right that the line between good and evil passes through every human heart, Than Shwe appears to have a remarkable ability to simply block out, justify, or remain indifferent to the moral implications of his actions.

In setting out her mission, Holland attempts to explain the way in which "a man who once favored simplicity became a greedy potentate ... If today he is too cynical to notice that his countrymen are starving because of his failings and excesses, where did his pessimism originate? Was he always a ruthless person or did he gradually become power-crazed?"[18] With a similar objective, I seek to chart Than Shwe's journey from simplicity to power, although no singular point of transformation is identified. I leave it to the readers to draw their own conclusions.

When he became the senior general in 1992, Than Shwe was greeted by some as a potential moderate,[19] and hopes were raised that the regime would change. Ambassadors who met him in his early years as head of state focused on his projection of geniality and affability, traits he can still display when he so desires. As this book, to an extent, demonstrates, Than Shwe's life and career—developed first within the system of multi-party democracy and then subsequent military control in Burma—serves as an example of Lord Acton's old adage, "Power corrupts and absolute power corrupts absolutely." As his power increased, even before he became Burma's leader, Than Shwe's better qualities of quietness and simplicity gave way to avarice, as he ensured the provision of wealth and prestige for his family and friends, again not unlike history's other dictators. Yet throughout his military career, even in the days when he was considered to be unassuming by some around him, there is no evidence to suggest that Than Shwe ever questioned the brutality of the then dictator Ne Win, the logic of Burma's military coups, or the purging of his contemporary military officers seeking a return democracy to the country. He carried out duties assigned to him without apparent objection, and gained a reputation as the consummate insider and "yes-man."

Today Than Shwe's core objective is maintaining military power and control. He is determined that the military retain a role in politics. He is also eager to protect his legacy, which is motivated by a particular interpretation of Burmese history and the example of past kings.

In trying to better understand this man, I traveled to Bangkok, Chiang Mai, and Mae Sot in Thailand, and to Kunming and Ruili in China, as well as to places as varied as Singapore, Malaysia, and Dubai, along with Tokyo and Nagoya in Japan, and to several cities in the States, including Washington DC, Rockville, Seattle, and Los Angeles. Interviews were also conducted with Burmese exiles living in Kentucky, Illinois, and Texas. The journey also included travel within Burma itself, including the old capital of Rangoon, and even into Than Shwe's new capital, Naypyidaw, as well as London and Sheffield, UK.

While this is a book about Than Shwe and an effort to unmask the man, it is, of course, also a story about contemporary Burma. The material about Than Shwe has come partly from interviews with people who have known or met him, and partly from published materials. Some, it has to be said, is based on rumor and reported anecdote, rather than concrete fact, though I try to be careful to differentiate in each case. Furthermore, I have set Than Shwe's life story in the context of modern Burma under military rule in the years since independence, and interviewed many of his regime's victims.

This book cannot be positioned as *the* definitive life story of Than Shwe. If it were, it would rightly be shot down by critics, since I have not been able to verify everything I have been told with as much painstaking research as I would ideally wish. Moreover, there are significant gaps in Than Shwe's curriculum vitae. The linguistic barriers posed by the fact that I am not a Burmese speaker have further impeded my research. I am privileged to have received invaluable assistance from native Burmese speakers in translating documents and interviews, but I am aware that there is untapped source material in Burmese, some of which I have not been able to access.

Despite all these obstacles, my main hope is simply that those seeking to learn about Than Shwe will no longer have to pore through pages of documents, press reports, and second-hand interviews to locate basic information about Than Shwe's life. By compiling some of the available material into this book, I hope that much more of the world will learn about Than Shwe. My objective is to help remove the mask of obscurity that has surrounded his eighteen years of dictatorship. At the same time, I hope this book, through its examination of Than Shwe and the history of his country, will serve as an introduction for those unfamiliar with Burma. Furthermore, I hope this book will provide a fresh angle on one of the world's most underreported humanitarian and human rights crises, and that it may inspire other researchers to dig deeper and uncover more information about Than Shwe. My aim is to lift the veil on at least some of the "opaqueness" that Andrew Selth, an analyst of Burmese military affairs, says extends "to the highest levels of government, where many important issues seem to be decided by individuals, notably regime leader Senior General Than Shwe." Selth poses a challenge, and one which in my small way I have attempted to meet: "The personal views and perceptions of the armed forces leadership are little known by outsiders and poorly understood . . . There is still little understanding . . . of what Than Shwe is thinking about the country's—and his own—future, yet that is crucial to any outcome."[20] While for many around the world this is true, it is also important to note that for those who follow Burma closely, Than Shwe's thinking and actions are better understood than some suggest.

Lastly, I hope this book will support the continuing struggle of the Burmese people to rid themselves of dictatorship once and for all, so that they have the freedom to build a life of peace and justice for which they have already sacrificed so much, and which is promised to them in the Universal Declaration of Human Rights.

FIG. 2. *Than Shwe inspecting a camp set up for displaced persons following the devastation wrought by Cyclone Nargis. Photo by Pete Pattison.*

1

FROM POSTMAN TO TYRANT

I managed to take five photographs before a firm hand grabbed me. I wasn't surprised. I had not gotten permission to take his picture. But photographers have a saying: "It's better to apologize than ask permission." I got ready to say sorry.

A BRITISH JOURNALIST slipped into the Irrawaddy Delta less than a month after Cyclone Nargis devastated Burma. He had asked a taxi driver to show him the damage caused by the storm in Rangoon, Burma's largest city, but the driver took him instead to a small camp for people displaced as a result of the natural disaster. The camp was in Hlaing Thar Yar Township in the suburbs of Rangoon.

The man he was photographing is the head of Burma's military regime, Senior General Than Shwe. The journalist had no idea he would get so close to one of the world's most ruthless dictators until just minutes beforehand. "The taxi driver went to ask whether I could visit the camp, and when he returned he told me in an awed voice that General Than Shwe was about to arrive," he recalled. "This was the general's first visit to meet victims of the cyclone, over two weeks after the storm devastated the country's coastline." For understandable reasons, the taxi driver was not prepared to hang around, but the journalist decided to wait.

"Before long a convoy of vehicles swept up to the camp—four-by-fours with blacked-out windows and trucks packed with well-armed soldiers. The motorcade was longer than the line of tents Than Shwe had come to inspect. As the general and his entourage spilled out, I strode purposefully up to him and began to take pictures."

What happened next portrays both the paranoia and the incompetence of Than Shwe's regime. "The soldier who seized me led me out of the camp and quietly but firmly told me not to move. The interrogation began. 'What was I doing here? Where was I from? How did I know the general was visiting?' Quite understandably he couldn't believe that I'd happened upon Than Shwe by chance. As he questioned me, I gently reached into my camera bag, removed the memory card from my camera and hid it in the base of the bag. If I was going to be deported, I was taking these photos with me."

While the soldier was questioning the journalist, General Than Shwe had walked the length of the forty blue tents, inspecting facilities. Then he prepared to leave, and the soldier guarding the unwanted, unexpected foreign visitor became distracted. "In the commotion, I quietly slipped behind the watching crowd, leapt into a passing taxi, and escaped."

So who is Than Shwe and how did he become the dictator of Burma? Little is known about his childhood, except that he seems to have been born on February 2, 1933, near Kyaukse in central Burma.[1] Kyaukse itself is both a district and a township, somewhat analogous to a county seat in the United States. Some versions say Than Shwe was born in a village called Minzu,[2] while a source close to a businessman reputed to be close to Than Shwe claims that he was born in a small town called Nyaung Chay Dauk, which the source says has since been incorporated into the city of Kyaukse. Either way, the fact that he was born and grew up somewhere in Kyaukse has been confirmed by the Burmese military in a document that states, "Senior General Than Shwe said that he was born and brought up in those areas."[3]

Dry and flat, Kyaukse is famous for its Elephant Dance, which was heavily promoted during the regime's "Visit Myanmar Year" in 1996. People dress in elephant costumes, and two white plaster elephants are on display at the entrance to the town. Little more than thirty miles from Mandalay, Burma's second major city and historic capital, Kyaukse is on the main railway line between Rangoon and Mandalay. Liable to flooding from the Zawgyi River, which flows from Shan State to the Irrawaddy, Kyaukse is inhabited by multiple ethnic groups, but especially Burman and Shan. In 2000 it was reported that at least five hundred people were killed in a town close to Kyaukse when a dam was opened to prevent it from breaking. Like much of central Burma, the culture is traditional and largely Buddhist. In the eleventh century King Anawrahta built a pagoda in Kyaukse. Nearby is the town of Pakokku where protests led by Buddhist monks in September 2007 began.

According to the source who worked closely with one of Than Shwe's favored business associates, Than Shwe's family were farmers, most likely raising rice paddy. Kyaukse is rural and known for its agriculture, farmland, and animal husbandry. Many of its citizens are farmers, without any higher education. The area is also known for producing turmeric, mango, onions, corn, and beans. In Burmese history, Kyaukse is famous for a complex system of irrigation that has enabled more than one rice crop to be planted each year.[4] Much of the agriculture is produced for domestic consumption, while these days some is exported as well.

Despite its close proximity to Mandalay, Kyaukse, like many rural communities, has been isolated in terms of access to international news and information. In the 1950s, there were "very few . . . forms of telecommunications," according to Than Khe, a student leader from Kyaukse who subsequently fled to the Thailand-Burma border in the late 1980s and joined an armed student rebellion against the Burmese dictatorship.

The two years preceding Than Shwe's birth were a turbulent time in 1930s Burma. They were dominated by a rebellion against British colonial rule led by a traditional medicine man known as Saya San. Sometimes written Hsaya, meaning "teacher," Saya San was shocked by the poverty he had observed on his travels around the country. According to Michael Charney, Saya San had published books urging the Burmese people to reject expensive Western medicine and instead use traditional Burmese treatments, arguing that they were both more reliable and cheaper.[5] In 1925 Saya San was commissioned by the General Council of Burmese Associations to conduct an inquiry into rural concerns, particularly "peasant complaints about the collection of taxes."[6] His report expressed particular outrage at the reported mistreatment of farmers and disrespect for Buddhism, and called on people to resist paying taxes. At what Thant Myint-U calls "the specially chosen and auspicious time" of 11:33 p.m. on December 22, 1930, Saya San declared himself king of Burma and launched an armed rebellion against the British. His army, which began with several hundred men, grew to over three thousand. It was, according to Thant Myint-U, "a passionate, desperate revolt and was not put down until the spring of 1932." The colonial government had to deploy more than eight thousand troops by 1931, and brought in seven battalions to crush the revolt. Saya San was captured and hanged for treason. He was represented in his trial by Dr. Ba Maw, who would later become the first prime minister under colonial rule.[7]

The British colonized Burma in three stages, following the three Anglo-Burmese wars that occurred in 1824–26, 1852–53, and 1885. Until 1923 Burma was governed from India, and was not regarded as a separate entity. However, on January 1, 1923, a new constitution was introduced for Burma, a governor appointed, and a Legislative Council elected. The separation of Burma from India was completed in 1935, two years after Than Shwe's birth. Another new constitution was introduced and came into effect in 1937. For the first time in the eyes of the British, Burma was a "distinct, separate colony."[8]

One wonders to what extent these historical events influenced Than Shwe, even in the first few years of his life when he would have been too young to absorb them consciously. He is known to be extremely nationalistic, and often condemns Britain, despite being a Manchester United fan (his grandson is known to like David Beckham). Astrology and Buddhism are important influences in Burma, and like the auspicious timing of Saya San's rebellion, Than Shwe has timed major decisions very precisely, most likely in order to capitalize on the beliefs of many Burmese people. According to Carolyn Wakeman and San San Tin, "Superstition runs deep in Burmese culture, and at times of difficulty people commonly rely on supernatural powers. They consult soothsayers and astrologers who explain how to ward off harmful influences, remedy problems, and assure a peaceful life."[9]

Than Shwe's early formal education was probably limited, although he attained greater informal education much later in life, ironically as an instructor himself. According to official biographical details published by the regime, Than Shwe completed third grade at Kyaukse elementary school in 1942, and went on to the local high school.[10] The official biography claims he graduated from high school in 1951,[11] although other sources suggest he received far less education than that.

According to U Khin Kyaw Han, a civil servant who went on to be elected to Burma's parliament in 1990 before the ruling military regime annulled electoral results, Than Shwe, like many young Burmese boys, would have, at a young age, become a "novice" Buddhist monk. Buddhism originated in Bodh Gaya, India where the Buddha is believed to have obtained enlightenment. Eventually spreading throughout much of Asia, the Theravada school of Buddhism is practiced in Burma, Sri Lanka, Cambodia, Thailand, and Laos. In order to become a novice monk, a young Burmese boy must, among other things, memorize words of an initiation rite in both Burmese and Pali. This is followed by an elaborate ceremony that includes a meal, the shaving of the young boy's head, and the adornment of Buddhist robes, as well as a statement of commitment to take refuge in Buddhist life and to observe ten of the precepts of Buddhism. The precepts are mainly directed at monastic behavior and lifestyle. They include the commitment to refrain from killing living things, stealing, lust, dishonesty, consuming intoxicants, eating after noon, engaging in entertainment such as singing, dancing, or playing music, using fragrances, make-up, or decorative accessories such as garlands, sitting on high chairs and/or sleeping on soft beds, and accepting money for personal gain.[12]

Lay people are not expected to follow all the precepts observed by monks. Instead, lay Buddhists strive to follow a shorter list of precepts, which are worth mentioning since Than Shwe has pursued his life and career with disregard for several of them. They include refraining from killing, stealing, sexual deviance (mainly adultery), dishonesty, and intoxication.

Buddhist Burmese boys remain monks for an un-prescribed period of time. Many remain novice monks for only a few days, while others stay for weeks or even months. For most young boys the ordination ceremony, known as "*shinbyu*," and the time spent serving as a monk are both a period of excitement and their first experience in the denial of some worldly desires. Many novice monks are glad to spend some time away from their parents, describing their time at the monastery as enjoyable. Westerners unfamiliar with Buddhist practices might understand the initial time in the monastery as a rough equivalent of a church retreat. The initiation of a novice monk serves for many Burmese boys as a coming of age event, after which they are expected to play a more mature role in their family. And, it must not be forgotten that the ceremony is very important to the parents, who earn great merit when their children become novice monks.

Some international observers find it difficult to reconcile the teachings of a religion focused on peace and spiritual enlightenment with the brutal practices carried out by Than Shwe's military regime, given how strongly Than Shwe and other generals claim to identify with Buddhism. The explanation is quite simple. Than Shwe justifies attacks on monks in his own mind by either labeling them "bogus" monks[13] or by disrobing them.[14] At the same time, military officials quite often use the blanket of Buddhism to defend, and deny, their own human rights abuses. One seasoned advisor to the US embassy in Burma in the 1970s and 1980s said, "I once had a meeting with a general in Burma and pressed him about the killings of political dissidents. Instead of responding to my question, he simply denied everything, saying, 'We're Buddhist, we don't kill.'"

In a remark that created waves of criticism in his own country, the late former Thai prime minister Samak Sundaravej controversially endorsed a similar position in 2008. As reported in *The Irrawaddy*, "Soon after taking power earlier this year, Samak visited Burma and returned gushing about the country's good-hearted rulers. The Burmese generals are 'Buddhists . . . they meditate,' he famously remarked. He added: 'Burma is a peaceful country.'"[15] Samak was subsequently removed from power on corruption charges.

The regime's English-language, state-owned media does not publicize Than Shwe's time as a novice monk in Burma, although, given his constant visits to monasteries,[16] it can be safely assumed that he served as a novice monk or *koyin*. It is more difficult to determine Than Shwe's level of formal education. It is not at all clear that he graduated from high school. Than Khe, whose father was a high school teacher in Kyaukse before Ne Win took power in 1962, when there were only two high schools in the township, said that his father knew everyone at the schools, but that he had "never heard of Than Shwe or his family."

Yet Aung Saw Oo, a Burmese dissident and historian, points out that Than Shwe would have needed a high school education in order to qualify for his later work sixty miles south of Kyaukse at the post office in Meiktila, where Than Shwe claims to have served for one year.[17] Clerk jobs at the time would have been seen as a step up the economic ladder from Kyaukse's main agricultural work, but a post office job would still have been considered entry level. According to Aung Saw Oo, "These jobs were for the middle class as a matter of circumstance. Children of farmers mostly did not graduate from high school since they were needed on the farms, and since a high school diploma was needed for a post office job, one could surmise that Than Shwe was from the middle or upper class in Kyaukse." However, he adds, "a postal clerk was the low end of the middle-class jobs. It was an ordinary job, and high school teachers, for example, were much more respected."

Yet another explanation by a close associate of one of Than Shwe's top business cronies suggested that Than Shwe had grown up in a rural area or small town but moved into Kyaukse in order to attend school. According to this source, his family was unable to afford a Kyaukse home, so Than Shwe lived with a family of extended acquaintances. One of the children of Than Shwe's host family was U Thaung, currently serving as the science and technology minister. Still other sources inside Burma suggest that Than Shwe's parents and U Thaung's parents were actually related, and that Than Shwe and U Thaung could have been childhood friends. U Thaung, one of the military regime's fiercest critics of democracy leader Aung San Suu Kyi, is at present reportedly leading efforts to obtain nuclear technology and know-how from Russia, and arranging to send Burmese military students there to study.[18]

Than Shwe was not the first of Burma's dictators to serve in the post office. The country's dictator from 1962 to 1988, Ne Win, also began his professional career as a postal clerk. "Postal clerks basically operated as they do now—accepting orders, shipping packages, and handling money," according to Aung Saw Oo, who also points out that the post office could have served as Than Shwe's first introduction to notions of corruption. Corrupt practices may have included paying extra "fees" to send money or simple theft of funds by post office staff. "Back then, there was some corruption, of course, but nothing like now where the entire business system is corrupt," he added. "But Than Shwe would have seen the opportunities, for sure."

U Khin Kyaw Han, an elected member of parliament from Yenangyaung Township in the Magwe Division, concurred with this assessment. "I knew many postal clerks in my township. You needed a high school education, but the clerk job was simple and not sophisticated. The postal clerks also managed money transfers, which these days have become an important opportunity for corruption. In the early days, however, you didn't have that same level of corruption."

Than Shwe does not speak publicly about his family and it is uncertain how many siblings he has. A Thai diplomat believes he was an only child, claiming that if he had brothers or sisters the Thai Foreign Ministry would know about them. However, former UN Special Envoy Razali Ismail says Than Shwe told him he had a brother or brother-in-law that had joined the Communists and was still in jail, while Than Khe believes Than Shwe may have had at least one elder sister who became corrupt in the Kyaukse area after her brother came to power. Than Khe recalled a story he heard from one of friends about Than Shwe's supposed elder sister: "Before Than Shwe became the dictator, his sister was very poor and operated a small grocery in Kyaukse. After Than Shwe became head of the army, the military seized property and bungalows from the people of Kyaukse, including my friend's father. Than Shwe gave the property to his sister, which she turned into guesthouses and got rich." Yet another source, the one close to one of Than Shwe's business associates, claims that Than Shwe's father had been married before and that Than Shwe has five or six siblings, although he said it is not clear which are his own full brothers and sisters and which are from his father's previous marriage. According to this source, most remain in Kyaukse.

As leader of Burma, Than Shwe has drawn on his ties to Kyaukse. In addition to U Thaung, who possibly grew up in the area, former Lieutenant General Maung Bo is also from the region, according to a defector. Ever since Than Shwe came to power, he has showered support on his hometown, supporting the building of factories, palm plantations, and dispensaries.

To show their support for Kyaukse, Than Shwe, U Thaung, and Minister of Industry-1 Aung Thaung have attended events in the area, including visiting bicycle, cement, footwear, and even candy factories.[19] Typically at such openings, Than Shwe barks orders to workers and managers about the need to improve efficiency, with his remarks reported in the state-owned newspaper, the *New Light of Myanmar*. The sanitized newspaper accounts of Than Shwe's visits to factory openings in Kyaukse and elsewhere in Burma generally involve Than Shwe giving "instructions" to Burmese throughout the country.

Than Shwe, himself, apparently did not devise the idea of expounding on topics of which he had no expertise. Burton Levin, the former US ambassador to Burma (1987–90), remarked that in the lead up to Burma's 1988 national demonstrations, before Than Shwe had gained control over the country, then dictator Ne Win did the same thing. "The content of the press and television [in Burma] consisted largely of paeans of praise to the military and mind-numbing accounts of Ne Win's inspection tours, which invariably ended by noting that Ne Win had provided 'proper instructions' to deal with whatever the task at hand. Although the inanities daily encountered in the media provided unintended amusement, they also provided wonderment about a leadership capable of viewing such insults to the intelligence of the Burmese people as beneficial to its interests."[20]

Than Shwe's steady rise through the military establishment apparently did not convince those living in his home area to support military rule. The only two parliamentary constituencies that comprise Kyaukse voted in the country's last election in 1990 for the National League for Democracy (NLD), the party led by Aung San Suu Kyi.[21] A year after the election, Aung San Suu Kyi won the Nobel Peace Prize. Both U Aung Kyaw Oo and Kyaw Win, allies of Aung San Suu Kyi, were elected with support of the people of Kyaukse. Aung Kyaw Oo received an engineering degree from Rangoon Institute of Technology and worked in Rangoon from 1980 to 1983, before returning to Kyaukse. Kyaw Win, an NLD organizer, was a high school teacher in Than village before the elections.[22]

As Than Shwe was undergoing his schooling, Burma was plunged into a world war. Aung San, leader of Burma's struggle for independence, founded the Burma Independence Army (BIA) with twenty-nine others, who became known as the Thirty Comrades. Trained by the Japanese, the BIA helped Japan prepare to invade Burma, in the hope that Japan would liberate the country from its colonial rulers. On December 8, 1941, Japan declared war on Britain and over the next three years overran much of Burma. The BIA took part in many of the Japanese campaigns, particularly against the ethnic groups in Burma that had sided with the British, and, subsequently, the Americans. As Thant Myint-U describes, "The bloodshed began in the western Irrawaddy Delta. Units of the Burma Independence Army, swollen with fresh recruits and patriotic pride, had just arrived alongside the black-booted Japanese and were beginning to disarm Karen soldiers as they were returning home." Many of the Karen were Christians who belonged to the colonial army, and drew the suspicions of the Burman nationalists. "Over the next many weeks, the BIA, thinking that its worst fears of Karen treachery were coming true, started daily executions of Karen suspected of disloyalty to the new order. Dozens, if not hundreds, were murdered. The Catholic Mission headquarters as well as an orphanage were burned to the ground."[23]

The Kyaukse of Than Shwe's youth was an important location at the beginning of the initially unsuccessful British and American efforts to defend Burma. When he was nine years old, the Japanese invaded Kyaukse with the aid of the BIA.[24] Already forced out of Rangoon far to the south, the British under General William Slim and General Harold Alexander held an important meeting with the commander of the American forces "Vinegar Joe" Stilwell at Kyaukse on April 25, 1942, as the Japanese forces, aided by Aung San's BIA, swept northward from Rangoon.[25] Stilwell had hoped to hold the Japanese on a line between Prome and Toungoo, but Japanese forces overran the defenses relatively easily.[26] It was at Kyaukse that Slim and Stilwell decided on a full retreat, heading north along the railway line towards Mandalay. The Japanese were right on their heels and entered Kyaukse, then Mandalay, and then proceeded further north. Ultimately, Stilwell attempted to evacuate troops by air, but when that was no longer possible, he walked 150 miles out of Burma starting near Shwebo north of Mandalay and ended up in Manipur, India.[27] Stilwell's long march out of Burma could not have been achieved without significant help from Burma's ethnic nationalities, particularly the Kachin, Chin, and Naga, who had worked closely with the British in the attempt to repel the Japanese occupation. Included in the group was Dr. Gordon Seagrave, a legendary missionary and medical doctor known as "Dr. Cigarette" to the Burmese with whom he worked because of his prolific chain-smoking.[28] Seagrave later played an important medical role as a lieutenant colonel under Stilwell in the recapture of Myitkyina.

After Slim and Stilwell reentered Burma and began to undermine Japanese rule with the help of many of the same ethnic minorities, the commander of Japanese forces Heitaro Kimura established Kyaukse as the "chief supply center for a large part of their army." The town was "easily defensible" due, in part, to the fact that Japanese had been fleeing there from all over Burma. Slim surrounded the town, moving in from the northwest, west, north, southwest, as well as the east, and on March 30, 1945, Kimura and the Japanese forces abandoned Kyaukse. Japan left over two thousand dead in the area. The battle proved decisive. After the fall of Kyaukse and the previous fall of Meiktila in the south, Slim said that "Kimura's only hope now was to extricate himself, fall back to the south, and collect what troops he could to hold us off from Rangoon."[29]

The Japanese occupation of Burma had been as brutal and barbaric as it had been elsewhere. According to John Pilger, an estimated sixteen thousand British and Allied forces died on the Burma-Siam railway, but perhaps as many as a hundred thousand Burmese of different ethnicities were killed.[30] Captain Tony Bennett witnessed the horrors that the ethnic groups suffered at the hands of the Japanese because of their allegiance to the Allies. In one village, which had been tireless in providing the British with intelligence about the movements of the Japanese, their help led to "an appalling tragedy." According to Captain Bennett, "Somehow or other the Japanese found out about it, and a short while before the war ended, when we were miles away in another area, they went to exact retribution. The men returned from Moulmein to find the village destroyed and all those in it dead. Old men, women, and children had been stuffed down the village well, some of them not yet dead."[31]

Ever since the Second World War, one British soldier has stood out, in particular, for sacrificing his own life to try to stop the Japanese torture of Burma's ethnic peoples. Major Hugh Seagrim, epitomized in the biography *Grandfather Longlegs*, knew that hundreds of Karen were suffering because of their allegiance to the British and, specifically, to him. By the end of 1943, over 270 Karen had been killed and the Japanese threatened to eliminate a further thousand unless Seagrim gave himself up. As one account puts it, "When Seagrim heard of the suffering they were enduring, he knew it was because of him. He could not bear it any more, and decided to give himself up."[32] He sent a messenger to the Japanese to inform them that he would surrender if they stopped the slaughter of the Karen. The Japanese captured him, but meted out vengeance on the Karen nonetheless. "As he gave himself up, Seagrim pleaded with the Japanese to spare the Karen and take him alone, but they ignored his request."[33]

In 1942 the Japanese disbanded the BIA and formed the Burma Defense Army (BDA) based in Pyinmana, the site of Than Shwe's new capital six decades later. On August 1, 1943, Japan granted Burma formal independence, although it turned out to be only nominal. The BDA's name was again changed, this time to the Burma National Army (BNA). Aung San's hopes that Japan would free Burma were misplaced. According to Mary Callahan, "Most of the available memoirs of these Pyinmana days speak of the harshness of the Japanese training methods and the physical and mental stress on the recruits [into the BDA]."[34] In mid-1944, frustrated at the Japanese occupation, Aung San supported the formation of the anti-Japanese "Anti-Fascist Organization," later reformulated as the "Anti-Fascist People's Freedom League," and made preparations to switch sides and join the Allies to help expel the Japanese. News of Aung San's dissatisfaction with the Japanese leaked to the forces of Slim and Stilwell. By 1943 Slim reported hearing that Aung San was unhappy with Japanese rule,[35] and on March 27, 1945, the Burma National Army rebelled against the Japanese forces and killed many Japanese officers. General Aung San reacted later than many to Japan's domination of Burma.

The Kachin, numbering several million, had proven crucial allies in the campaign to defeat Japan in northern Burma, as had the Chins, who had fought in General Orde Wingate's "Chindits." Known as "levies," the Kachin fighting force killed many Japanese troops, and carried out effective guerrilla warfare under the initially loose direction of the British.[36]

The northern Burma campaign was considered important by Stilwell and the Allies because the airfields at Myitkyina in Kachin State could be used to help re-supply China, which Japan was attempting to strangle by cutting its international lifelines. Before the United States carried out its "island hopping" tactic as the primary offensive strategy against Japan—by over-running numerous small islands closer to Japan in order to establish landing strips that could be used to launch aerial bombardment of Japan— military advisors had hoped to use China as the key jumping-off point in direct attacks on Japan.[37] Stilwell's division that was responsible for taking Myitkyina from the Japanese came to be known as "Merrill's Marauders," a phrase popularized after the Hollywood movie of the same name. Stilwell's push into northern Burma cost many American lives, but he remained resolute in his campaign to win control of Myitkyina and open the important Ledo Road supply route, inspired by the Latin phrase he kept in his office: *Illegitimi non carborundum*, a mangled expression that is supposed to translate into "Don't let the bastards grind you down."[38]

Despite owing much to the Kachin, Chin, Rakhine, and Burma's other ethnic nationalities in the struggle to end Japanese fascism during the Second World War, the United States policymakers and general public have, for the most part, long-since forgotten their heroic allies that were willing to fight and die for freedom. Instead, the US has left the Kachin to be crushed at the hands of Burma's successive military regimes. The American betrayal of their erstwhile allies ultimately left many Kachin decades later no choice but to ally, albeit tentatively and for a limited period, with the overwhelmingly armed, China-backed Communist Party of Burma (CPB)[39] just to ensure their survival.

In the south of Burma, the campaign against the Japanese was led primarily by General William Slim, who, after initially pulling out of Burma at the start of the conflict, reinvaded and captured Rangoon on May 3, 1945. Slim and the British were strongly supported by a different ethnic group, the Karen, who have now been largely abandoned by the British government as Than Shwe's regime attempts to crush Karen efforts to pursue self-determination. Indeed, the abuses heaped on the Karen people by Burma's military regime are among the worst in Burma.

The timing of Aung San's decision in the third week of March 1945 means that when Slim ultimately forced the Japanese from Kyaukse on March 30, the Allies may not have been viewed as a "liberating army" by everyone in the Kyaukse area. Unlike the ethnic areas in eastern and northern Burma, Kyaukse was a predominantly Burman area, and the local population, who had not been conscripted into the Allied forces, was not necessarily as sympathetic to the returning colonial British and invading Americans. Most likely, the original Japanese invasion of Kyaukse and the retreat of Stilwell in 1942 would have been celebrated by many in the Kyaukse area, in part, because their national leader Aung San had been working with the Japanese at the time. In theory, many Kyaukse residents may have celebrated the reinvasion of Kyaukse by the British in 1945 as another "victory" had they known that Aung San had switched allegiances, or had their frustration with the Japanese grown severe. However, given that Aung San's explicit rebellion against the Japanese had taken place only days earlier, it is likely that people in Kyaukse may have been unaware, and may still have despised their British colonial masters. At any rate, by the time he was twelve years old, Than Shwe had seen his hometown area ruled by the British, then the Japanese, and then the British again. Three years later, he would witness his hometown seized yet again by Karen and Kachin defectors from the post-independence Burmese military.[40]

With Japan having lost much of central Burma, the fall of Rangoon came shortly thereafter. On August 14, 1945, the Second World War ended. Two months later, on October 24, Japan formally surrendered in Burma.[41] The United States and Britain, alongside ethnic minorities such as the Kachin and Karen, had so thoroughly decimated the Japanese forces that by the time the Burma Defense Army explicitly rebelled against the Japanese, the Allies had the upper hand and Japan was heading for a decisive defeat in Burma.

While the Burmese junta has attempted to claim that its *tatmadaw* military predecessors were responsible for gaining Burma's independence, others feel that the Second World War also paved the way for Burma's freedom. According to Ronny Nyein, a graduate of Burma's elite Defense Services Academy, "If the Second World War had not occurred, the young Burmese patriots may have encountered a much longer and more difficult push for independence."

Not long after the war, Britain made attempts to restart its colonial administration, but according to Christina Fink, "Burmese nationalists were insistent on independence and organized widespread strikes to make their point. Without Indian troops or the financial resources to maintain a large British force, the colonial government could not easily enforce submission and finally relented."[42]

Aung San began negotiations with the British, but simultaneously warned the Burmese people of the need to be prepared for another fight, if the British didn't accede to Burmese desires for independence.[43] In January 1947, he led a delegation to London for talks with Prime Minister Clement Attlee, and an agreement was reached for independence within a year. However, Burma's major ethnic minorities did not attend the discussions, and some members of the British parliament objected to what they saw as a British sell-out of their erstwhile wartime allies. Referring to the Aung San-Clement Attlee Agreement, Burma scholar Josef Silverstein points out that "to those in [the British] Parliament who believed that the government owed some sort of debt to the loyal minorities in Burma, this seemed an irresponsible way of fulfilling an obligation."[44]

A month later, Aung San attended the Panglong Conference, which brought together representatives of the Shan, Kachin, and Chin ethnic nationalities to discuss their status in an independent Burma. The Karen also attended, but as observers. Under British rule, Kachin, Chin, and Shan ethnic areas were governed separately as "Frontier Areas," and these ethnic nationalities were resistant to the idea of a unitary state dominated by the Burman majority. The Karen also sought some form of autonomy, or even separation, but their status was more complicated, in part because many Karen-dominated areas were part of what some considered Burma proper, including in the Irrawaddy Delta.[45] At the same time, Aung San's negotiations with Attlee had remained pointedly ambiguous over the question of the Karen people and other ethnic nationalities—a move many Karen saw as a direct betrayal of what they had believed was British support for an independent Karen state. While the British government never formally promised independence or autonomy for the Karen, individual British soldiers serving in Burma during the Second World War certainly made such pledges, and were encouraged to do so by their superiors in order to secure the Karen's allegiance and support in the war against the Japanese. The debt owed to the Karen, who sacrificed much for the Allies, was never repaid and their loyalty was betrayed.[46]

Under the terms of the Panglong Agreement, which included a "principle of equality" among ethnic groups, the Shan, Kachin, and Chin would have "full autonomy" in the Frontier Areas. A subsequent constitution granted the Karenni and Shan the legal right to secede after ten years. Silverstein called the agreement "a major landmark in the struggle for nation unity."[47] The Karen refused to sign and boycotted the subsequent elections in April for a constituent assembly that would draft Burma's new constitution. According to Silverstein, the Karen position in the lead-up to independence "confirmed the continued existence of fear harbored by the Karen and the Burman over the excesses of violence each committed against the other during the war."[48] In Thant Myint-U's words, for the Karen, "the memories of bloodletting were too fresh, and their hope for British and American help was too strong. They insisted on a separate Karen state within the British Empire, looking perhaps to the example of Pakistan."[49]

Despite his failure to persuade the Karen to join national reconciliation efforts (with many subsequent opportunities lost by others as well), Aung San is regarded by most Burmese people as a unifying figure that could have kept Burma together and in peace. While the legacy of the BIA's behavior toward the Karen during the Second World War was bloody, Aung San's participation in the Panglong Conference could have been taken as a sign of his commitment to finding a just solution to the question of ethnic rights in Burma. Whatever the case, the "course of Burma's modern history" was changed completely on July 19, 1947.[50] While Aung San was chairing a meeting of the Executive Council, the interim government established with the agreement of the British in preparation for independence, gunmen armed with Sten guns drove into the Secretariat's compound at 10:30 a.m. A few minutes later, they burst into the council chamber, shooting one guard on the way. As the doors opened, Aung San stood up—and was immediately shot dead. The gunmen sprayed bullets across the room, leaving only three survivors. Aung San and most of his government-in-waiting were assassinated.[51] Theories abound as to who killed Aung San, but one of his longstanding rivals, U Saw, was soon accused, tried, and hanged. U Nu, the only council member who had not been at the meeting, took over.

On January 4, 1948, the British flag was lowered for the last time and Burma became a truly independent nation. U Nu, former chairman of the Rangoon Student Union and a close colleague of Aung San, became the prime minister of Burma, and the BIA was feted by much of the general population as the heroes of independence.

At the same time as the people of Burma were struggling with ethnic relations in their country, as well as the death of their national hero, segments of the Communist Party of Burma, which had been functioning as an above-ground political party based in Rangoon, took up arms and went "underground" soon after independence, seeking to overthrow the Burmese state.[52] Of the original Burmese revolutionaries, some had

Communist sympathies, while others believed firmly in socialism (Aung San had originally planned to travel to China to seek help from Mao before he changed course and went to Japan),[53] while still others were influenced by the Japanese rightists or the British colonialists. Before and during the early days of independence, many key leaders, including large segments of the national army's Burma Rifles,[54] defected to join the Communists or the ethnic peoples' movements. The subsequent fighting resulted in a major loss of life, increased political polarization, and the justification needed to vastly increase the size of the state army. The legitimate questions surrounding the status of the ethnic nationalities, as well as the threat to state power posed by the CPB, helped set the stage for the next sixty years of war and conflict.

Within months, the country was torn apart by civil war, as both the Communists and the Karen separately rose up in armed struggle. These two groups seized major cities such as Mandalay, Maymyo, and Prome and areas of Insein, a suburb of Rangoon. By early 1949 half the government troops had mutinied.[55] Ne Win replaced Smith Dun, a Karen, as commander in chief, who was apparently removed solely on the basis of his ethnicity, even though he had remained loyal to U Nu's democratic government. He then began the task of rebuilding the Burma Army, or *tatmadaw*. Than Shwe was not quite fifteen years old.

The Karen, at least, had reason for rebellion, apart from abuses committed during the war and feeling that they were sold out by the British. Pitched battles between the Karen and the *tatmadaw* began after Burmese police officers entered eight churches simultaneously on Christmas Eve 1948, murdering more than eighty churchgoers.[56] That, combined with numerous other attacks and brutal massacres of Karen civilians by militias, resulted in many Karen taking up arms under the auspices of the Karen National Defense Organization (KNDO).[57] Some attacks on the Karen were arguably unrelated to the U Nu government; although in some instances troops from Ne Win's 4th Burma Rifles were involved. For example, the 4th Burma Rifles went into Maubin in the Irrawaddy Delta and burned down the American Baptist Mission School.[58] In apparent response to these attacks on civilians, the KNDO seized the town of Insein that now houses the country's notorious prison for political prisoners and dug in, until it was eventually driven out after a long and bloody siege that lasted a little over three months.

In the process of the battle, Karen civilians and KNDO soldiers fled with elements of the national army's Karen Rifles who defected, and attempted to backup the Karen at Insein. They were also poised for an all-out invasion of Rangoon. At the same time, many Karen and other minorities were expelled from the military, either out of fear that they would aid the Karen resistance or—perhaps more likely—because they dominated much of the military hierarchy and were still resented for being "rightists" that had worked closely with the British throughout the war at a time when Aung San had joined the Japanese. This "rightist" perspective on the Karen, which contrasted greatly with the leftward leanings of Aung San, U Nu, and others,[59] was underlined in the post-war period when it was the Karen and the Kachin Rifles that recaptured many areas that had been briefly seized by the CPB.[60]

In addition to the human rights abuses committed by the civilian militias on the Karen population, the fact that the Karen dominated much of the area helped justify the Karen assault on Insein. Indeed, the Karen were a major part of the population in many of the areas surrounding Rangoon to the east in what was to become Karen State, to the north in Nyaunglebin, and to the west and southwest in the Irrawaddy Division, also known as Burma's "delta" region. Thus, their push for an independent homeland in the area was not without demographic merit.

One of the ethnic minority leaders to respond to the cry for help at Insein was Naw Hseng. Before attempting to help the Karen holed up at Insein, Naw Hseng—a decorated Kachin commander that had distinguished himself as part of the anti-Japanese Kachin "levies" before joining the post-independence state army—was helping lead the government's efforts to crush the Communists north of Rangoon. Naw Hseng was ordered by armed forces chief Ne Win to travel south to Toungoo from Pyinmana, where he had been attacking the Communists as part of the national military, but on the way he switched sides, refusing to attack the other ethnic minorities that had been his allies during the war. For a variety of reasons, Naw Hseng headed north toward Mandalay instead of south toward Rangoon and Insein, capturing several towns including Kyaukse on February 21, 1949. Than Shwe, who would have been about sixteen years old at the time, could have been in high school. On June 26, 1949, the government reasserted control over Kyaukse, after Naw Hseng had headed south nearly eight weeks earlier when he realized that his seizure of several towns between Mandalay and Rangoon had done nothing to help the Karen entrenched at Insein.[61] Naw Hseng was ultimately defeated and fled to neighboring China.

The move by the U Nu government to reassert control over Kyaukse represented the fifth change of government in Than Shwe's sixteen years of life. Four of the five changes of government came through violence. The exception was the final transition to independence from the British. For a future leader like Than Shwe, who has focused, in part, on maintaining the territorial unity of Burma and who has been adept at using violence to obtain his goals, the lessons of the effectiveness of overwhelming force cannot have been lost. However, there is no concrete evidence that reveals the full extent of his thinking during the invasions of Kyaukse.

Five years later, apparently after completing some schooling and his year as a postal clerk, Than Shwe decided to join the *tatmadaw*. He was selected as part of the ninth intake (the ninth consecutive class) of the Officer Training School (OTS) in the old colonial hill station of Maymyo just northeast of Mandalay, now known as Pyin Oo Lwin. The area had served as a vacation destination in colonial Burma, replete with tennis courts, golf courses, and swimming pools for British officials to escape the heat of the plains.

The OTS had been founded much further south in Mingaladon in 1942 to train cadets from the BDA's camps in Pyinmana, Mandalay, and Rangoon. But while the Japanese believed that training an officer corps would be its best hope of controlling the Burmese army, Callahan claims that the OTS instead "proved to be an institution that provided space for the army's growing nationalist identity to ferment," adding that "ultimately, the OTS served as a training ground not for pro-Japanese officers and cadets, as the Japanese military intended, but for politically unified, anti-Japanese cells that formed laterally and vertically among the classes being rushed through the various training programs offered there." Selection of cadets was controlled not by the Japanese but by former members of the Thirty Comrades, such as Burma's future dictator Ne Win. The selection process was harsh, and was designed above all to test both tenacity and mental toughness.[62]

The year after Than Shwe entered the OTS, the then leader of Burma's armed forces founded the country's Defense Services Academy (DSA), modeled on America's West Point military academy[63] and designed, in part, to stop ethnic nationalist movements.[64] Efforts to build "a first-class fighting force, capable of repelling external aggression" were detailed by Ne Win in a memo in August 1951.[65] Lieutenant Colonel Aung Gyi (who later would become a member of the National League for Democracy under Aung San Suu Kyi) was tasked with leading a planning committee to advise the government on a new structure for the army. He recommended that, given the precarious situation of the Rangoon government, at least 40 percent of the government's budget should be devoted to military expenditure.[66] The reorganization of military training, including the creation of several new training establishments such as the DSA, was, in Callahan's words, "perhaps the most remarkable result of these early efforts at military reform."[67]

The DSA opened in Bahtoo in 1955, and primarily attracted high school graduates between the ages of sixteen and nineteen. In 1957 the DSA and OTS swapped locations, with the DSA moving to Maymyo and the OTS relocating to Bahtoo. Seven years later the OTS moved again to Hmawbi and then back to Bahtoo in 1991.

According to Khin Maung Nyunt, who was a student in the first "batch" of DSA students and now resides in the United States, an education at the DSA entailed a multiyear curriculum based on two separate tracks: science and the liberal arts. Liberal arts students studied economics, history, geography, the history of war, and other topics. Science students studied mathematics, chemistry, physics, and engineering. Engineers often studied at the DSA for two years and then transferred to Rangoon University to complete their technical studies. While the OTS was mainly designed to educate tough, frontline soldiers, the DSA, in coordination with the University of Rangoon, aimed to create more sophisticated leaders with an understanding of military history, among other topics.

Entry into the DSA was initially highly competitive. According to Khin Maung Nyunt, thousands of applicants from all over the country applied for only fifty-four available positions. Each applicant had to take a written exam, followed by exams related to endurance, speaking abilities, and personal health.

Gaining admittance to the OTS, in contrast, was much easier and culminated with appointment as a non-commissioned officer (NCO). According to Maung Aung Myoe, the OTS today recruits primarily from university graduates and non-commissioned officers, while the DSA draws on high school graduates, and subsequently awards university degrees to its students. However, in 1953 most of the OTS recruits, like Than Shwe, were NCOs, and "only a very small percentage of cadets had high school or higher level education."[68] That changed only in the 1960s.

Of the entire cabinet of the current military regime, known as the State Peace and Development Council (SPDC), the number two general, Maung Aye, along with Than Shwe's ally U Thaung, are the only two left from the original batch of DSA graduates. Ever since the DSA and OTS were created, the *tatmadaw* has been subject to various forms of factionalism and division, but not enough ultimately to break the unity of the military. The influence and the rivalries of these two institutions are exemplified among the top leadership in Burma today. While Than Shwe is an OTS graduate, his deputy, Maung Aye, is from the first DSA intake. Khin Nyunt, prime minister and intelligence chief under Than Shwe until he was purged in 2004, was from the twenty-fifth intake of the OTS. Modern institutional rivalry that could play out in stresses on military unity is diminished, in part, by the fact that Than Shwe has for many years been largely responsible for the career development of senior ranking officers, and has promoted young, handpicked soldiers, thereby hoping to earn lifetime loyalty. Rivalry between OTS and DSA graduates has, at various times, been matched by a divide between field commanders and military intelligence. Yet, despite hopes by many Burmese dissidents, rivalries over "who graduated from where" have not seriously emerged in recent years and have tended to dissipate during times of crisis in Burma, as the military unites to retain power.

While at the DSA, Khin Maung Nyunt met and became friends with Maung Aye, who is now serving as the second most senior general after Than Shwe. Khin Maung Nyunt said in the 1950s Maung Aye was "pretty straightforward and straight-laced. He did not drink, did not smoke, and seemed honest." In contrast, Aung Lynn Htut, one of the most senior intelligence officers to defect from the military regime, met Maung Aye much later in his political life. He said that the Maung Aye he knew in 2005 was quite different from the friendly fellow student Khin Maung Nyunt had met in democratic Burma during the 1950s. While working at the Burmese embassy in the United States from 2002 to 2005, Aung Lynn Htut was often required to shop for expensive suits for Maung Aye and Than Shwe, purchased mainly from the high-end Nordstrom's at Tysons Corner shopping center in the wealthy enclave of McLean, Virginia. When the United States imposed financial sanctions on Burma after the military regime attacked Nobel Peace Prize recipient Aung San Suu Kyi in 2003, Aung Lynn Htut was temporarily unable to obtain suits for Maung Aye and Than Shwe, but the US State Department subsequently allowed accounts to reopen and it is believed that the purchases continued.

Since Than Shwe completed his training at the OTS without a college degree, Khin Maung Nyunt says that his only option was to enter the army upon graduation. At the OTS Than Shwe would have met mostly high school graduates, but also some college educated students who had applied directly, having already studied in college, and other "rank and file" entrants who, some with years of previous military experience but little education, could still attend the OTS. Had Than Shwe graduated from a university, he may have entered other services apart from the army.

As an OTS cadet, Than Shwe is likely to have studied subjects such as military science, according to Maung Aung Myoe, as well as "section-level and platoon-level commands and staff duties."[69] According to Sein Thaung, a 1973 graduate of the OTS, four primary conventional battlefield tactics were taught at the school in the 1970s, which included offense, defense, withdrawal, and marching. With the exception of the notorious "Four Cuts" counterinsurgency campaign introduced in the 1960s, tactics of guerrilla warfare were not addressed in depth in the early years of the OTS, since the main activity of government troops was securing larger areas controlled by armed groups, Sein Thaung said.

Ronny Nyein points out that one important lesson learned by all graduates of both the DSA and the OTS was the basics of battlefield engagement. Nyein says that one lesson, in particular, seems to have taken root with Than Shwe: the use of "search fire." The term refers to the tactic of firing weapons in the general direction of a secluded enemy in the hope that the enemy will fire back, allowing the initial shooter to ascertain the position of the enemy. Nyein says that the military regime under Than Shwe has adapted this tactic to suppressing Burma's democracy movement. When demonstrators organize street marches calling for an end to dictatorship, the regime often allows the demonstrations to develop for a few days, or even a few weeks, in order to encourage all elements of the opposition to reveal their positions, and only then does the military crack down with overwhelming force. Such a theory does appear to have played out in reality on numerous occasions, for instance, when students organized mass demonstrations in 1996, when the opposition National League for Democracy planned a national meeting of party members in 1998, and when Buddhist monks took to the streets in protest in 2007. In each case the military paused and allowed the demonstrations to develop before cracking down. In this way, suggests Nyein, the military uses "search fire" tactics to coax the opposition into the open where it can be dealt with more effectively—perhaps similar to how some observers interpret Mao Zedong's campaign in China known as "Let a Hundred Flowers Bloom."

After graduating from the OTS, Than Shwe's exact position in the armed forces is unclear. In February 1991 the *Working People's Daily*, one of the military regime's state-controlled newspapers and a predecessor of the current *New Light of Myanmar*, ran a series of stories about the history of the leadership of the armed forces in Burma, including helpful lists of every single leader of light infantry divisions, regional commands, and even those that had been expelled from Ne Win's Revolutionary Council since 1962.[70] The newspaper articles contained greater detail than Than Shwe's official curriculum vitae, which states that he served as a second lieutenant at the No. 1 Infantry.[71] For example, the *Working People's Daily* biography states that upon graduation Than Shwe served at the 1st Burma Regiment as a platoon commander. According to a military officer who served in the *tatmadaw* at the time, Than Shwe must have served as an infantry soldier, and most likely with a regiment that would serve as his "mother regiment" throughout much of his career, probably the 1st Burma Regiment. As for the location of his initial posting, Than Shwe may have operated in the areas around Hpa-an in what is now Karen State. (This assumption is drawn from the knowledge that Than Shwe's wife is from Hpa-an and it was during this time that he apparently met her. On the other hand, he could have operated in the areas of southern Burma, including Pegu and Rangoon, or even as far north as Meiktila in central Burma, where he was reported to be much later in the 1950s). The 1991 *Working People's Daily* article reported that Than Shwe was appointed as a platoon commander in July, only a number of months after reporting to the OTS. At the time, OTS training only lasted for a period of between six and nine months, since the Burmese military faced a serious short-age of officers for its expanding ranks.[72]

According to OTS graduate Sein Thaung, Than Shwe would have imme-diately put to use the original purpose of OTS training: to teach young cadets how to lead small groups of soldiers in battle. Almost all OTS grad-uates that entered the army became platoon commanders ranked as a second lieutenant. As a platoon commander in the infantry, Than Shwe essentially was a leader of ground troops. Instead of pursuing a career in specialist divisions handling artillery, tanks, services, or ammunition, Than Shwe appears to have been assigned as a frontline soldier. A platoon, at the time, was comprised of thirty-five troops divided into three sections. Some of the less successful graduates of the OTS would have commanded section-level groups within a platoon, which was basically a group of ten rank-and-file soldiers. Setting aside the thirty soldiers that made up the three sections of a platoon, the remaining five were officers that included a platoon sergeant, a platoon runner, and a platoon commander—in this case Than Shwe. Subsequently, Than Shwe was promoted to full lieuten-ant, likely still with the same regiment, which enabled him to assume the post of company commander, most likely overseeing three platoons and a total of 105 soldiers.

One of Burma's primary international "enemies" in the early 1950s was China, which was funding and supporting the CPB, although not to as great a degree as during the late 1960s. At the same time, the years pre-ceding Than Shwe's entry into the OTS were marked by ongoing struggles against the country's ethnic minorities. Battles in the Karen areas included the push to over-run the KNU headquarters at Papun east of Rangoon across the Gulf of Martaban, as well as in the rural areas surrounding Thaton and Hpa-an.[73] Before Than Shwe entered the OTS, the two main challenges to the central government—the ethnic armed resistance groups and the Communists—reached the apex of their territorial control around

Rangoon. The Karen had lost control of many of their urban centers in the delta to government forces, although they were certainly not defeated and retained control of a significant area, including to the east of Rangoon. By the time Than Shwe entered the OTS in 1953, U Nu's government had largely secured the capital, gaining significant ground over the insurgents, while Ne Win had reformed the *tatmadaw* in order to launch further counteroffensives against the Karen. The *tatmadaw* became a force of its own, in some important ways beyond the control of U Nu's elected government. According to Callahan, "By 1953, the *tatmadaw* alone claimed responsibility for defining who was an enemy of the state and deciding how enemies and threats would be handled."[74]

Then, just as the ability of the Karen and the CPB to threaten seizure of Burma's most important urban areas was being contained, a new threat emerged from the shadow of China's civil war. Kuomintang troops fleeing the Communist victory in 1949 crossed the border into the jungles of northern Burma. For U Nu's fragile government and for the *tatmadaw*, this was alarming, as it brought with it the threat of a Chinese Communist invasion. The US, and perhaps others, including the Taiwanese, supplied airdropped aid and equipment to the Kuomintang, and Burma became a base for anti-Communist forces to try to retake control of China.[75] This was not what the *tatmadaw* had in mind.

Khin Maung Nyunt confirms the Burmese fear at the time of a Chinese invasion against the Kuomintang or in support of the CPB, reporting that in the mid-1950s when Than Shwe was at the OTS, the key "enemy" of the Burmese government was China. All prospective officers such as Khin Maung Nyunt learned that Chinese support for the CPB, as well as the presence of the Kuomintang tempting a Chinese invasion, were primary threats to Burma's independence. Cadets were taught that the second most dangerous threat to Burma's independence was the country's ethnic minorities. While Khin Maung Nyunt points out that ethnic minority leaders have long since changed their stance from seeking independence to participating in a federal state of Burma, it is believed by many that cadets are still taught that Burma could fall apart at any minute without the strong arm of military rule.

It was while serving in the infantry that Than Shwe met his wife-to-be, Daw Kyaing Kyaing, and they married in 1956. Sources based in

Thailand who knew Kyaing Kyaing at a young age reported that she was a widow whose husband had been an officer who was killed in battle. Kyaing Kyaing was from the Pa-O ethnic group, although she may have been half-Chinese. Born in Shwe Gon Township between Hpa-an and Thaton, almost directly west of Rangoon across the Gulf of Martaban in Karen State and close to the border with Mon State, she may have already had a son with her first husband. Rarely when a fellow officer is killed in battle, does another officer marry and look after his fallen comrade's widow. But most Burmese believe Than Shwe and other officers drew lots, essentially a lottery, to decide which of them should marry Kyaing Kyaing—Than Shwe won. Other reports indicate the marriage may have been arranged by the commanding officer, while rumors suggest that Than Shwe had already been married, or at least involved with another woman previously, and had fathered a child. But when Than Shwe married Kyaing Kyaing, he is rumored to have abandoned his son and the child's mother. Unconfirmed sources that had previously been close to Than Shwe state that, about forty-five years later, in 2000, former Secretary-3 General Win Myint from Kyaukse arranged a secret reunion for Than Shwe and his abandoned son, without Kyaing Kyaing's knowledge.

According to the Burmese dissident and historian Aung Saw Oo, Kyaing Kyaing's name was formerly Daw Ma Kyaing. Aung Saw Oo makes this claim based on a visit to a Buddhist pagoda in Burma in the early 1980s where Than Shwe and Kyaing Kyaing had made donations prior to Than Shwe becoming the ruler of Burma. His wife's name was listed at the pagoda as Daw Ma Kyaing. Aung Saw Oo reports that the name Daw Ma Kyaing suggests a rural or "country girl" existence in Burma, as compared to the more regal-sounding Daw Kyaing Kyaing, which he says she likely chose when Than Shwe rose to power.

The Pa-O are one of Burma's ethnic nationalities, believed to be a subgroup of the Karen. They are estimated to number less than a million in total, and primarily inhabit three separate areas: the hills around Inle Lake in southwestern Shan State, the Thaton area of Mon State, and the Sittang River Valley north of Toungoo, Karen State. Legends suggest that the Pa-O originated in Central Asia and migrated first to the Thaton area east of Rangoon. They are devout Buddhists, although their Buddhism is mixed with the animism that they had previously followed. While the Pa-O in

Shan State have tried to preserve their identity and culture, it is generally believed that lowland Pa-O from the Thaton area, where Kyaing Kyaing comes from, have largely become "Burmanized." That may, in part, explain why Kyaing Kyaing has done little to promote ethnic autonomy, and has certainly shown no sympathy for the Pa-Os who have continued to fight an armed struggle since 1947, even though the Pa-O National Organization was established in the Thaton area of Lower Burma.[76]

Not long after marrying Kyaing Kyaing on February 21, 1957, Than Shwe was promoted to acting captain. According to the *Working People's Daily*, this occurred after Than Shwe had seen "active service" in Karen State and areas east of the Salween River in southern Shan State, while earlier serving as a platoon commander and company commander.[77] While impossible to confirm, this statement indicates that it is possible that Than Shwe engaged in combat against the Kuomintang (KMT) as well as the Karen. The areas east of the Salween River in southern Shan State represented a stronghold for the KMT, and the Shan ethnic minority had not yet taken up arms in a substantial manner—something that eventually did happen. The Karen State was home to Karen efforts for self-determination, where the Karen held much stronger military positions than in the delta region. The CPB, at the time, was largely confined to central Burma and, to some extent, the Yoma mountain ranges. If the *Working People's Daily* is to be believed, it would be less likely that Than Shwe was fighting against the Communists.

A major question that has often arisen around Than Shwe's military service is the extent to which he participated in actual fighting. Indeed, Than Shwe's role while allegedly serving as a platoon commander and company commander in Karen State and southern Shan State in the 1950s has never been fully defined by the Burmese military regime. Some former soldiers in the *tatmadaw*, now living in exile, report rumors that Than Shwe never actually saw active duty in the 1950s or at any other time, but this cannot be confirmed. Without a doubt, the *tatmadaw* was engaged in active duty in the late 1950s against the country's ethnic minorities, the CPB, and the KMT. This, of course, does not necessarily mean that all soldiers were engaged in actual combat. Some evidence could suggest that Than Shwe did not participate in actual fighting, or at least did not serve with particular distinction. Two key points make this case. Given the promulgation of militaristic ideology by the Burmese military, and particularly by Than Shwe, it would seem strange for him to downplay battlefield successes in his official curriculum vitae. Further, Than Shwe has received none of the top battlefield awards associated with honor or valor in fighting. One of these honors is the *Aung San Thuriya*, a rare award named after Aung San. Two others include *Thiha Thura* and *Thura*, with *Thura* being the lowest ranking of the three. Other military leaders in the present regime, such as the third-ranking leader Shwe Mann, have won the *Thura* award, and subsequently earned the right to place the term in front of their name. Than Shwe has received none of these awards.

Many observers have asked over the years why Than Shwe's military uniform is covered with medals and awards, which may seem to indicate his involvement in active fighting. According to Thant Zin Myaing, a *tatmadaw* veteran and DSA graduate, all soldiers earn a medal for participation in a major operation, including frontline soldiers as well as those that provide support and intelligence, even the leaders of the operation back in military headquarters. Although I have not deciphered the medals on Than Shwe's chest, many of them could have come simply from Than Shwe's association with battlefield operations, not actual fighting. Similarly, some of the medals plastered across the chests of Burma's top generals come not from active battlefield experience, but from ordering others into battle later in their careers. Other medals include citations noting length of military service. According to Thant Zin Myaing, it is important to note that before 1988 the *tatmadaw* did not give out many medals simply for participating, in some way, in a military operation.

On the other hand, during the 1950s, Than Shwe may indeed have seen and participated in regular battles. There is some limited contextual evidence to suggest that this is the case. First, soldiers in the *tatmadaw* often rose through the ranks based, in part, on their battlefield experience, and Than Shwe certainly rose consistently upwards through the military hierarchy. Indeed, some former military officers report that battlefield experience not only helped provide the impetus for promotion, but that it was a necessity. Underlining this possibility, Than Shwe served in many military positions that would have placed him in the capacity to command and control military operations—positions often given to those with battlefield experience. For example, his time served in the

88th Light Infantry Division as well as with the 1st Burma Regiment in support of, and possibly under, the 77th Light Infantry Division would have placed Than Shwe in command positions overseeing pitched battle. Additionally, Than Shwe served in geographical locations in which troops under his command operated in areas where active fighting took place. For example, he was apparently based in conflict areas in Karen State in the 1950s and Shan State in the late 1960s and early 1970s, and against the China-backed CPB throughout the early 1980s. Lastly, one former CPB soldier claimed to be aware of Than Shwe's presence in the conflict areas, although he indicated that Than Shwe had gone into hiding during one particular battle.

The conflicting claims about Than Shwe's combat experience might be explained by the fact that he may not have spent as much time fighting as other high-ranking officials. Yet, Khin Maung Nyunt reports that in order to be promoted to captain, a second lieutenant at the time would have had fighting experience. However, OTS graduates such as Than Shwe, upon reaching the rank of captain, could become a headquarters company commander responsible for home base operations, but not engaged in fighting. In contrast, many DSA graduates such as Maung Aye and others would be assigned to fighting units until they were promoted to full company commander and even thereafter, thereby placing them in direct combat operations for as many as ten or eleven years. Since Than Shwe served as a low-ranking officer for only four or five years, and since a portion of this time may have been as a headquarters company commander away from battle, it may be that he was only fighting for a few years— much less than others in the military. Indeed, he may not have avoided combat, but simply fought much less than others.

At some point during his period serving at a low rank in the military, Than Shwe is reported to have spent two or three months at Meiktila, local headquarters for an important military detachment. Apparently serving as an intelligence officer, Than Shwe reported often to Lieutenant Colonel Tin Htoon. Tin Htoon described Than Shwe as "relatively boring," with a clear addiction to chewing betel nut, the seed of an Areca palm tree that is wrapped in betel leaf and infused with lime or other flavors.[78] The nut can quickly turn one's teeth bright orange and contribute to oral and pharyngeal cancers. Generally viewed as a vice, Tin

Htoon disliked betel nut and ordered Than Shwe to clean his mouth before attending meetings.

Tin Htoon remembered Than Shwe as an unremarkable soldier. His primary responsibilities were with the Psychological Warfare Department within the Ministry of Defense, which had been founded in 1952 as the Psywar Directorate by Aung Gyi and Lieutenant Colonel Ba Than.[79] Staffed by three young Burmese soldiers and civilians working under Aung Gyi, the Psychological Warfare Department would ultimately formulate the ideological justification for General Ne Win's military coup in 1962 and ensuing brutal governance. The Department also served as the intellectual backbone or "think tank" for the Ne Win regime, and was tasked with countering Communist ideology. Time and time again, officials of the Psychological Warfare Department found a way to justify Ne Win's rule in their amalgamated interpretation of Burmese culture, socialism, and Marxism.

At the outset, according to Chit Hlaing, one of the three young staff members at the Department, one person was assigned to work on psychological warfare and propaganda, mainly focused on undermining the CPB as well as various ethnic groups seeking autonomy, another was assigned to focus on the economy, and the third—Chit Hlaing himself—was assigned to study Marxism and Soviet communism in order to determine whether "it was appropriate to apply them to the Myanmar scenario."[80] Each worked under Ba Than, the leader of the newly created Education and Psychological Warfare Department.[81] At the same time, two of their superiors, San Lwin and Pe Kyi, traveled to the United States to study the psychological warfare activities of the US Army. They were not the only persons to receive US military training. Maung Aung Myoe reports that between 1953 and 1963, eighteen officers trained at the US Staff College in Ft. Leavenworth.[82] The American training apparently was not decisive in creating a desire for democracy and freedom, since San Yu and Kyaw Tin, who both staunchly supported Ne Win's dictatorial rule for decades, were among those who received training.

According to the *Working People's Daily*, on February 26, 1958, the year U Nu was forced to hand over power to a military-led caretaker government under the commander in chief Ne Win, Than Shwe was appointed to the Office of the Director of Education and Psychological Warfare, where Chit Hlaing was working.[83] Than Shwe spent six months at the Director's office, probably based at the Southern Command headquarters at Mingaladon, a suburb of Rangoon, before being transferred to the Northern Command in Mandalay.

Chit Hlaing claims to have worked alongside Than Shwe at the Central School of Political Science later in the 1960s. However, it is unclear from the records how closely the two men would have worked together in 1958. In his writings, Chit Hlaing does not mention working with Than Shwe in 1958. It is also unclear whether Than Shwe actually underwent training in psychological warfare during this six-month period in 1958, or whether he simply worked at the Psywar Directorate. It is possible that his "psy-ops" (psychological operations) training came during his subsequent post in Mandalay. The *Working People's Daily* biography simply explains that Than Shwe was "attached to the office" of the directorate—not a definitive statement that he was taking classes.[84] To add to the confusion, even though the *Working People's Daily* reports that Than Shwe spent six months with the Office of the Director of Education and Psychological Warfare, his official curriculum vitae makes no mention of this placement. Instead, it states that Than Shwe moved directly from the No. 1 Infantry where he had served in the 1950s to the Psychological Warfare Unit (1) where he served as "quartermaster," i.e., someone who maintains the quarters of soldiers, being responsible for supplies, transfers, and logistics. If this was the case, then Than Shwe may not have received any formal psy-war training alongside Chit Hlaing, and the two men may not have met until later at the Central School of Political Science.

However, a source that taught the opening psy-war training course has no doubt that Than Shwe took part. "Than Shwe was definitely among the first batch of psy-war students," he said. Hans-Bernd Zoellner believes Chit Hlaing did indeed teach Than Shwe at some point, calling him "a teacher of many leading members of the still ruling *tatmadaw*, the most prominent among them being Senior General Than Shwe." Zoellner reports that Chit Hlaing and Than Shwe's relationship continued well into the future, saying that Than Shwe "cared for his teacher some years ago when the former instructor at the military's Psy-War Department had to undergo eye surgery."[85] According to Chit Hlaing, the first batch of students for psy-war training were selected by San Yu, a close ally of

Ne Win who would go on to become president of Burma in the 1980s.[86] However, Ronny Nyein points out that it may have been Chit Maung, a parliamentary secretary in the Ministry of Defense, who approved Than Shwe's participation in psy-war training.

Chit Hlaing notes that the first psy-war training course for officers started at Mingaladon on December 1, 1957, and claims that during this democratic period, Ne Win ordered students to stay far away from party politics, instructing them that: "The *tatmadaw* should study political science, but should strictly stay away from political parties. The *tatmadaw* should stand to safeguard the constitution." However, most Burmese people, and some scholars, dispute the contention that the military was intent on staying out of politics. Mary Callahan writes that in 1956 a commanding officers conference culminated in an "ideological statement" that "was the culmination of several years of psywar programs aimed at politically isolating the enemies of the Burmese state."[87] Callahan believes the Psywar Directorate's programs, whether deliberate or not, helped bring the *tatmadaw* firmly into domestic politics. It called on the military to engage in "explicitly political tactics" and oversaw the military's "expansion into non-military national affairs, most of which was managed and overseen by officers connected with the Psywar Directorate."[88] At any rate, even if Chit Hlaing is correct that the *intent* behind the 1956 statement was to support democracy, he certainly was soon proven wrong. Not long thereafter, Ne Win would seize power in a military coup.

There is nothing to dispute the notion that Than Shwe would have been surrounded by psy-war practitioners, whether during training in psy-war or during his time in Mandalay. Chit Hlaing writes that psychological operations activities "waged a continuous ideological struggle," aimed "mainly at armed insurrection of rebel parties of all colors." He claimed the main mission of the operations—to "weaken the political influence of the CPB, and to defend the principles of parliamentary democracy"—was achieved. Chit Hlaing also writes that "materials covered in the [psy-ops] courses consisted of propaganda principles, economic principles, basic elements of Psy-War, practical aspects and political sciences."[89] It has also been suggested that Than Shwe could have overseen the production of cartoons and caricatures of the military's enemies, especially the CPB leaders, as part of the propaganda effort.

While the main focus of psy-ops training may have been to set the framework for undermining non-state actors, especially the Communists, Chit Hlaing also claimed, perhaps with some merit, that the military did not aim to undermine all leftist movements. Indeed, the "*tatmadaw* had already accepted socialist economy as a preferable system."[90] After Ne Win seized power for a second time in 1962, he quickly moved to nationalize major businesses in the country and cut off Burma from international interactions under what his regime dubbed the "Burmese Way to Socialism." Chit Hlaing himself was a well-known leftist sympathizer from the revolutionary days, and a member of the Nagani Book Club that had distributed Communist literature in the pre-independence period.

It is this part of Than Shwe's training—psychological operations—for which he is well known. If the *tatmadaw*'s successes against the CPB were any positive measure, and psychological operations played an important role, then the *tatmadaw* must have been doing something right. However, it must be said that some observers say the significance of Than Shwe's participation in psy-war is overstated. According to the DSA graduate Ronny Nyein who worked in the War Office (military headquarters) alongside Than Shwe, the primary purpose of low-level psychological warfare units was simply to attract young Burmese men to join the military. In this respect, as a very low-ranking official, Than Shwe is likely to have held meetings with potential recruits and helped set local recruitment guidelines to meet desired troop levels. In such an administrative position, it may be that Than Shwe was not involved in true psychological warfare, although this seems unlikely.

The propaganda promulgated by the War Office at the time, which centered, in part, on maintaining the territorial integrity of the nation, has deeply infused Than Shwe's rhetoric since he became leader of Burma in 1992. Nearly every speech he gives publicly underlines this core theme. At the same time, his possible early experience in recruiting members to the *tatmadaw* was put to use after 1992 when he led the efforts to double the size of the Burmese military. In under a decade, Than Shwe expanded troop levels from just over a hundred fifty thousand to a staggering four hundred thousand, though some speculate that current troop numbers could be far less. It was also at this time that the number of forcibly conscripted child soldiers in Than Shwe's armed forces increased dramatically.

According to multiple interviews with former members of the Burmese military, there were virtually no children in the armed forces prior to the 1990s. However, in tandem with Than Shwe's increase in the size of the military, Human Rights Watch reported that the number of child soldiers swelled to possibly as many as seventy thousand.[91]

Once in Mandalay and having completed his work at the Psywar Directorate, the *Working People's Daily* reports that Than Shwe worked at the headquarters of the Northern Command, serving under Brigadier General Aung Shwe, who, many years later after resigning from Ne Win's administration, would join the National League for Democracy. Than Shwe then reportedly served under San Yu, a lifelong ally of Ne Win, who was a founding member of the military regime that seized power in 1962. San Yu was relieved of duties for one month in 1961, but was the man in charge in the north at the time of Ne Win's coup, and would remain so for nearly a year after the coup. In his capacity as commanding officer of the No. 1 Mobile Psychological Warfare Company based out of Mandalay, Than Shwe would have worked closely with San Yu.

According to a source whose family member served as a military officer in Mandalay, psychological warfare staff members were largely focused on creating anti-Communist propaganda, including movies, plays, and performances. These activities were designed to sway the Burmese population away from Communist sympathies.

At the same time, a mobile psychological unit was somewhat different from a standing intelligence officer. Mobile units often participated in mop-up operations after battle, during which they would take several steps to try to win the hearts and minds of local villagers, including convincing the local villagers that the *tatmadaw* had their best interests in mind. Khin Maung Nyunt says that mobile units would organize infrastructure repair, such as the building of houses and schools destroyed in the battle, the provision of basic assistance to farmers, and the repairing of dams and irrigation trenches. The mobile units would also organize classes for villagers, designed to teach them about the importance of the *tatmadaw* and especially about the democratic constitution.

Even though Than Shwe's time spent in psychological warfare may or may not have represented the utilization of genuine psychological strategies, he has proved expert at using divide-and-rule tactics, successfully capitalizing on splits in the armed opposition groups, as well as creating fake democracy groups in an attempt to usurp the popularity of Burma's legitimate democratic struggle. Whether or not Than Shwe developed a facility for using such tactics as a psychological warfare staff member, he certainly would have learned these tactics from decades of observing Burma's previous dictator, Ne Win, in action.

FIG. 3. *Than Shwe and his wife Kyaing Kyaing in Sri Lanka. Photo by AFP.*

2

THE LAND OF GREEN AND ORANGE

IN NOVEMBER 2008, a Burmese poet, Saw Wai, was jailed for two years for writing an eight-line Valentine's Day poem published in the popular magazine, *The Love Journal*. The poem, entitled "14th February," at first glance reads as a simple romantic verse. Its lines include: "You have to be in love truly, madly, deeply and then you can call it real love. Millions of those who know how to love, Laugh and clap those gold-gilded hands." However, the authorities were not slow to spot the hidden meaning. The first word of each line of the poem spells out in Burmese the following: "Power Crazy Senior General Than Shwe." Saw Wai was charged with damaging "public tranquility."[1]

For almost five decades, Burma has been ruled by military regimes intolerant of dissent. Since the age of nineteen Than Shwe has spent his entire life in this system. In 1962 Ne Win assumed power for a second time, deposing the democratically elected government of U Nu by force. Than Shwe, reported to be a supporter of the coup, became an instructor and then a dean at the Central Institute of Political Sciences, which was to promulgate the ideology of Ne Win's military regime.

While some Burmese regarded Ne Win's earlier rule from 1958 to 1960 as a move towards stability, the public's attitude quickly soured. The second coup d'état and the subsequent two decades are seen as some of the most bloody and repressive years in Burma's history. On March 2, 1962, at 8:50 a.m., Ne Win informed the nation through a radio broadcast that the military had taken power. In the early hours of that morning, soldiers entered the homes of every government minister and placed them under "protective custody."[2] The former president of the country, Sao Shwe Thaike, who was the *sawbwa* (chieftain) of Yawnghwe in Shan State, was arrested and died later that year in prison. One of his sons, Sao Mye

Thaike was shot dead when the army raided his home. The previous night, just hours before the coup, Ne Win was seen attending a performance of a Chinese ballet.

The Revolutionary Council was established and mainly led by Ne Win's allies from the 4th Burma Rifles.[3] U Saw Oo, one of the key staff members of the Psy-War Department, was appointed information minister.[4] Within a few months, the Revolutionary Council drew up its guiding ideology, which it called "The Burmese Way to Socialism." Described by most commentators as a peculiar mix of Marxism, nationalism, and Buddhism grounded in an intolerance of dissent and an extreme nationalism, the ideology was detailed in a document with the same name, and in another, even more peculiar paper, "System of Correlation of Man and His Environment."[5] One former Western diplomat summed it up as "an amalgam of Karl Marx and Groucho Marx." In the document, headed "Top Secret," the Revolutionary Council defined its guiding principles and then, in a section entitled "Reorientation of Views," the paper described its approach:

In marching towards [a] socialist economy it is imperative that we first re-orientate all erroneous views of our people. Fraudulent practices, profit motive, easy living, parasitism, shirking and selfishness must be eradicated. We must educate the people that to earn one's living by one's labor and to see dignity in one's own work comes into vogue.... Attempts must be made by various correct methods to do away with bogus acts of charity and social work for vainglorious show, bogus piety and hypocritical religiosity, etc., as well as to foster and applaud bona fide belief and practice of personal morals as taught by ethics and traditions of every religion and culture....

The Revolutionary Council will therefore carry out such mass and class organizations as are suitable for the transitional period, and also build up a suitable form of political organization. When political organizational work is carried out socialist democratic education and democratic training will be given to the people so as to ensure their conscious participation. (The Revolutionary Council believes and hopes that there will come about democratic competitions, which will promote socialist development within the framework of socialism.) The aforesaid are in outline the belief, policy and program of the Revolutionary Council of the Union of Burma.[6]

Chit Hlaing took notes on Ne Win's thoughts as he prepared to outline the "Burmese Way to Socialism." According to him, the entire process of defining the regime's ideology, which was to dominate Burma for twenty-six years, was based on a few months of research, several meetings with Ne Win, two days of discussion with Revolutionary Council members, and five drafts of the defining paper, completing the effort by the end of April. Ne Win told Chit Hlaing that he was willing to work with every-one, with one major Orwellian caveat: "So long as they don't oppose us, we will make use of them."[7] He also insisted that the document "must criticize parliamentary democracy ... and the criticism must begin with the British parliament."[8] Martin Smith notes that Aung Gyi, an associate of Ne Win at the beginning of the coup, later criticized the "stunningly simplistic way in which Ne Win's whimsical 'Burmese Way to Socialism' evolved," mainly as an ad-hoc ideology to justify his rule as a response to the appeal of communism and ethnic autonomy.[9]

At the time of the coup, Than Shwe was serving in the Northern Command headquarters in Mandalay, where he had been sent in August 1960. A few months later, he was promoted to commanding officer of a mobile psychological warfare company that was connected with the Northern Command headquarters. When the 1962 coup took place, the entire mili-tary structure and leadership was shaken up, and Than Shwe's leader at the Northern Command, San Yu, was later promoted. There is no avail-able evidence that Than Shwe objected to the coup in any way, and his subsequent career indicates that he is in favor of the military playing a leading role in politics.[10]

Unlike most political parties, which form on the basis of principles, Ne Win was a man in search of justification for his rule. This is borne out by the fact that Chit Hlaing says that the ideology of the Burma Socialist Program Party (BSPP) was formed *after* the party was started, in response to a question from Than Shwe: "We have formed a party. And you are planning training courses, aren't you? Under the circumstances, we need a guiding philosophy for the party. It's true the economy is the priority in our program. But we do need theory. What preparations have you made in this respect?"[11]

On July 1, 1963, the Central School of Political Science was opened with Chit Hlaing as chief instructor. After a brief stint at the Southeast Command in Moulmein (reportedly less than a week), on December 8 Than Shwe moved to the Central School of Political Science. "The Burmese Way to Socialism"—pioneered by the psy-ops headquarters—would form the basis of his teaching curriculum. Saw Myint directed the school together with his close colleague Chit Hlaing, both of whom had written the justification for Ne Win's seizure of power, the principles of the "Burmese Way to Socialism," and the ideology of the Burma Social-ist Program Party. At about the same time, Ne Win's regime opened a school for the Defense Services to provide command in-service train-ing courses. These schools were reported to have trained at least 44,173 civilians and servicemen, while the party created lots of propaganda rooted in the "Burmese Way to Socialism."[12] Yet the general secretary of the party reported that the participant quality and results of the training were poor, and party members finished their training "puffed up with arrogance thinking they alone were the most learned."[13] This damning report, published in 1966, came roughly three years after Than Shwe had been teaching in the program.

The historian Aung Saw Oo says that in order to teach the "Burmese Way to Socialism" instructors would first teach classes about capitalism and then communism, explaining why each was wrong. Then, students would learn how to attack intellectually both capitalism and socialism, concluding that the "Burmese Way to Socialism" was the only way for-ward. According to a source who worked in a senior position at the school at the time, Than Shwe served initially as an instructor in party ideology, and then became the head of the history department. He taught various aspects of history, all related to the "Burmese Way to Socialism" and all with the related purpose of justifying Ne Win's dictatorship. His posting in the history department may explain why in subsequent years diplomats who have met Than Shwe have been subjected to extended lectures on a single particular interpretation of Burmese history. It may also explain Than Shwe's own fascination with Burma's ancient warrior kings and his construction of a new capital regarded as a "royal" seat. According to one

senior source, the history Than Shwe taught was largely propaganda—
rewritten for his, and the regime's, own purposes.

While certain historians cite Than Shwe's involvement in psychological
warfare as the basis for his ability to maintain power in Burma, it may be
more likely that his time as an instructor gave him the intellectual foun-
dations he needed to advance his career. In fact, with the exception of
his graduation from high school (which possibly never took place at all),
his perfunctory study of warfare at the OTS, and a few possible months of
psy-war training, Than Shwe was virtually uneducated until he became
an instructor at the Central School for Political Science. He had no college degree, and went almost immediately from the military field into a
position of teaching history. The idea that Than Shwe never had much
formal schooling is widely believed by the Burmese population. One
military officer currently serving in Burma pointed at a portrait of Than
Shwe in 2009 saying: "Our leader is a very uneducated man." On seeing
a picture of Aung San, he said: "He was a very great leader."

In order to effectively teach the dialectical materialism that included
both so-called "Burmese" materialism and socialism, Than Shwe needed
to understand the topics at least enough to inform his students. Tellingly,
the Central School for Political Science was not run explicitly by the *tatmadaw*, but rather by the Burmese Socialist Program Party. Maung Aung
Myoe writes that the importance of instilling propaganda into the population became more important after the coup: "More institutions were
introduced to indoctrinate both civil servants and military personnel."[14]
Trainees were required to study the "System of Correlation Between Man
and His Environment," the BSPP's ideology, as well as military tactics and
training. Weekly discussions on socialism were required at the platoon
level, while monthly discussions were held at the battalion level.

The "Burmese Way to Socialism" resulted in the almost immediate
introduction of laws aimed at reducing, even eliminating, foreign influence in Burma's economy and society.[15] The first victims of the regime's
policies of nationalization were Chinese, Indian, Anglo-Burmese, and
Westerners who had chosen to remain in the country after independence. Their businesses were seized, their visas not extended, and many
were forced to flee the country. Foreign aid agencies and advisers, non-
governmental organizations (NGOs), such as the Asia Foundation and the

Ford Foundation, and foreign missionaries were all expelled. The teaching of the English language in schools was banned.[16] Fulbright scholarships were terminated, and the Johns Hopkins School of Advanced International Studies, which had a campus in Rangoon, was closed. All major businesses and industries were nationalized, and private enterprise was prohibited. Ironically, given his personal predilection for such pursuits, Ne Win banned ballroom dancing, horse racing, gambling, and beauty contests.[17] On a personal level, Ne Win sought out women with gusto, even sending soldiers to the frontline so that he could pursue their wives, according to a senior advisor to the US embassy working in Burma in the late 1970s and early 1980s. Ne Win married five times.

Student protests against the coup and against the repressive nature of the regime were met with brutal force by the military, setting a precedent for the subsequent crackdowns in 1967, 1970, 1974, 1988, 1996, and 2007. On July 7, 1962, while Than Shwe was apparently still serving as a psychological operations officer in northern Burma, the army raided Rangoon University where hundreds of students were meeting, and the next morning the Student Union Building, where Aung San and others had begun the movement for independence in the 1920s, was blown up.[18]

Throughout this time, the Burmese military regime continued to use manuals copied from the United States. An American advisor to the US embassy said that the General Staff College where senior-level generals were trained was modeled on its American and British counterparts. When this same advisor visited the Defense Services Academy in the late 1970s, he said: "The students were spending more time on politics than on military affairs. The academy had transitioned to becoming a school to train political and governmental leaders." The advisor also pointed out that by the end of the 1970s, "The DSA and OTS were no longer practically training to defeat an armed enemy. [Instead], they sought to demonstrate to the people of Burma that they were willing to crush anyone and everyone."

Ronny Nyein, the DSA graduate, agrees. "When I was in the navy we were called in to deal with some demonstrations in a particular township. The lieutenant in charge told his commanding officer he could stop the demonstrations if he could have permission to kill three of the demonstrators. The commanding officer told him 'yes,' so that is what they did. I have never seen such cruelty like that, it was not necessary at all but that is how they deal with problems." The American advisor believes that, as a result of the top-down military system, "you are simply not going to find generals that will support democratic change."

By 1966 and 1967, it is unclear how Than Shwe's career had advanced. One possible trajectory, advanced by the regime's curriculum vitae of Than Shwe, is he became the quartermaster general of the Light Infantry Division 101. However, this story is undermined by the fact that there was no Light Infantry Division 101 at the time, and no "quartermaster general" position at the infantry or division level—there was only one single "quartermaster general" for the entire army, and Than Shwe certainly did not hold that position.

Alternatively, the *Working People's Daily*'s biography of Than Shwe reports that he did not serve at a light infantry division, but at a light infantry battalion, as the acting commander of the headquarters company.[19] This may explain the discrepancy. Each infantry battalion at the time was comprised of approximately five companies, with usually one company responsible for matters relating to the headquarters of the battalion. In that capacity, the company responsible for headquarters could be interpreted by some as containing quartermaster duties. Therefore, the official curriculum vitae and the *Working People's Daily* biography may overlap, notwithstanding somewhat divergent information. Given the overlapping sets of information in both biographies (neither of which may be correct), one quite likely possibility is that Than Shwe served in the capacity of quartermaster within the battalion, and also as head of the headquarters company. If this was the case, his new position did not entail battlefield service, but coordinating supplies and other matters for mobile troops.

More important than his exact position at this time, however, was what was taking place in Burma's war against the CPB and ethnic minorities. In the mid 1960s, the *tatmadaw* devised a plan to flush out armed groups via a brutal campaign against armed resistance groups known as the "Hpyat lay Hpyat" or "Four Cuts" campaign, which continues to this day.[20] The campaign is designed to sever armed opposition from its grassroots support in the rural population by cutting off supplies of food, funding, recruits, and intelligence. The military carries it out with brutal efficiency against the local population, burning rice fields, executing suspected sympathizers, cordoning off roads and waterways, and generally making local travel difficult. At the same time, in many areas the *tatmadaw* has for decades carried out mass relocations of villages to areas closer to existing *tatmadaw* military bases where they could be carefully watched for signs of support to the resistance. Anyone refusing to relocate would be considered an enemy and shot immediately.[21] Over the years, millions of refugees and internally displaced persons have fled their homes in Burma as a result of actual or threatened tactics that appear to be similar to the Four Cuts campaign. Needless to say, the campaign itself was defined by human rights abuses, and some of the world's worst atrocities have transpired as a result. International organizations such as Human Rights Watch, Amnesty International, Christian Solidarity Worldwide, EarthRights International, and WITNESS, as well as smaller, regionally and locally based groups such as the Free Burma Rangers and many ethnic human rights groups, have documented severe atrocities associated with Four Cuts-style scorched-earth attacks. Of particular concern are the rapes of ethnic minority women carried out alongside Four Cuts operations, documented in gruesome detail by researchers such as the Shan Women's Action Network, the Karen Women's Association, the Women's League of Chinland, and the authors Betsy Apple and Veronika Martin.[22]

That Than Shwe apparently served as quartermaster at an infantry battalion does not necessarily prove that he was initially involved in these atrocities. Indeed, as a quartermaster or leader of a headquarters battalion he may not have had any direct involvement, simply staying on his base. At the same time, Than Shwe appears not to have been involved in the initial defense against a legitimate threat to the people of Burma launched by an almost completely different CPB in early 1968.

The areas in lower Burma where Than Shwe worked in 1967 and 1968 were far from northeastern Burma where the CPB maintained its strongest positions. The CPB's positions close to Rangoon had substantially weakened so much over the years that they maintained only a handful of small bases in the hills near Rangoon and presented no existential threat to Burma, even though the Four Cuts campaign was applied in the area. However, on January 1, 1968, the CPB launched large attacks on *tatmadaw* positions in Shan State. The CPB had previously coordinated with the

Chinese Communist Party but had difficulty in receiving supplies due, in part, to their inability to command a supply line to the Chinese border. This attack, and those to follow, was different from previous battles between the *tatmadaw* and the CPB because, now ensconced near the Chinese border, the CPB could readily arm, refuel, and prepare itself from Chinese territory. The supply line it had earlier failed to create was simple along the Chinese-Burmese border with the Chinese Communist Party directly providing supplies, ammunition, and respite from battle.

These attacks were not simply different because of the CPB's ability to procure supplies from China—this was a different CPB almost entirely. The invasion itself was organized and led largely by the Chinese. Many of the soldiers were not Burman Communists from the central plains areas but Chinese volunteers.[23] The state-controlled media in Rangoon labeled the attacks a "foreign invasion," not without some justification.[24] While the CPB had been in weak standing throughout much of Burma, the well-armed invasion from China quickly succeeded in overrunning numerous towns and cutting key transportation routes used by *tatmadaw* soldiers. Realizing they could not resist the superior forces of the Chinese-backed CPB, many local ethnic groups grudgingly accepted the leadership of the CPB and were subsequently used as cannon fodder in fights between the CPB and *tatmadaw*.

Than Shwe's *Working People's Daily* biography suggests that he was not involved in the initial fighting against the stronger CPB in northeastern Shan State. Instead, it appears that, after being promoted to acting major he served alongside the 77th Light Infantry Division in the exact areas where the Four Cuts campaign was being employed against ethnic minorities, as well as remnants of the CPB in lower Burma. As a result of a new promotion, Than Shwe reportedly "saw active service" in Karen State and the delta and Bago Yoma areas in operations launched by the 77th Light Infantry Division.[25] The light infantry divisions (LIDs), which some describe as modeled on the US 82nd Airborne (without the air power), or more accurately the US 7th Infantry and 10th Mountain divisions, were designed as mobile units that could move about the country and carry out attacks as called for by the *tatmadaw* leadership. According to Martin Smith, the LIDs reported directly to the headquarters of the military instead of to the regional commanders in order to ensure there was no sympathy shown for those under attack. "The intention was deliberate. As counterinsurgency 'shock-troops,' they have few qualms about local sensibilities," argues Smith.[26]

Years later, Ne Win and Than Shwe were to utilize troops without an allegiance to the local population in a similar way, when they brought in out-of-town troops to suppress Burma's 1974 student demonstrations, 1988 national uprising, and the 2007 Saffron Revolution. The 77th Light Infantry Division was the first to be created, followed by the 89th and 99th divisions. Than Shwe spent significant amounts of time working within or alongside both the 77th and 88th LIDs.

Yet Than Shwe's battlefield performance, if any happened at all, was apparently not strong enough to send him to the front against the CPB. Instead, he followed the more traditional movement of officers rotating between the War Office and field operations, and was moved back to the War Office after just a year of involvement in regions associated with the Four Cuts campaign. He rose through the ranks quietly but efficiently. On January 27, 1969, Than Shwe was promoted to full major, and a year later became second general staff officer (G2) at the office of the commander in chief, who was still Ne Win. The staff officers ranked from G3 up to G1, with G1 being the highest posting. Serving as a G2 placed Than Shwe near the epicenter of decision-making within the Burmese military apparatus, and gave him a chance to see the War Office in action. According to a retired officer who served in the War Office at the time, Than Shwe worked in a chain of command that reached all the way to Ne Win. Under Ne Win served his close confidante San Yu, under whom Than Shwe had previously served in the Northern Command and who selected the initial group of students for psy-war training that included Than Shwe.

Within the War Office, Than Shwe worked as a G2 in a section of the operations branch that passed paper between *tatmadaw* positions throughout Burma and the military leadership. According to the retired War Office official, several times a day regional commanders, light infantry divisions, and others would send reports from their field positions back to headquarters near Rangoon. The reports were sent via telegraph to a station near the base of the Shwedagon Pagoda in Rangoon, and were then forwarded to the War Office headquarters. Than Shwe's job was to oversee a few officers operating at the lower G3 level, each of whom would receive reports from different areas of the country. Every morning the G3s would create maps of locations of any combat activities, noting particular statistics such as the number of deaths of government troops, the number of opposition casualties, and any territory gained or lost. G2 officers, like Than Shwe, and their superiors would then decide whether the information merited passing on up the chain of command.

During this time, the Four Cuts counterinsurgency campaign was being carried out against the ethnic minorities in the delta region and the Pegu Yomas. Than Shwe is likely to have seen the reports, especially since he had recently served alongside the 77th Light Infantry Division. At the same time, the most serious existential threat against Burma, the China-backed activities of the reconstituted CPB, preoccupied the minds of most planners in the War Office, and it is highly likely that Than Shwe oversaw field reports from areas of fighting against the CPB. After countless losses, in early 1972 the *tatmadaw* won a seminal victory at the Kunlong Bridge in northwest Shan State with the aid of 105mm Howitzer guns that the United States had supplied to U Nu's government in the 1950s.[27] Nevertheless, intense fighting against the CPB continued for eleven years after the 1968 incursions, and even lasted into the late 1980s. At one point, the threat was so severe that Ne Win invited his erstwhile opponent U Nu and other former democratically elected leaders for talks on resolving the China problem. However, when U Nu proposed a return to multiparty democracy, Ne Win rejected the move and U Nu subsequently went into exile, where he lived until the early 1980s.

Than Shwe's next career move followed the trajectory of several military officials at the time. Having rotated back and forth between the field and administrative positions in the *tatmadaw* headquarters, he once again moved away from headquarters to a field leadership position—this time as a battalion commander of the 1st Burma Regiment, the same place where it is believed he may have started his career after Officer Training School.

Back in the field from 1971 to 1975, Than Shwe worked alongside the 88th Light Infantry Division. According to the *Working People's Daily*, most of Than Shwe's activities were focused in Shan State on operations launched by the 88th Light Infantry Division, presumably against the CPB, and included areas such as Monse/Narle in northern Shan State,

Kengtung/Mong and Khat/Mongoung east of the Salween River, as well as various areas in southern Shan State.[28] In this position, Than Shwe was likely to have had five companies under his command, having probably led one of these companies, or a comparable one, when he previously served as quartermaster at the battalion headquarters. In the field, Ne Win's regime at the time cut deals with drug traffickers in order to help repel the CPB—relationships that continue to dog Than Shwe's government to this day.[29]

While serving at the War Office as a G2 or in his next position as a battalion commander at either the 1st Burma Regiment or Infantry Battalion 1, Than Shwe is believed to have formed a relationship with Aye Ko, which some Burmese dissidents suggest was crucial to his career development.[30] Aye Ko, the second commander of the 88th Light Infantry Division, moved into that position either while Than Shwe served in the War Office or beforehand. Aye Ko also served as head of the Northeast Command and was known as a loyalist to Ne Win, particularly because, according to Ronny Nyein, he had begun his career in the Burma Rifles where many of Ne Win's allies started their careers. Than Shwe's position is likely to have put him in direct communication with Aye Ko. Later, when a failed coup attempt against Ne Win resulted in the purge of dozens of military officials, Aye Ko served as vice chief of staff of the army under Chief of Staff Kyaw Tin from the 4th Burma Rifles, and was in a position to further promote the advancement of Than Shwe to assume the leadership of the 88th Light Infantry Division, a position Aye Ko had earlier held himself. Than Shwe continued to move up the ranks, and while serving as battalion commander he was promoted to lieutenant colonel on September 7, 1972.

During this time Than Shwe worked closely with Sein Thaung, who had graduated from the OTS at the top of his class, after completing a degree at Rangoon University. Sein Thaung was a G3 intelligence officer assigned to the commander of the 88th LID, Myo Aung. The 88th LID was based in Magwe, but Than Shwe served in a forward division headquarters in Kutkai, Shan State, only a short distance from Lashio. At the time, there were fewer divisions than at present in Burma, so the posting was quite important. Than Shwe is believed to have commanded approximately 777 troops. According to Sein Thaung, Than Shwe played no role in fighting since he had developed a reputation as a poor wartime commander. Instead, his troops were a reserve force used for providing security at road crossings, digging ditches, and hauling supplies.

— Sein Thaung worked closely with Than Shwe during this time, and describes him as "not very smart, very quiet, and always willing to say things to please the commander. He always wanted to be near the commander to try to tell him what a good job he was doing. But Myo Aung, and really no one, was impressed." During operations against the CPB, intelligence officers junior to Sein Thaung used to brief both the 88th LID commander as well as the battalion commanders. Sein Thaung reported that while most commanders asked many questions, probing the intelligence officers' assessments, Than Shwe remained silent, looking even sullen, as officers debated and discussed military options. Sein Thaung noted that Than Shwe drank from time to time, but not prolifically, and could usually be seen with a cigarette hanging from his mouth. He was not known to smoke cheroots, the Burmese cigars common throughout the country.

Sein Thaung's criticism of Than Shwe as a quiet leader lacking any kind of dynamism is consistent with the views expressed by many other former *tatmadaw* officers. The critique is borne out, in part, by the fact that many other officers had achieved positions superior to Than Shwe in a much shorter period of time. While Than Shwe was never known to oppose authority, his apparent silence did not get in the way of a slow but steady rise through the ranks. Indeed, four years after his posting in Shan State, he was brought back to the War Office at a more senior position—a first general staff officer (G1) in the operations branch that oversaw both the G2s and G3s below him, as they processed reports from the field and sent out orders related to battlefield operations.

It was Than Shwe's new position as a G1 at the War Office that proved to be a watershed moment in his career. An unexpected series of events rooted in major student protests against military rule in the early 1970s, and culminating in a coup plot against Ne Win in 1976, placed Than Shwe on a rapidly rising career path that would result in him being well positioned to take over the country nearly two decades later. And, as often seems to happen in Burmese history, his rise was a result partially of his willingness to kowtow to authorities, but also just plain luck.

When Than Shwe was promoted to G1 in the War Office, General Tin Oo (who would later go on to become a leader of Aung San Suu Kyi's National League for Democracy) was serving as commander in chief of the armed forces. Than Shwe worked in the operations bureau, directly under Colonel Maung Maung. Tin Oo, as the leader of the military, made all major decisions on battlefield engagements, including both attacks and counterattacks. It was the job of Maung Maung to carry out these orders, and communicate directly with the mobile light infantry divisions as well as the regional commands. Each light infantry division—there were three in total at that time, numbered 77, 88, and 99—had over seven thousand troops, in theory. The light infantry divisions were comprised of ten battalions, each made up of 777 troops. In reality, the light infantry divisions probably had fewer troops, but 7,770 was the goal. The regional commands, seven in total, were comprised of a much larger number of troops. The regional commands held positions such as forts, headquarters, and forward positions, while the light infantry divisions could be moved all over the country according to need. The LIDs fought both the CPB as well as nationalist parties of the Karen and other ethnic groups, such as the Karen National Union.

Than Shwe was the highest-ranking official that served directly under Maung Maung as a staff member in the War Office, and therefore was involved in the execution of Tin Oo's plans. The operations bureau often worked twenty-four hours a day, responding to orders concerning the logistics of moving troops, ammunition, supplies, and family members.

Tin Oo was a popular leader among many officers in the War Office, and had even earned a reputation as a reformer. He was also popular among civilian reformers. While claiming to be protecting the Burmese people from Communist rule, Ne Win's regime had violently crushed its own people. Numerous high profile and widespread student demonstrations took place in Burma in the early 1970s, with the aim of bringing an end to the country's military dictatorship. The death of U Thant, the Burmese-born former UN secretary-general, proved a catalyst for one of that period's most prominent student movements.

In April 1974, students at Rangoon University organized demonstrations calling for a return of student rights, such as the right to form a representative student union. The protests, while small, followed in the tradition of student protests of 1967 and 1970, as well as those against the military coup in 1962, which Ne Win crushed by dynamiting the student union building and reportedly killing hundreds of students peacefully protesting inside. The military responded with force to the early 1974 demonstrations, arresting hundreds of dissidents. In May, workers in Myit Nge of the Mandalay Division organized protests that spread throughout many major urban areas. The workers were calling primarily for improved workers' rights, as well as action to address rapidly rising commodity prices that came about as a result of the "Burmese Way to Socialism." The workers' uprising was similarly crushed by the Ne Win regime, and between thirty and forty workers were killed, according to Aung Saw Oo. Undeterred, students at several Rangoon universities seized on the death of U Thant to organize further demonstrations against Ne Win's rule.

According to Mya Win, a medical student at the time at the Institute of Medicine 1 in Rangoon, student leaders were looking for an opportunity to protest against Ne Win, and U Thant's death provided the occasion. Several hours before the burial, U Thant's coffin was placed on display in Kyeikkasan Stadium, a home to horse racing before Ne Win banned the sport. Thousands of students poured into the stadium, and, having planned to make their move, literally grabbed U Thant's body and coffin and took it back to Rangoon University. The students were angered that the body of U Thant, an ally of previous democratic leader U Nu and, therefore, disliked by Ne Win, would be buried in a traditional cemetery, instead of somewhere more honorable. The move grew into major demonstrations involving dozens of schools in much of the country, and Ne Win responded with force, arresting thousands of students and killing others. Mya Win was lucky enough to escape the carnage.

Ne Win closed many schools and universities as a result of the U Thant protests, only angering students further. When the schools reopened in 1975, students again protested in June, on the anniversary of the previous year's uprising. The next year in March 1976, students organized protests to commemorate what would have been the hundredth birthday of one of Burma's most respected political leaders Thakin Kodaw Hmaing, who had served as a leader of Burma's Dobama Movement that led efforts to end British rule in Burma. Thakin Kodaw Hmaing had worked closely alongside the country's independence hero Aung San and authored some of

Burma's most well-known stage plays, news articles, and poems.[31] Again, the military cracked down on the demonstrators.

By this time, Ne Win, who professed to have taken power in order to hold the country together, was despised by much of the population. Piling on the pressure, in the summer of 1976, Kyaw Zaw, one of the original Thirty Comrades that helped lead Burma's independence struggle, fled from Burma and began broadcasting in-depth interviews about Ne Win via the CPB's radio station. In the interviews, according to Martin Smith, Kyaw Zaw revealed that General Aung San had considered removing Ne Win from the military because of his "fascist" tendencies. Kyaw Zaw himself called Ne Win "morally depraved."[32]

According to Mya Win, during many of the demonstrations throughout the mid-1970s students and other leaders would shout chants against Ne Win such as "Ne Win and San Yu, we don't like you, U Tin Oo, we like you." San Yu, who had helped pilot the advancement of the psychological warfare program, was serving in the 1970s as commander in chief of the *tatmadaw*, before Tin Oo's appointment in 1974, and was known as a hardline defender of Ne Win's regime. San Yu had also been a member of Ne Win's original Revolutionary Council that was established when Ne Win seized power in 1962.

While his heroics on the battlefield played a role, Tin Oo's popularity is attributed by democracy activists to his willingness to speak out against Ne Win's policies, especially with regard to cracking down on demonstrators. Although Tin Oo may never have made such pronouncements in public, he regularly confronted Ne Win's hardline cronies at high-level meetings of the Burma Socialist Program Party. Word of Tin Oo's reformist tendencies quickly leaked out to the general population, and student and workers' leaders looked to him to possibly replace Ne Win and usher in a new era of reform in the country.

Ne Win—always fearful of any threat to his rule—swiftly removed Tin Oo. Working closely with another person also named Tin Oo, who was head of military intelligence (often known as "MI" Tin Oo), Ne Win devised trumped-up charges of corruption against Tin Oo, which he used as a pretext to remove him from power. Specifically, according to a former Burmese intelligence official now living in the United States, Tin Oo's wife was charged with accepting free items, including door hinges from

Thailand that Tin Oo had used in the construction of his home. In reality, according to the intelligence official, Tin Oo knew nothing of the door hinges. His wife had placed an order for the goods from Thailand, and an intelligence official from the BSPP based in Thailand, Colonel Wan Tun, arranged for their delivery. When Tin Oo's wife attempted to pay for the hinges, she was repeatedly told not to worry, that all had been taken care of. In retrospect, many believe that Tin Oo, in this way, was set-up by Ne Win and the intelligence chief "MI" Tin Oo. When the moment arrived for Ne Win to make his move, the photos of the door hinges from years earlier miraculously appeared at the behest of the intelligence chief. Tin Oo denied all the charges against him but offered his resignation anyway, and it was accepted.

Before his resignation, Tin Oo made moves to transfer power to a new commander in chief, Kyaw Htin, who had been one of three top leaders serving directly beneath him (the three were vice chiefs of staff of the army, navy, and air force). Kyaw Htin had served as the army's vice chief of staff.

As Kyaw Htin prepared to take over as commander in chief, anger at the effective dismissal of Tin Oo reverberated throughout parts of the military establishment. Many military leaders by this time had grown deeply disenchanted with Ne Win's rule, together with the economic devastation heaped on the country by the "Burmese Way to Socialism." The frustration reached a boiling point, especially with Ohn Kyaw Myint, who served as the personal assistant to the new commander in chief, Kyaw Htin. According to one of the officers involved in the plot, Ohn Kyaw Myint and several other young officers began plotting a coup to remove Ne Win, and created a complex plan that apparently included taking over the country's radio station, surrounding the homes of key BSPP leaders, assassinating Ne Win and San Yu, and then stepping back and handing the country over to civilian rule. Like many democracy activists in Burma, Ohn Kyaw Myint and the rest of the coup plotters were staunchly anti-Communist and in no way sympathetic to the CPB, but were also firmly opposed to the brutal practices of Ne Win that included the execution of Burmese student protestors, the imprisonment of political activists, and the demonization of democratic rule. Many people supported U Nu, the country's last democratically elected prime minister, and fervently hoped to convene a high-level meeting of Burmese politicians that would reorient the country towards the path of freedom.

Despite the involvement of dozens of top military officials, Than Shwe was never invited to join the efforts. His marginalization was amplified particularly by the fact that his direct superior, Maung Maung, was one of the coup's key leaders. Throughout the military structure, Ohn Kyaw Myint and the other coup plotters worked closely with many military leaders as well as their assistants. In the case of Than Shwe, however, his help not only was never sought, it was purposely avoided. According to one of the coup plotters that was close to Tin Oo, Than Shwe was viewed as an "idiot" that "would immediately inform on everyone else if he knew of the efforts." Yet, the same coup plotter points out that the operations offices under Than Shwe were so busy pushing paper that it would have been difficult, in any case, to recruit Than Shwe to the coup effort.

In the end, the coup attempt never even happened. According to the source that had worked on the coup plot, the move, originally intended to occur on Armed Forces Day, March 27, 1976, was delayed after the head of the military's central command moved a group of soldiers away from their position in front of the government's main national radio station. The coup leaders had planned on including those troops in the coup, and now the leaders needed to reach out to the new troops stationed in the same location. Meanwhile, one of the coup participants, Captain Win Thein, approached Minister of Mines Than Tin to seek his support for the effort. Than Tin promptly informed Ne Win and the coup leaders were arrested. The plot was over.

Ohn Kyaw Myint, realizing he was going to be arrested by "MI" Tin Oo, fled to the American ambassador's compound and sought a meeting. According to the *New York Times*, US Ambassador David Osborn or one of his staff refused to allow him into the house, instead driving him back into town in an embassy car "in line with current anti-terrorist security practices . . . to remove any possible threat to the ambassador." The next morning, Osborn contacted Burmese officials to inform them that a man claiming to be a Burmese military officer had requested asylum and that he had been told: "The embassy would have no choice but to hand him over to the authorities if they asked for him." However, Osborn refused to give the identity of Ohn Kyaw Myint to Ne Win's regime. Perhaps the

United States, deeply involved in fighting communism in Southeast Asia, could not be seen as undermining the Ne Win government, which, despite its professed commitment to socialism, was pulling out the stops to defeat the CPB. Many Burmese, to this day, question the veracity of Osborn's refusal to identify Ohn Kyaw Myint, especially after the *New York Times* reported it had "learned independently" that Osborn had not contacted the Burmese Foreign Ministry regarding the incident, as would have been standard practice, but instead communicated with the Burmese intelligence chief "MI" Tin Oo.[33] Adding to the mystery, "MI" Tin Oo led the efforts, on behalf of Ne Win, to arrest the dissident military officials.

Refused assistance by the US embassy and possibly informed upon, Ohn Kyaw Myint was arrested shortly thereafter, tried before a military court, and hanged. The other coup plotters were also tried and sentenced to long terms in prison, though some were subsequently released during general amnesties granted by Ne Win (these amnesties were used in an attempt to woo dissidents to turn themselves in, such as U Nu, who had fled to the jungles and taken up arms against Ne Win's regime). Tin Oo and others were released as part of the amnesties.

In one fell swoop, Ne Win, perhaps with the assistance of the American embassy, had inadvertently helped to clear the path for Than Shwe's rise to power. The 1976 coup attempt was one of those flukes of history, the implications of which would not be fully understood for years to come. With many of the most charismatic military leadership having attempted to usurp his rule, Ne Win placed a new priority on personal loyalty. It was clear that going forward he would brook no dissent from popular critics like Tin Oo, but instead rapidly elevating "yes-men" such as Than Shwe. Indeed, cleared of a major chunk of dissent from within the military apparatus, the next twelve years of military rule saw Ne Win increasingly distant from the Burmese population. His behavior grew more erratic, and his policy decisions resembled little in the way of standard governance. By surrounding himself with an insular group of military cadres, he would make a series of decisions that ultimately led to his own downfall. No one benefited from this more than Than Shwe, the farm boy from Kyaukse.

The attempted coup was not the only momentous event Than Shwe was to witness. While in the office of the commander in chief, Than Shwe dealt with both the ethnic nationalities' push for autonomy as well as the CPB's major attacks against the *tatmadaw*. According to numerous sources that served in the *tatmadaw* at the time, the CPB by this time had become the strongest army in Burma, with at least ten thousand troops under arms. Following earlier attacks in the 1960s, by the mid-1970s the CPB was launching major attacks in an attempt to secure ground that it had lost in previous years east of the Salween River and elsewhere. The CPB was well stocked with arms and munitions from China, even though the Chinese government also courted Ne Win's military regime. The practice, according to Henry Kamm of the *New York Times*, was well accepted at the time. The Chinese government often dealt with foreign governments under which it supported Communist insurgencies. Kamm wrote: "Peking contends that good relations with the Burmese government are independent of the friendly ties with the Burmese Communist Party."[34] In this case, the Communist Party of China supported the CPB while the Chinese government simultaneously reached out to Ne Win's regime.

The attacks by the CPB had devastating effects, with the Communist forces claiming to have killed over five hundred troops, including the deputy commander of the 99th Light Infantry Division. Martin Smith found evidence suggesting the attacks were carried out from the east side of the Salween River. It appears that the Communists crossed over to the west bank near Tangyan and attacked areas controlled from Rangoon.[35]

While Than Shwe was still serving in the War Office under Kyaw Tin and Aye Ko, he witnessed the reprimand of Tun Yi, the regional commander of the entire Eastern Command that was based out of Taunggyi. Tun Yi was initially viewed as a successful military leader, even though he had not succeeded in entirely defeating the Communists. Among other military campaigns, he led the one at Kunlong Bridge, aided by America Howitzer guns, which marked a major victory against the China-backed CPB in early 1972. However, Tun Yi stumbled upon one significant political roadblock. According to Aung Saw Oo, as the head of the Eastern Regional Command (one of the two commands most important in fighting the CPB), Tun Yi failed to edit a regional party conference proceeding that criticized the socialist system. Consistency of message and complete support for Ne Win's professed ideology were a necessity for obtaining promotions, and Tun Yi had failed to fully comply. His error was especially problematic in the wake of the failed assassination of Ne Win, which had been rooted in dissatisfaction with the regime's disastrous economic and political policies. Such a mistake by Tun Yi would simply not be tolerated.

Tun Yi was a headstrong military leader who had carried out orders from Ne Win without dissent. He had been nicknamed "Napoleon" by the first batch of DSA students, according to one of them. It was a moniker that stuck with him throughout his life. But although Tun Yi was committed to defeating the CPB, it appears that Ne Win wanted to make an example of him, without losing one of his more valued fighters. According to Aung Saw Oo, instead of sacking him from the military, Tun Yi was suspended from his post and transferred to the Institute of Defense near the War Office in Mingaladon. As such, he worked in a position beneath Than Shwe, who was still serving as a general staff officer at the War Office. Perhaps confident in his rising stature for having not participated in the coup attempt or perhaps wanting to show his exemplary loyalty, Aung Saw Oo says that Than Shwe treated Tun Yi badly.

Shortly thereafter Than Shwe was granted another promotion, as were many officers that had not participated in the coup plot. Offered a leadership position, Than Shwe left the War Office in early 1977 and became either acting divisional commander or tactical commander of the 88th Light Infantry Division, which was participating in the fight against the CPB in Shan State. This position has been described by the military regime as the "deputy commander" of the 88th Light Infantry Division, but others have explained Than Shwe first served as tactical commander and was then promoted to deputy commander. In this capacity, he and his commander likely had nearly eight thousand troops under their control.

Then, events outside of Than Shwe's control benefited his career again. The 88th Light Infantry Division, as well as other divisions, had made very little progress against the CPB. Angered at the continuing defeats, Ne Win moved to sack two leaders of the anti-Communist military effort, including the leader of the Northeast Command, Min Naung, and, more importantly for Than Shwe's career, Myint Lwin, the lead commander of the 88th Light Infantry Division. As Martin Smith has noted, Min Naung was not only recalled from the front, but was "demoted to head of the country's fire service department," a humiliating move intended to "send a warning to other senior military officers."[36] Clearly, Ne Win sought a decisive defeat of the CPB.

Than Shwe's star was on the rise due, in part, to the fact that he had not angered any of his direct superiors. Next in line in the rankings, he became the full commander of the 88th Light Infantry Division on March 29, 1980. While focused on fighting the CPB, this posting was not purely a military endeavor. According to Ronny Nyein, LID commanders were required to be members of the Burma Socialist Program Party. On his official curriculum vitae, Than Shwe was elected to the Central Committee at the BSPP's Fourth Party Congress in 1981—a position that was important to advancement in the *tatmadaw* after the 1976 coup plot. While an honor for Than Shwe, membership in the Central Committee also served a dual purpose for Ne Win—it allowed him to intensify his oversight of commanders via the military chain of command as well as the party infrastructure.

According to Aung Saw Oo, those working for Ne Win such as Aye Ko had faith in Than Shwe's political loyalty but doubted his military prowess. In order to ensure that his orders were carried out by Than Shwe and others throughout the military apparatus, Ne Win established two new positions, with the title "Military Operation Commander." Appointed to fill the spot as commander of the Northern Operation Command was none other than Colonel Tun Yi, who Than Shwe had mistreated while serving at the War Office. Essentially, Than Shwe had been promoted and then practically demoted, through the appointment of an additional layer of superior officers. Than Shwe got the message—as in the past, he kowtowed to his new superiors and showed great deference, fearful of Tun Yi's direct ties to the War Office and his influential reputation.

Than Shwe never made substantial gains against the CPB. According to one DSA graduate who served in the 66th Light Infantry Division that often aided the 88th Light Infantry Division, "Than Shwe was a total failure. He made no progress at all against the Burma Communist Party." Aung Kyaw Zaw, a former CPB soldier and son of one of the Communist leaders, described Than Shwe as "a very incompetent soldier" who "lost so many battles."

"Operation King Conqueror" was launched on November 19, 1979, in response to attacks on the *tatmadaw* by the CPB, and with the aim of capturing the Communist headquarters at Panghsang "before Christmas."[37] Although the *tatmadaw* failed to achieve that goal, they regained control of Mawhpa and established a forward base at Loi Hsia-Kao Mountain, thirty kilometers west of Panghsang.[38] In August 1980, Keyes Beech, a journalist for the *Los Angeles Times*, visited Taunggyi, the headquarters of the *tatmadaw*'s Eastern Command close to where Than Shwe headed the 88th Light Infantry Division (the Northeast Command was based further north in Lashio). He reported that the *tatmadaw* had suffered massive casualties in its offensive against the CPB across the Salween River into northeast Burma, an area near the Chinese border. Beech wrote that the *tatmadaw* lost between four and five thousand men in the fighting, and that tourists had seen scores of injured Burmese being hauled off planes in Rangoon.[39] *The New York Times* appeared to confirm these reports, writing in August 1980 that Burmese government sources put the casualties at five hundred dead and two thousand wounded.[40]

At the time of his leadership in the 88th LID, Than Shwe's sole goal was to fight the CPB. However, nearly all the operations he participated in failed. Aung Kyaw Zaw, the former CPB soldier, says Than Shwe only had one battle victory in his entire time fighting the CPB, and that was on April 11, 1980, when his troops, under the command of Aung Phone, were able to defeat a CPB battalion at Mon Yang. The *tatmadaw* had been fighting the CPB in Mon Yang since 1975. Finally in the space of three or four hours, the *tatmadaw* captured three or four posts, although they still did not capture the CPB's main camp in the area. Nevertheless, the loss was a blow to the CPB. "We lost so many people. Within one hour, we buried at least seven people, including three company commanders and a battalion commander. There were at least 120 casualties. It was the biggest loss in our history, and Than Shwe's only victory—so he is very fond of Aung Phone." Aung Phone later became the forestry minister and, despite serious allegations of corruption, was protected by Than Shwe.

With the exception of this one victory, Than Shwe's troops faced defeat after defeat at the hands of the CPB. Aung Lynn Htut, the former intelligence officer who worked at the Burmese embassy in Washington DC and who had also served in the 66th Light Infantry Division, said that Than Shwe's failures were due, in part, to his poor leadership, but also a lack of weapons. The CPB had access to weapons supplies up and down the

Chinese border, and the few journalists who visited the area often commented on the scale and scope of available weaponry, which included automatic weapons, rocket launchers, set artillery pieces, and ammunition. In some ways, says Aung Lynn Htut, the *tatmadaw* was simply outgunned. At the same time, China assisted the CPB with its transportation needs, allowing CPB members to enter China from northern Burma and then travel further south to where other CPB bases were located. In this way, CPB members could avoid the difficult path of traveling through areas controlled by the *tatmadaw*.

Because the CPB held defensive units and plentiful weaponry across the border in China, sources also confirm that Than Shwe apparently could not at that time use the full range of the Four Cuts policy that had proved devastating against the civilian populations in the delta region, south and west of Rangoon. The Four Cuts had also been used by the *tatmadaw* in the Pegu Yomas, but with an arguably diminished level of brutality. Again and again, Than Shwe carried out offensive and defensive attacks against the CPB, and again and again, he failed.

However, Than Shwe's failures were not simply due to a lack of equipment. Aung Kyaw Zaw claims that as a result of one six-day battle, which started on June 20, 1980, near the Laos border, the Communists occupied one of the 88th Light Infantry Division's outposts and captured a significant supply of guns, artillery, and ammunition. After the outpost was overrun, the vice chief of staff, General Tun Yi, sent in Brigadier-General Hla Oo, who was in charge of the No. 1 Special Command to Taunggyi. Hla Oo ordered Than Shwe to leave his post in Kengtung and move his troops into Khangtang and the Loi Mwe Valley. Than Shwe heeded the command but switched off his radio for two days. "He went to sleep in the valley," says Aung Kyaw Zaw. "He didn't want to fight." When he finally switched on his radio, the CPB intercepted the communications, and what they heard must have sounded hilarious to them. "Hla Oo was scolding Than Shwe. 'Why did you switch off the radio?' he asked. Aye San, the eastern regional commander, and Hla Oo were very angry with Than Shwe. They told him to take off his badge and his rank, and hand them over to senior officers. They told him he was incapable of doing his job. Than Shwe sounded very afraid, but came up with the excuse that he was worried about CPB intercepting his communications."

Yet, unlike Min Naung and other commanders, Than Shwe was neither sacked nor demoted for his repeated battlefield failures. Instead—as is often the case in Burma—he was promoted, perhaps for his loyalty. Aung Kyaw Zaw says, "Ne Win did not like good soldiers. He only liked followers, dull people like Than Shwe, not leaders. Than Shwe was dependent on Ne Win and very obedient."

It is not possible to determine who exactly saved Than Shwe's career at this point, given his failures on the battlefield. Since Ne Win had placed a new premium on personal loyalty after the 1976 coup attempt and given that Than Shwe's career path had been similar to Aye Ko's, it may be that Aye Ko advocated Than Shwe's promotion. As an active member of the BSPP, Than Shwe participated in numerous party meetings and apparently firmly understood the tenets of the "Burmese Way to Socialism," especially after having taught them at the Central School for Political Science, thereby exhibiting his loyalty to the existing power structure and its leadership. Ronny Nyein supports this speculation: "Aye Ko was Than Shwe's mentor, and Than Shwe was his pet." Additionally, Nyein points out that Than Shwe was the youngest LID commander at the time, and if Aye Ko was seeking support for his position at the helm of the *tatmadaw*, one way to ensure loyalty was to promote younger officers who would then feel beholden to their superiors.

The 1976 coup plot was not the only reason that Ne Win, Aye Ko, Kyaw Tin, and San Yu were seeking loyalty from the younger officers. At the BSPP's Third Party Congress, Ne Win suffered a difficult political setback. At all previous Party Congresses, which took place every four years beginning in 1969, the thousands of party delegates choosing the leadership of the BSPP had always awarded Ne Win the top number of votes. However, in February 1977 several Central Committee members of the BSPP, including Tun Lin, Than Sein, Tin Win Nyo, and Tin Aye Kyaw, led an effort to unseat Ne Win from within the party structure. Frustrated with the stagnating economy, Ne Win's erratic leadership style, and, as many argue, apparent leftist tendencies, they recruited party members to vote for other candidates. Instead of receiving the most votes and, therefore, the presumed chairmanship of the party, Ne Win came in further down the ballot. Striking back, Ne Win held an extraordinary Party Congress months later and engineered a victory. In the process and aftermath, he arrested many of the members of the Central Committee that had attempted to diminish his power. Aung Saw Oo, who was in prison at the time, remembers being moved from his cell to make space for the newly incarcerated Central Committee plotters.

Ne Win faced another challenge from within the military apparatus in the early 1980s. His intelligence chief "MI" Tin Oo had quietly begun amassing power from within the intelligence structure in order, many suspect, to eventually remove Ne Win. "MI" Tin Oo was in a prime position to build personal loyalty through the recruitment of replacements because Ne Win had tasked him with finding "dirt" on the BSPP Central Committee members that had not voted for him at the 1977 Party Congress. By 1983 Ne Win's frustration with "MI" Tin Oo came to a head, and he was unceremoniously removed, along with many other intelligence officers who were perceived as loyal to "MI" Tin Oo. While Ne Win had successfully removed a rival from within the military apparatus, the purge also came with a major downside. In 1983 North Korean government agents carried out a brazen bombing attack that killed four South Korean ministers visiting Rangoon. Burmese intelligence had failed to learn of the plot in advance, thus prompting many to suspect that the dismantling of the intelligence structures had effectively permitted such an attack. An interim intelligence chief served for a very short period of time, followed by the appointment of Khin Nyunt, who was to play a leading role in Burmese politics for nearly two decades until he was purged by Than Shwe, ironically in almost the exact same style that "MI" Tin Oo had been removed by Ne Win.

Amidst the political backdrop of the 1976 coup plot, the 1977 Party Congress defeat, and the removal of intelligence chief "MI" Tin Oo in 1983, Ne Win made several key moves to shore up his complete dominance in Burma. First, many civilian members of the BSPP Central Committee were replaced with military officials, a plan initially executed by intelligence chief "MI" Tin Oo. Second, seeking to avoid a repeat of the 1977 Central Committee vote debacle, Ne Win moved to ensure that township and district level party leadership positions were stacked with members of the military rather than civilians, thus ensuring that in future Party Congress sessions he could use the military chain of command to guarantee his victory. Finally, Ne Win sought to promote regional commanders who were known to be loyal both to the military and to himself. Than Shwe, known as a "yes-man" soldier and acolyte of Ne Win's top associates Aye Ko and San Yu, seemed a perfect candidate. Despite Than Shwe's failures on the battlefield, his loyalty ensured the ongoing allegiance of Ne Win's close associates, particularly, many suggest, Aye Ko. At the same time, Than Shwe's age—fifty years old—made him quite junior in the military apparatus. Utilizing a tactic that Than Shwe himself would follow years later, Ne Win sought to promote junior commanders in what many believe was an attempt to ensure their loyalty as a measure of gratitude for major career advancement.

In 1983 Than Shwe was promoted from commanding the 88th Light Infantry Division to a much higher posting—the head of the entire Southwest Command based in Bassein, now called Pathein, in the Irrawaddy Division, where he eventually became a brigadier general. This took him away from the frontlines, as there was no large-scale active fighting in this area at the time. According to one man who knew him well at this point in his career, Than Shwe was one of the most humble and approachable of the regional commanders. "He was a very nice guy," said this source, who worked for him and now lives in exile. "He got on well with everybody. He was very friendly. His wife and his family were also very nice. They did not take advantage of his position at that time. They lived like ordinary people, not like other commanders. We could go to their house anytime. When he traveled, he would often wear plain clothes, and only changed into his military uniform when he was near an army camp. He would chat to people freely. I was surprised when he became vice president after 1988, and then head of state. It is strange realizing how a person can change so much. I think he changed due to power."

This description of Than Shwe is clearly at odds with what we know of him now and what was reported of him earlier, but it is confirmed by another person that knew him at the time, who describes him as "a moderate person, who lived an ordinary life. His kids went to school in an army truck." One of his activities as regional commander included opening volleyball tournaments. One observation made by this source was that Than Shwe was extremely loyal to the military and to the BSPP. "He never talked about the country and its prospects with me. He seemed only focused on pleasing the higher officers and leaders. He always praised the leaders, and never showed any ambition. He was certainly proud of being a soldier. He followed BSPP orders very carefully." As regional commander Than Shwe was also chairman of the BSPP in the region, and so would regularly meet with local BSPP officials when traveling around the delta. "He often gave long speeches, sometimes for two hours nonstop. He was very keen on talking about politics, and telling people the BSPP line. He would talk about the party's policies and targets, in agriculture or development. He talked a lot, sometimes long into the night, but did not listen much."

Than Shwe was the youngest regional commander. He was known to observers, at the time, as someone who never smoked or drank, and apart from suffering hay fever, he was in good health. Although not regarded as particularly intelligent, he read the propaganda newspapers avidly. A keen golfer who had learned how to play from his intelligence officer Kyaw Win while serving in the 88th LID, he taught some of his subordinates to play. He resisted the trappings of his position at the time, and was often given GQ sports shirts as gifts. Although they were very fashionable, he never wore them. Instead, he allowed other officers to take them to resell.

Still a betel nut chewer, Than Shwe had two privates who accompanied him at all times. They were responsible for his betel nut supplies. According to one of his former staff members, the two privates carried a box around whenever they traveled with him and would prepare the betel nut for him. One day, however, Than Shwe abruptly announced he had given up the habit, and he was never seen chewing betel nut again.

Than Shwe's later displays of devout Buddhism and the influence of astrology were not in evidence at this time, according to his former staff member, supporting the contention that Than Shwe does not make major decisions based on astrology. But one passion he showed in the delta continued in his later years: an enthusiasm for infrastructure projects. "He was very keen on improving accessibility to the delta," said the former staff member. "Because so much of the delta is river, he always said we needed to build more bridges and more roads. He was very interested in development."

This was a passion he shared with Indonesia's dictator, General Suharto. Journalist Richard Lloyd Parry says of Suharto that development was "the third pillar" of his regime and the one in which he took the most pride.

"Factories and clinics and electricity grids" delighted the Indonesian dictator. "Suharto revelled in these achievements; he was never happier than at the inauguration of a new power station or on the production line of a condom factory," Lloyd Parry writes.[41] Than Shwe was just the same, but an important difference is that he has focused much more on basic infrastructure such as roads and production plants, and also on exporting Burma's natural resources, instead of using them for the good of the Burmese people. The construction of a major road between Rangoon and Mandalay especially caught his attention. Than Shwe's former staff member recalls that Than Shwe often went to see how the road was developing. "It was the first highway in the western part of the Irrawaddy, and like most roads, it was built by the Ministry of Construction in a joint-venture initiative with the Japanese. He would talk to the engineers and to the village heads to encourage the construction of the road. He got on very well with the engineers." Than Shwe developed a habit in his capacity as local commander of offering orders and advice on every subject imaginable, typically on issues about which he knew very little. In addition to construction, he showed a particular interest in agriculture, giving instructions to the farming population, in line with the goals of the Ne Win government, even though his entire professional career had been in the military.

Than Shwe's ability to focus on construction and infrastructure projects, as well as the rice trade (the government had a monopoly on this trade at the time) was made possible because the Irrawaddy Division, the delta region of Burma to the west and south of Rangoon, had been largely pacified. Previously a stronghold of support for both the CPB and the Karen resistance, earlier commanders of the division had carried out the brutal Four Cuts counterinsurgency campaigns. Razing villages, murdering scores of innocent civilians, and relocating civilian populations next to military encampments, the *tatmadaw* had crushed virtually all military resistance in the region. The execution of the "Four Cuts" policy was led in part by Aye Ko, who is rumored to have facilitated Than Shwe's transfer to the Irrawaddy posting.

While military officials who knew Than Shwe at the time believed him to be an honest, if quiet and ineffective, commander, the civilian population saw another side. According to one source who grew up in the area, Than Shwe oversaw the wedding of his daughter Kyaing Than Shwe to a young soldier named Thein Naing. According to this source, who was a close friend of the young soldier, Thein Naing's parents were purposely excluded from the wedding since Than Shwe believed it would be inappropriate to associate with a lowly farming family. Even when Thein Naing's parents were seriously ill, the source said, neither Than Shwe nor his wife made an effort to visit the couple, an extremely rude affront in traditional Burmese culture. Nevertheless, Thein Naing has done well under Than Shwe. He now reportedly serves as the Mingaladon region air commander, and is widely expected to be appointed head of Burma's air force in the future. Like Than Shwe's other relatives, he has been richly rewarded for his loyalty.

It was during his time as southwest regional commander that Than Shwe's name first appeared in the state-run newspaper, the *Working People's Daily*. On November 10, 1983, the paper ran an article about Than Shwe opening a ceremony on agriculture and livestock,[42] and then on December 7 inspecting the harvest.[43] On January 9, 1984, he is reported to have visited a timber-purchasing camp, and to have held discussions with "the working people" on "matters relating to organization, social affairs, successful implementation of the economic plan, and transport and communication affairs."[44] The first known photograph of Than Shwe was published in the *Working People's Daily* on April 28, 1984, where he is seen leading a co-ordination meeting on the cultivation and production of crops in the Irrawaddy Division.[45] Although an earlier picture on January 30 shows a soldier that appears to be Than Shwe, the quality of the photograph is not good enough to confirm the soldier's identity. In neither picture is the soldier wearing many medals, perhaps further advancing suspicions that the medals that adorn Than Shwe's uniform today were awarded for longevity of military service, not for active combat service. Some Burmese dissidents joke that Than Shwe has not actually won any awards or medals, but simply awarded them to himself when he reached a senior position in the regime.

Although the newspaper tended only to report on the regime's supposed successes as well as the activities of top members of the military and the BSPP, the reports of Than Shwe at this time give an outline of his activities. Accordingly, it appears that this period began to define Than Shwe's future rule, particularly influencing the content of the new constitution that was drafted almost twenty-five years later. As regional commander, Than Shwe showed the same interference with the media and the judiciary, and he permitted the same culture of impunity in regard to human and civil rights violations that he presides over as head of state today.

Than Shwe turned his attention to the media and the judiciary while serving in the Southwestern Command. In November 1983, he hosted a meeting on journalism that was aimed at "bringing out literature beneficial to the working people"—a euphemism for censorship rules and exercising military control over the media.[46] The meeting was held with journalists to "explain" government practices, but like many such meetings later held by the Than Shwe regime, journalists reported that the purpose was to instill fear and encourage self-censorship, so that their reporting would extol the virtues of the military.[47] In late 1983, Than Shwe held a meeting with judges in the Irrawaddy Division where he delivered a speech that was meant to assert, once again euphemistically, the military's intention to exert control over the judiciary.[48]

These were the early signs of Than Shwe's later rule. Burma's new constitution, introduced in 2008, stipulates that parliament will have no oversight responsibilities with regard to the military, and all members of the military will have complete immunity from prosecution for any act carried out under state orders. In sum, the military will exercise its own legal affairs in direct contravention of the Geneva Conventions and in complete disregard of the Rome Statute of the International Criminal Court.

Forced labor was widespread under Than Shwe's regional command, according to multiple sources that lived in the region during that time. Even the *Working People's Daily* acknowledged the use of forced labor. On December 30, 1983, over thirty-six hundred "volunteers" participated in the digging of a "15,725 foot-long drainage ditch on both sides of the Southwest Command Headquarters Road."[49] Nay Lin, who was raised in the Irrawaddy Division, recalls that such "volunteer" efforts were in no way voluntary. Indeed, the United States Department of Labor in the late 1990s launched a comprehensive investigation into the use of forced labor by Than Shwe's regime. Interviews with dozens of "volunteer" laborers confirmed the practice was not voluntary.[50] In June 2000, the International

Labour Organization (ILO), a UN agency, invoked Article 33 of its constitution for the first time in its eighty-year history, effectively authorizing the imposition of international sanctions on Burma. Two years earlier, an ILO commission of inquiry into forced labor in Burma found that hundreds of thousands of Burmese had been subjected to the practice, a violation of prohibitions against slavery under the ILO Charter.[51]

As a regional commander, Than Shwe also developed the habit of inflating claims about his success in improving people's lives. On December 24, 1983, he held a ceremony to "mark total victory over illiteracy in the entire Irrawaddy Division."[52] The regime arranged for twenty two-thousand people to attend the event. Using military language, the *Working People's Daily* reported that "working people converged on the venue in six columns ... together with standard bearers."[53] That Than Shwe had emerged victorious in a campaign to eradicate illiteracy is highly suspect. Nay Lin, who was a young student at the time, reports he knew "many, many" people who could not read, and there was "no chance" that 95 percent of the population was able to read. U Mya Win, a medical student from the same area, offers a similar conclusion, with a caveat: "Definitely, 95 percent of the people were not literate. There is no chance [of that]. Perhaps 95 percent of the people could read a word or two. The surveys measuring reading were skewed to produce victory, not to show accuracy."

Twenty-five years later, Than Shwe would again show a predilection for exaggerated claims and falsifying government statistics when his regime announced that 92 percent of the people had voted in favor of the new constitution in a national referendum held in May 2008, in which supposedly 99 percent of voters had turned out to vote. Foreign diplomats denounced these figures, particularly as the vote occurred a little over a week after Cyclone Nargis had destroyed the livelihoods of an estimated two million people.[54] A year later at a meeting in Naypyidaw, Than Shwe claimed that Burma had made remarkable progress since Cyclone Nargis, and was enjoying a rice production surplus, with annual output of 1,600 million baskets of rice (one basket equaling 33 kilograms). This was an increase from 1988, when annual output was 600 million baskets, and he forecast production to rise to 2,000 million baskets. These figures were released by the regime at the same time as a UN World Food Programme (WFP) official expressed concern about food shortages, particularly in the delta. The WFP spokesman said, "Even some farmers who own dozens of acres of paddy are unable to feed themselves."[55] Three months after the cyclone the UN Food and Agriculture Organization (FAO) said 63 percent of paddy fields were still under water, 85 percent of seed stocks had been destroyed, and 75 percent of farmers lacked sufficient seed to prepare for a new harvest.[56] Than Shwe, however, declared that "due to remarkable progress in the agricultural sector, the nation had not only self-sufficiency but also a surplus in food."[57] Most experts dispute these agricultural production levels.

While some noted Than Shwe's modesty and quietness, his record as regional commander did not win the endorsement of ordinary citizens in the Irrawaddy Delta. In elections held in Burma in 1990, just a few years after Than Shwe had left the Southwest Command, the National League for Democracy won fifty of the Irrawaddy Delta's allotted fifty-two parliamentary seats. Of the remaining two seats, the military-backed party won only one, while the remaining seat was won by an independent candidate allied with the NLD.[58]

Even though Than Shwe may have behaved like a tin-pot dictator and presided over a brutal rule in his region, it is perhaps the very characteristics that those close to Than Shwe noted—modesty, a quiet humility, a simple ordinary life, loyalty, no displays of ambition, and an interest in infrastructure projects—that actually contributed to his rise. According to a Reuters profile of Than Shwe, part of his success in winning power over his rivals is that "he proved less threatening."[59] As one man, who knows the regime well, put it: "Than Shwe kept quiet—he knew that if you show off too much in the military, you are likely to be chopped."

FIG. 4. *Clockwise from the top: A pro-democracy banner in a camp for internally displaced peoples, Karen State; a regime propaganda billboard in Rangoon; a regime propaganda billboard on the wall of the old royal palace, Mandalay. Photos by Benedict Rogers.*

3

THE DEMOCRATIC CHALLENGE

ACCORDING TO SPECIALISTS in palmistry, most people have three "skin creases" in their palms. The top line across the palm of our hands is the "heart" line, indicating compassion. The middle line is the "head" line, representing intellect and career path. The third is the "life" line, relating to health. Look at a photograph of Than Shwe on Armed Forces Day in 2007 published in *The Myanmar Times*. He is waving with his palm outstretched. Look closely at the palm of his hand. Unlike most people, he only has two lines—a head and a life line. In a palm reader's eyes, Than Shwe lacks sympathy and compassion.

As pro-democracy protests swept Burma in 1988, Than Shwe was at the center of a regime that killed an estimated three thousand people. In 1985 he was promoted from southwest regional commander to deputy chief of staff of the armed forces and deputy minister of defense. Part of the responsibility for the 1988 massacres, therefore, lies on his shoulders.

Discontent began to surface after Ne Win's sudden decision, based on numerological or astrological advice, to demonetize 25, 35, and 75 kyat notes on September 5, 1987. Students began protesting the following day, as thousands of people lost their savings overnight. The universities were closed for a month. Trouble continued to brew, but the spark that ignited the movement was lit on March 12, 1988. The incident itself was relatively minor: a brawl in the Sanda Win teashop following an argument between customers over what music to play. One of the customers hit a student over the head with a stool. The police were called in, arrests were made, but the people who had attacked the students were released the following day. One was the son of a local BSPP official, and his release caused outrage among the students. Protests began, led by students from the Rangoon Institute of Technology (RIT), with riot police firing at the demonstrators.

Several were killed, and on March 13 soldiers and police raided the RIT campus.[1] The seeds for the ensuing turmoil of 1988 were sown.

On March 16, Rangoon University students gathered on the White Bridge on Prome Road calling for an end to dictatorship. The authorities responded with extreme brutality, beating at least one hundred people to death. Eyewitnesses claim that female students were taken away and gang raped. In the following days, students were rounded up and arrested, and in one especially horrific incident, forty-one students suffocated to death in an overcrowded police van on the way to prison. Their bodies were reportedly cremated the next day.[2] Students dubbed the bridge "Red Bridge" in recognition of the student blood that had spilled.

Although the regime responded to the protests with extreme force, the demonstrations unsettled the leadership. Ne Win resigned from his formal positions on July 23, 1988, making an unprecedented apology for past mistakes, and Sein Lwin, the general believed to be responsible for the White Bridge incident and known as the "Butcher of Rangoon," succeeded him. Sein Lwin was also believed to have been responsible for dynamiting the Rangoon University Students Union in 1962, and suppressing protests in 1974. His appointment caused more outrage for the students, who began another round of protests, rallies, and the publication and distribution of anti-regime posters and pamphlets. As David Steinberg noted, "No move could have been better calculated to enrage the students."[3]

Protests continued throughout the end of July and early August and, according to Steinberg, "perhaps at its height, a million people had demonstrated in Rangoon, the capital, with a population of about two million at that time."[4] Than Shwe reportedly locked his family at home, complaining they were "scared to death."[5] One of his daughters told Htein Lin, a fellow student at Rangoon University who later became a political prisoner, that she was really concerned about the students, and did not want anyone to know she was Than Shwe's daughter. She was studying law and nursing at the same time. "She didn't like my group," Htein Lin recalls. "She knew I was a rebel. I was very wild—I smoked, took drugs, drank— and she warned others not to hang out with me. She said she believed people would come to attack and kill her family. She was very depressed, and was convinced her whole family was going to die."

Adding to the rumor mill that swirled throughout the country, the United States moved naval ships into the waters around Burma, sparking highly unlikely stories at the time, which continue to be circulated internationally, that the US was considering a possible invasion to restore democracy. Burton Levin, then US ambassador to Burma, says this could not be further from the truth. Months before the 1988 uprising had come into full swing, the United States had begun preparing contingency plans for the evacuation of US embassy personnel from Burma, along with staff from other embassies (the United States was the only country capable of removing people by helicopter on a large scale). For this purpose, says Levin, the US sent a Seventh Fleet task force to the region to prepare for possible helicopter evacuations, and informed the Burmese regime of the move. The Burmese foreign ministry called Levin in and asked him to issue a statement confirming that the US naval presence was purely for possible evacuation purposes. Levin says he issued a "very reassuring" statement. "We had no intentions of invading Burma at any time," adding, "but of course there were even rumors of US marines coming up the Irrawaddy."

The movement reached its peak during the events of August 8, 1988—a date now engraved in every Burmese person's mind—when a nationwide strike was launched. The strike was timed precisely for 8:08 a.m. on August 8, auspiciously marking the date of the fall of the Ava Dynasty in AD 1526, which correlated with 888 of the Burmese calendar.[6]

In his resignation speech just a little over two weeks earlier, Ne Win warned that: "When the army shoots, it shoots to hit; it does not fire into the air to scare. Therefore I warn those causing disturbances that they will not be spared if in the future the army is brought in to control disturbances."[7] August 8 was not by any means the first time the army had shot unarmed civilian protestors, but it was certainly one of the most bloody occasions. Hundreds were gunned down that night, and yet the demonstrations continued for several more weeks. By August 12, the regime admitted that one hundred people had been killed, but hospitals claimed at least three thousand deaths.[8] Steinberg notes that observers estimated that over a thousand died in the few days after the September 18th coup, while the demonstrations and other events leading up to the 1988 coup saw perhaps four or five times that number killed.[9] Bertil Lintner says,

"The regime responded with unprecedented brutality. Troops from the 22nd Light Infantry Division sprayed automatic rifle fire into crowds of unarmed protestors. Armored cars equipped with machine guns fired indiscriminately into Rangoon neighborhoods, killing scores of people inside their own homes."[10]

On August 12, Sein Lwin had resigned, bringing a temporary slowdown to the protests. A civilian prime minister, Dr. Maung Maung, a close friend of Ne Win and a lawyer who had helped draft the 1974 Constitution, was installed, but this did not placate the growing movement for democracy. Dr. Maung Maung's government eased some restrictions, including permitting the publication of newspapers, journals, and magazines, and for a few weeks free speech flourished in Burma. However, US Ambassador Levin, who reports that he met with the regime in mid-1988 along with then Congressman Stephen Solarz, says that Maung Maung was willing to make no concessions to international calls for restraint, and pointedly rejected a suggestion for the government to step down and create an interim civilian authority that could plan and carry out national elections. Instead, Maung Maung kept referring repeatedly to his desire to act in line with Burma's constitution, which had been unilaterally created by Ne Win's government fifteen years earlier. "It was a whole lot of [nonsense]," said Levin, "but of course, I knew at the time that [Maung Maung] had no real power."

Into the midst of this stepped Aung San Suu Kyi. As Aung San's daughter, she immediately carried a special place in the hearts of most Burmese people. She became "a moral beacon" across the country, in the view of one former Western ambassador. "She represented a line of continuity with her father, and so when anyone thought of her, they thought of her father." Aung San had been the founder of Burma's military and the leader of the struggle for independence. His daughter, people said, resembled him physically and, when she stood up to deliver her first public speech to a crowd believed to number as many as five-hundred thousand at the Shwedagon Pagoda on August 26, they believed they had at last found a leader who could restore democracy to the country. She became, as Lintner describes, "proof and torchbearer of the profound Burmese drive for democracy."[11]

Burton Levin says that Aung San Suu Kyi's ability to assume the mantle of the struggle for democracy was not solely due to her father's reputation in Burma: "It was her courage, charisma and the force and eloquence of her message that earned her the adulation, bordering on worship, of virtually the entire population and elevated her to the leadership of the anti-regime movement. The Burmese people felt that at long last someone was standing up for their rights."[12]

Aung San Suu Kyi lived abroad for much of her life, and was married to an Oxford academic, Michael Aris. She had worked at the United Nations in New York, studied in Kyoto, Japan, worked with her husband, a Tibet scholar, in Bhutan, and raised her family in Oxford. She had returned to Rangoon earlier in 1988 to nurse her dying mother, Daw Khin Kyi, and found herself propelled into Burma's political crisis. She described the movement as a "second struggle for Burmese independence," and offered her services as a mediator between the government and the students in a letter to the Council of State in early August.[13]

The tone struck by Aung San Suu Kyi was one of firm and passionate belief in democracy and human rights, balanced by an unambiguous willingness to enter dialogue with the generals. She advocated nonviolence and a peaceful transition. The generals could not have wished for a more reasonable opponent, and yet they repeatedly rejected her offers of dialogue. She expressed a simple desire to attempt to find some common ground. "How can we find out if there are places where we can meet, issues on which we can work together, unless we talk to each other?" she later told Alan Clements.[14]

Yet Aung San Suu Kyi did not refrain from criticizing the generals, and for the military regime any opposition was unacceptable. "My impression of them as a whole," she said of the generals, "is that they do not know what communication means. They don't communicate, either with the people or with the opposition. And I wonder whether they even communicate with each other." The regime, she added, was "afraid of dialogue." To this day, she said, "They do not and cannot understand what dialogue means. They do not know that it's a process that is honorable, that it can lead to happiness for everybody—including themselves. I think they still see dialogue as either some kind of competition in which they might lose, or as a great concession which would disgrace them."[15]

Instead of entering into dialogue with Aung San Suu Kyi and the students, the military seized direct power once again. General Saw Maung, a close ally of Ne Win, overthrew Maung Maung's BSPP government on September 18, and established an overtly military regime once again. Saw Maung did not make this decision alone. Indeed, according to an official working with Khin Nyunt at the time, Ne Win asked both Saw Maung and the then intelligence chief Khin Nyunt to take over the country and establish a military government. US Ambassador Levin believes that the military took direct control again because portions of the *tatmadaw* had begun to join the demonstrators. "The military itself had begun to crumble. Part of the navy and air force joined the demonstrators but when soldiers from the army showed signs of defecting, the generals stepped in. Perhaps they were fearful that the Burmese people would kill them." In essence, the military had never left government, but since 1974 a thin facade of civilian rule had been established, as the Burma Socialist Program Party replaced the Revolutionary Council and some government leaders took off their military uniforms. Now, the uniforms were back in the forefront.

On July 27, 1988, Than Shwe had been appointed deputy defense minister. During the crisis in 1988, Than Tun, who reported to Than Shwe, instructed Si Thu and his troops to initiate a number of scare tactics to create chaos among the public. A former Western ambassador claims that uniformed soldiers raided the German embassy's depot of aid supplies, and trashed a cigarette factory. According to a defector, scare tactics included distributing pamphlets, spreading rumors of widespread poisoning of the water supplies,[16] creating divisions among the opposition groups, releasing criminals from prison and "making people fear their surroundings by creating an unruly environment," thereby "creating a scenario where it was justified for the army to step in." It is not known to what extent Than Shwe himself was involved in this campaign, although given his favored divide-and-rule tactics and his background in psychological warfare, it would be no surprise if he was. Whatever the case, the plan worked and the military seized direct power once again, and Than Shwe was a major beneficiary. After Saw Maung's coup on September 18, Than Shwe became number two in the newly created State Law and Order Restoration Council (SLORC). Although Saw Maung and Khin Nyunt had been at the forefront of organizing the coup efforts, Khin Nyunt could not assume a position as one of the top two leaders of the new SLORC government, according to one of his close associates, and this helped to pave the way for Than Shwe's ascension. Even though Khin Nyunt had served for many years as intelligence chief, he had never led significant divisional or regional commands. In a military dictatorship, he simply didn't have the military experience to earn the support of the other top members of the SLORC and military apparatus. Therefore, the second position in the SLORC, the vice chairmanship, went to Than Shwe. Apparently, Than Shwe's appointment as vice chairman did not happen without some internal politics. Saw Maung hoped to maintain complete control over the SLORC apparatus, but Than Shwe wanted to play a leading political role apart from his position as army chief. According to a close aide to Khin Nyunt, Than Shwe had asked Saw Maung on two occasions, unsuccessfully, to assume the political portfolio. After Khin Nyunt lobbied on Than Shwe's behalf, Saw Maung eventually relented.

Saw Maung's new regime immediately imposed a curfew, a ban on gatherings of more than five people, and the prohibition of processions and protests. The brief flowering of free expression was over.

Soon after taking power, however, Saw Maung announced that Ne Win's earlier promise of a multiparty political system would still go ahead. Elections were promised, and on September 27 a new law for the registration of political parties was introduced. The Burma Socialist Program Party was dissolved, and a new party, the National Unity Party (NUP), was created. Dr. Maung Maung, the former civilian prime minister, recalls: "The [BSPP] government, being defunct, was redundant. We were redundant. Constitutionally, the Council of State could proclaim a state of emergency . . . which would mean turning over power . . . to the military. . . . We needed to look to the future, a future of enduring peace, harmony and peaceful changes. It was time to break out of the vicious circle of unrest, violence, insurgency, military intervention, ideological and factional disputes that has plagued the country since independence."[17] That, however, was wishful thinking. The NUP was new only in name, and consisted mostly of the same old faces.

The promises to honor the election results were unambiguous. On September 22, 1988, Khin Nyunt told foreign military attachés, "The *tatmadaw* would systematically transfer power to the party which comes into power after successfully holding the general elections."[18] The following day, Saw Maung said, "The fact that we have formed a government with very few people is evidence that we have absolutely no desire to hold on to state power for a prolonged period."[19] On Armed Forces Day, March 27, 1989, Saw Maung pledged that "after the election the Pyithu Hluttaw representatives elected by the people will form a government in accordance with the law ... We, the *tatmadaw* personnel, will go back to the barracks."[20] On July 5, 1989, Saw Maung reiterated his promise: "I will transfer the power according to the law. If a government could be formed with a majority of votes, then I will hand it over. I agree with it." A new constitution would be required, but it would be up to the new government and those elected to draft it.[21]

Later in September 1988, Aung San Suu Kyi joined forces with a coalition of student leaders, democracy activists, intellectuals, writers, and former soldiers to form the National League for Democracy (NLD). She became the party's general secretary, with the vice chairmanship going to Tin Oo, the former commander in chief of the armed forces who had been purged and jailed by Ne Win following the 1974 protests and the suspected coup plot in 1976. Aung Gyi, another former soldier, became chairman of the NLD. He had published open letters criticizing Ne Win earlier in the year. Unfortunately, a split developed between the two men and Aung Gyi later resigned from the NLD.

Daw Khin Kyi, Aung San Suu Kyi's mother, died on December 27, 1988. The funeral was held on January 2, 1989, and it drew thousands of well-wishers. Then in the early part of 1989, Aung San Suu Kyi and the NLD began preparations for an election campaign. She toured the country and "tens of thousands of people turned out to see her."[22] In June 1989, the regime changed the name of the country, from Burma to Myanmar. However, Aung San Suu Kyi, the democracy movement, and the leaders of the ethnic nationalities still prefer "Burma" to be used. The United States, United Kingdom, several other countries, and many newspapers have respected their wishes. The democracy movement's insistence on continuing to use Burma, even two decades after the name change, reflects their argument that the regime had no mandate to change the name of the country.

The regime began to get nervous about the effect Aung San Suu Kyi was having on the people, and so it resorted to tactics of harassment, intimidation, and threat. The most serious, and the most celebrated, of these acts came on April 5, 1989 as Aung San Suu Kyi toured Danubyu, fifty miles from Rangoon. As she and her supporters walked down the street, they came face-to-face with a row of soldiers, their rifles pointed directly at them. In an extraordinary scene, the captain ordered Aung San Suu Kyi and her supporters to leave. At first, he ordered them to walk on the side of the road, not down the middle, but then he warned that he would shoot even if they continued down the side of the road. Recalling the event, Aung San Suu Kyi said, laughingly: "Now that seemed highly unreasonable to me . . . I thought, if he's going to shoot us even if we walk at the side of the road, well, perhaps it is me they want to shoot. I thought I might as well walk in the middle of the road."[23] Defiantly, she told her supporters to stay back, and she calmly walked towards the troops, their guns trained on her. The captain commenced a countdown to shoot.

Clearly, her status as Aung San's daughter, combined with her international prominence, caused the regime to think twice before assassinating her, although they have come close to it on several occasions. Seconds before the captain was about to give the order to shoot, a major rushed onto the scene and ordered the troops to lower their guns. He became embroiled in an argument with the captain. "We just walked through the soldiers who were kneeling there," she recalled. "And I noticed that some of them, one or two, were actually shaking and muttering to themselves but I don't know whether it was out of hatred or nervousness."[24] Exasperated, the captain tore the insignia off his shoulder and threw it on the ground.

By June it was clear in the regime's mind that Aung San Suu Kyi spelled trouble. On July 20, she and U Tin Oo were placed under house arrest. A media campaign began in an attempt to discredit Aung San Suu Kyi, particularly focused on the fact that she was married to a foreigner. "The papers regularly carry cartoons depicting her as a black-toothed witch manipulated by foreigners seeking to harm the interests of the Myanmar people," Roger Mitton reported.[25] Regime officials refused to use her full name, and one described her as "someone who crawled out from under a stone."[26] Several thousand NLD members were arrested and Aung San Suu Kyi began a hunger strike, demanding that she be moved to prison alongside her supporters.

While she remained under house arrest, plans for the elections went ahead. Although the regime did everything it could to restrict the NLD and other pro-democracy parties' ability to campaign, the election day itself is generally regarded to have been free and fair. As Lintner writes, "Probably believing that its year-long propaganda campaign in the *Working People's Daily* against the NLD had been effective—and evidently underestimating the degree of hatred towards the military that still existed—the SLORC decided to allow an astonishing degree of openness following months of repression."[27] On May 27, 1990, the people of Burma went to the polls and courageously voted for freedom. The NLD won 392 of the 447 seats it contested, amounting to 82 percent of the total parliamentary seats. The military-backed NUP won just ten seats. "The SLORC was probably as taken aback as almost everybody else; it was utterly unprepared for an NLD victory of this magnitude," concludes Lintner.[28]

What happened shocked perhaps only those unfamiliar with Burmese history, and set the course for Burma's political crisis for the next two decades. Instead of acknowledging the result and beginning a transfer of power, the regime refused to accept electoral defeat. Elected members of parliament were imprisoned or driven into exile, and the regime argued that the ballot was not for a parliament, but for a body to draw up a new constitution. The regime had completely reneged on its promises.

Saw Maung ruled for another eighteen months, with Than Shwe as his deputy. A former Western ambassador who had met Than Shwe and other members of the junta at least five times recalls that he was very quiet when attending meetings with Saw Maung. "Than Shwe joined in the smiles, like a good number two, but it was not easy to know whether he really wanted to smile," he says. Saw Maung and Khin Nyunt were engaging and talkative, but Than Shwe generally said nothing.

Concerns about Saw Maung's mental health grew within the regime. One former Western ambassador said Saw Maung was "more than a little deranged," and another describes him as "erratic and unstable." He was a heavy drinker, who also suffered from diabetes. In a golf tournament with other generals, he reportedly screamed, "I am King Kyansittha!,"*

---

* King Kyansittha (AD 1084–1112) was the second Bagan Dynasty king, son of King Anawrahta.

and threatened those around him with his pistol.[29] In a speech broadcast on television, he repeated his reference to King Kyansittha, assured the people that he was not a practitioner of black magic, and announced that martial law equaled "no law at all."[30]

According to one British newspaper report, Saw Maung suffered a nervous breakdown and toward the end of 1991, he was unable to fulfill his duties. "Doubts about General Saw Maung's mental state have been public knowledge for months, according to the diplomats," *The Times* reported. "These were aroused by a series of rambling, incoherent speeches. After becoming violent, he was put in the hospital for a time. He is said to have injured himself kicking furniture and throwing himself about. Some foreign dignitaries visiting Rangoon were told they could not meet him because he had a tooth ache."[31]

John Casey, writing in *The Daily Telegraph*, said that Saw Maung was "a buffoon." At a press conference lasting several hours, Saw Maung tried to explain the difference between Christianity and Buddhism. "A Buddhist says 'Oh Lord Buddha!' if he meets with something dangerous; but a Christian says 'Oh, my God'!" was his simple explanation. In a verbal attack on Aung San Suu Kyi, he reportedly said that she must never be allowed to hold power in Burma because she married a foreigner. "The Prince of Wales—what was his name?—had to abdicate because he married a foreigner, Mrs. Simpson. That is our law too," he concluded.[32]

In 1991 Aung San Suu Kyi was awarded the Nobel Peace Prize. According to *The Times*, "One senior diplomat who has known General Saw Maung for several years said he thought [this] was a breaking point for the general, because he realized that the honor for Daw Suu Kyi shamed him."

Saw Maung's apparent illness continued and in April 1992 he resigned. *The Times* reported: "The increasingly eccentric behavior of Saw Maung, 63, who led the group of military officers who seized power in 1988, had fuelled rumours that he had suffered a nervous breakdown or some other mental illness. Many of his speeches were almost incoherent."[33]

A former Western ambassador says that at the time, most diplomats expected that Saw Maung would be removed. There is speculation that Than Shwe and Khin Nyunt initiated this, as well as a little-held belief that Saw Maung was drugged, which may explain his extraordinary behavior.

Some speculate that Than Shwe, perhaps with Ne Win's tacit approval, was instrumental in drugging the top general. Ultimately, whoever may have maneuvered against Saw Maung, a power struggle occurred between Than Shwe and Khin Nyunt. As a close protégé of Ne Win and head of military intelligence Khin Nyunt was seen as the more likely successor, but Than Shwe, already next in line to Saw Maung in the hierarchy, came out on top. Some suggest that Khin Nyunt actually persuaded Than Shwe to take the top position, in the belief that Than Shwe would not last long and that he could outmaneuver him in due course. Although not as close to Ne Win as Khin Nyunt, Than Shwe was perhaps seen as a safer bet—less overtly ambitious, supremely loyal to the military, and more conservative. He also had two things in common with Ne Win: both had started out in life as postal clerks and both had demonstrated an adeptness for psychological warfare.

An alternative and perhaps more likely version is that Khin Nyunt and Than Shwe worked together to remove Saw Maung, though without drugging him. In early April 1992, an associate of Khin Nyunt reports that the two dispatched intelligence officials to meet with all the existing regional commanders. The intelligence officials reportedly carried letters signed by both Than Shwe and Khin Nyunt, and the regional commanders were ordered to open the letters and read them on the spot. The letters proposed the removal of Saw Maung from power, based on his increasingly erratic behavior. Without exception, all the regional commanders immediately agreed and the intelligence officials flew back to the War Office to report back to Than Shwe and Khin Nyunt. The two immediately created a radio broadcast that announced Saw Maung's removal from power—without ever informing Saw Maung directly. Saw Maung never put up a fight, and accepted his "resignation" without debate.

The same source, however, says that Saw Maung's wife Aye Aye Yee initially refused to accept the changes. Saw Maung lived in a compound at military headquarters, and Aye Aye Yee promptly entered the headquarters and launched into a tirade against Than Shwe and Khin Nyunt, screaming: "It is not your right to take power, you are not royalty!" Aye Aye Yee was removed from the premises, and the military headquarters assigned armed intelligence officials to prevent future incursions.

And so on April 23, 1992, Than Shwe became the SLORC chairman, the senior general, and the head of state. A former Australian ambassador to Burma recalls that at the time, "many saw Than Shwe as a 'short termer,'" a stopgap after Saw Maung's demise. He was "in between Maung Aye and Khin Nyunt," both seen by diplomats as more impressive personalities, but with Than Shwe, "there was no evident personality."

"He played the fool at the beginning, giving the impression of a parochial, grassroots, unambitious person, giving Ne Win the impression that he could trust him, that he was not hungry for power," argues a former Thai ambassador. "He was a mastermind—he fooled everybody."

Bertil Lintner says that soldiers in the Burma Army who knew Than Shwe laughed when they heard of his appointment because he was not regarded as the brightest of the bunch, although "he is said to be feared by his subordinates," according to *The Times*.[34] Soon after he became the leader, Than Shwe held a series of secret cabinet meetings at night. They became known as *nya kyaung* or "night school," with Than Shwe referred to as "headmaster." Some of those who attended are now his key lieutenants today—men like Thein Sein, the current prime minister, and Khin Maung Than, a senior official in the Defense Ministry.[35] Than Shwe's ascension to the top position was immediately followed by a large earthquake along the Chinese border, considered by many Burmese to be a omen of ensuing chaos and disaster for the nation. In addition, the flowering of bamboo for the second time in less than fifty years occurred—another ill-fated sign since it represents an ecological phenomenon that catalyzes rat infestation.[36]

Several months after Than Shwe assumed power, Ne Win came to visit him while he was playing golf with other generals at the military golf course in Mingaladon, according to a former Burma Army officer. Than Shwe was not a particularly skilled golfer, and former US Ambassador Burton Levin reports that the generals often cheated in their matches. "I have never seen a shot hit so far off the green and miraculously end up right near the hole," Levin notes. "It was obvious that the caddies and intelligence officers staffing their golf outing were moving the ball."

When they learned that Ne Win had arrived, Than Shwe and the other generals rushed back to the clubhouse to meet him. Even though Ne Win was no longer officially in power, he was still their former commander and therefore deserved a meeting at least. Than Shwe briefed Ne Win on all the infrastructure projects he had undertaken since assuming power, and Ne Win expressed his approval. Using a Burmese expression that roughly translates as: "When I was leader, the mat was on the ceiling—now, you have the mat on the ground," Ne Win indicated to his successors that they were doing the right thing. While Than Shwe owed no direct allegiance to Ne Win, obtaining the former dictator's blessing was clearly welcome. The meeting ended and the generals resumed their golf game.

The National League for Democracy wasted no time in reaching out to Than Shwe, and proposed numerous face-to-face meetings aimed at finding a solution to the military regime's refusal to transfer power to the democratically elected leaders of the country. While most of these exchanges remained private, NLD Chairman Aung Shwe sent a series of illuminating letters to Than Shwe beginning in December 1995 through to March 1997. The letters, representing insights into the thinking of the NLD, address several issues still relevant to Burma today. These include the regime's constant refusal to enter into genuine negotiations with the NLD aimed at a transition to democracy, Than Shwe's post-election delaying tactics designed to prevent the NLD from forming a national parliament, and his post-election pressure on individual NLD members aimed at forcing them to resign from the party or politics altogether. Aung San Suu Kyi, who at the time of the publication of the letters enjoyed a brief respite from house arrest, wrote in the introduction to the collection: "By studying these letters it is clear how the NLD's Central Committee has been carrying out its duties with vigor despite the hardships that members face on a daily basis."[37]

The letters were smuggled out of the country, and were then translated into English, since "being caught in possession of such a document of this nature would result in arrest, torture, and a lengthy prison sentence."[38]

After the election in response to the regime's refusal to allow the NLD to form a parliament, Aung Shwe repeatedly called for Than Shwe to enter into a constructive, binding dialogue, with the aim of a full transition to democracy. Aung Shwe was, in particular, concerned with the unilateral manner in which Than Shwe had ignored the result of the 1990 election and instead created a constitutional convention designed to marginalize the NLD and perpetuate military rule. Initially, over eighty members of the NLD were invited to participate in the convention, which Than Shwe had stocked with military allies and business cronies in order to prevent the NLD from having a strong say in the constitution drafting process. Aung Shwe complained to Than Shwe that when the NLD briefly withdrew from the convention in protest at the very few seats in the convention it held and the onerous restrictions placed on convention participants, the National Convention Working Committee, controlled by Than Shwe's regime, accused the NLD of "attempting to destroy the process of the National Convention." Aung Shwe repeatedly called for a more fair and open process, pointing out: "Our collective goals can be reached through dialogue and consensus between individuals and groups."[39] Than Shwe simply ignored the letter, and the National Convention continued without any NLD input.

In February 1996, Aung Shwe again appealed for "face-to-face dialogue" with Than Shwe and the military regime, and also sought to underline his case by articulating that dialogue had worked in other countries. "There are many instances where countries have successfully used dialogue to find solutions to internal conflicts and international hostilities," he said. Again, Than Shwe ignored the appeal. Than Shwe's refusal to enter into a genuine dialogue with the elected leaders of Burma continues to this day. Indeed, the constitution approved by the handpicked convention guarantees military control over the country, and it will be impossible for the constitution to be amended without the military's agreement.

The letters also pointed out that Than Shwe had used bureaucratic wrangling to deny the NLD the chance to form a parliament. These include unnecessarily prolonged scrutiny of election finances. Than Shwe himself notes that the evaluation of complaints about election finances was not completed until March 1996—nearly six years after voters had rejected military rule at the polls. Aung Shwe attempted to hold the regime to its own words, citing a press conference in which regime officials stated that while they could not specify when parliament would be convened, "we have no intention whatsoever of delaying it."[40]

US Ambassador Burton Levin confirmed Aung Shwe's contention that the military regime used various machinations to avoid recognizing the election results. "I remember the great sense of popular excitement when it became apparent that the NLD had won. Then over the course of the next few weeks the games began. Delayed vote counts were followed by a series of arcane procedures which soon made it evident that the regime had no intention of abiding by the results," he recalls. "One strongly suspects that the regime's original willingness to go ahead with elections was predicated on the belief that its puppet party would garner enough support from the countryside to emerge victorious. That the regime misread the situation so badly offered further evidence of its political insensitivity."[41] To this day Than Shwe has neither responded to Aung Shwe's complaints about the post-election period nor allowed the NLD to form a parliament and assume its rightful position in government.

The letters also illustrate the severe repression of democracy activists in the country, in particular, the "fabrication of evidence, forced resignations, loss of livelihood, imprisonment, the inciting of mob of violence, and forced porterage, all of which have been used by the SLORC to systematically destroy the NLD as an opposition voice."[42] The letters also cite countless examples of abuses carried out against individual NLD members. The overall goal of Than Shwe appears to have been to decimate the NLD membership and force as many members of parliament as possible to resign, using a variety of tactics to make this happen. Some political prisoners were transferred into "dog cells," notorious for severe punishment, NLD members were jailed or forced to resign from the party, and families of NLD activists were pressured to demand that they resign.

Aung Shwe and the NLD repeatedly urged Than Shwe to investigate the unlawful rulings and actions taken against the NLD, citing the regime's own set of laws. Yet the repression of the NLD continued throughout the 1990s, intensifying after Aung San Suu Kyi was released from house arrest in mid-1995. Clearly, as Than Shwe signaled from the beginning, he had no interest in democracy. He had waited a long time to assume power in Burma, and he would not be held back in his drive to cement military rule for generations to come.

4

THAN SHWE'S CRIMES AGAINST HUMANITY

ONE MAN WAS en route from his village in Toungoo, Karen State to a nearby town to buy food, when he was abducted by Burma Army soldiers. The soldiers tied his hands, dragged him through the jungle, tied him to a tree upside down, gouged his eyes out, and drowned him.[1] Three years later, the Burma Army struck again, this time attacking and occupying the village, burning houses, and looting property. Seven villagers were shot dead. The murdered man's widow fled with two of her five children, and walked for over a month to reach a camp for internally displaced persons (IDPs) near the border with Thailand. She was not alone.

In the same camp was another woman, whose fifteen-year-old son had been captured by the Burma Army. He had been tied to a tree, tortured, and beheaded.[2] A third woman had a similar tale to tell. Her husband had been caught by the Burma Army on his way home from his farm. He was carried through the village and then grotesquely mutilated. Soldiers tore his eyes out, and cut off his lips and ears. He died alone in the forest.[3]

This is what is happening in Than Shwe's Burma. And these are by no means isolated incidents. In recent years, numerous reports have been published documenting hundreds of extrajudicial killings as well as the widespread and systematic use of rape and sexual violence as a weapon of war, the forcible conscription of child soldiers, and the widespread use of forced labor. In Than Shwe's Burma, over twenty-one hundred political prisoners are in jail as of 2009, subjected to some of the worst forms of torture in the world. In a campaign of ethnic cleansing, as many as perhaps a million people are internally displaced, either in military-controlled relocation sites or on the run in the jungle. In the words of one report by a humanitarian relief team, they are "hunted and shelled like animals."[4] People are used as human minesweepers, forced to walk ahead of the military to clear the landmines, losing their limbs, and sometimes their lives, in the process. Civilians are shot at point blank range, and killed in other ways as well. In August 2009, the Shan Women's Action Network reported, "Over one hundred villagers, both men and women, have been arrested and tortured. At least three villagers have been killed. One young woman was shot while trying to retrieve her possessions from her burning house, and her body was thrown into a pit latrine. Another woman was gang-raped in front of her husband by an officer and three of his troops."[5]

When Than Shwe first took power, his appointment was cautiously welcomed by some in the international community, and there was some speculation that he was perhaps a "moderate." As Bertil Lintner says, "No one had any illusions that sullen, taciturn Than Shwe was a closet liberal with any grand schemes up his sleeve,"[6] but people were pleasantly surprised by the initial appearance of moderation. In 1992 the US State Department declared it was heartened by changes in Burma after 102 of 2,000 political prisoners were released. In testimony in the US Congress, an assistant secretary of state said he had seen "an unanticipated measure of conciliation" with dissidents. Under Than Shwe's leadership, the International Committee of the Red Cross (ICRC) and Amnesty International were permitted to enter the country and meet Aung San Suu Kyi.[7] Some restrictions on the opposition were relaxed, and a significant program of economic liberalization was introduced, primarily led by the economics minister General David Abel. Than Shwe also launched a crackdown on corruption within the regime.[8] His initial reforms did not amount to "any structural changes," as Lintner points out, but were designed to create "what a Rangoon-based diplomat aptly described as a 'dictatorship with a human face.'"[9] It would not take long for the human face to slip, and for Burma under Than Shwe to return to a bare-bones dictatorship.

Despite the initial upbeat assessments by some observers, Stephen Solarz, an influential congressman from New York serving on the House Foreign Affairs Committee, appeared to have a more accurate assessment of the realities on the ground, saying that the regime "should be under no illusions about what actions it needs to take before it will lose its international pariah status."[10] Any idea that Than Shwe might be a moderate was quickly abandoned. Military offensives against the ethnic groups greatly intensified, and prisons remained filled with dissidents and instruments of torture.

Than Shwe wasted no time in immediately consolidating his power. He plucked the most junior regional commander, Maung Aye, from the headquarters of the Eastern Regional Command to serve as his army chief—pointedly bypassing his only possible rival at the time, Khin Nyunt, who, as mentioned earlier, did not have the command experience anyway that others in the military would consider necessary to hold such a position. Furthermore, he did not appoint Khin Nyunt as vice chairman of the SPDC, thereby assuring his own complete control over the political positions of the junta (just as Saw Maung had initially refused to appoint Than Shwe as vice chairman of SLORC after 1988). The refusal to appoint Khin Nyunt came as a surprise to some in the intelligence apparatus and also to international embassies based in Rangoon. Yet Than Shwe's desire for political control was not to be underestimated.

Some international observers and media reports have pointed to the position of Khin Nyunt over the years and suggested that he was a possible reformer or moderate. However, according to a close associate of Khin Nyunt, he held no real power since all his major decisions had to be approved by Than Shwe, and Than Shwe always held complete control over the army, the true center of power. Khin Nyunt could operate within the confines of Than Shwe's power, but had Khin Nyunt tried to make a move to remove Than Shwe or attempted a compromise with Aung San Suu Kyi, Than Shwe could have easily called on the military to end Khin Nyunt's career, or his life. Aung Lynn Htut claims that intelligence officers under Khin Nyunt worked actively to sell lies to Western academics, who, in turn, believed whatever the intelligence officers said. "They were like 'pets' to us . . . Even Khin Nyunt essentially viewed [one such academic] as a lobbyist for us."

On February 15, 2006, the mutilated body of an unidentified person was found in the Bla Khi area of Karen State. The victim's throat had been slit and left hand cut off. Around the same time, reports emerged from Karenni State of continuing offensives. On March 27, more civilians were attacked. Saw Po De, a forty-year-old man, was beheaded in the village of Ker Der Gah. A nine-year-old girl, Naw Eh Ywa Paw, was shot, and her father and grandmother killed. "The people had fled the attacking

Burma Army who were sweeping the entire area . . . They did not know the Burma Army was waiting for them. . . . The shock of having a line of troops open fire at point blank range must have been tremendous," said a relief worker from Free Burma Rangers, a humanitarian organization. At least eleven civilians were shot dead. One of the survivors said: "The Burma Army waited in a prepared position to kill villagers. They waited until they were only ten yards away and opened fire on a man carrying his mother, as well as the families and children behind him. What kind of people, what kind of system, can do this?"[11]

Cynics dismiss such atrocities as merely inadvertent casualties of the regime's counterinsurgency campaign against the ethnic groups' armed resistance organizations. Others regard such abuses as the result of badly behaved frontline troops, rather than Than Shwe's specific responsibility. But how can the persistent targeting of elderly civilians, women, children, and men who have nothing to do with the armed resistance be justified as counterinsurgency? Given the widespread and systematic nature of these crimes, how is it possible for them to occur persistently and consistently with impunity on Than Shwe's watch unless they were approved by him? There may be little available evidence in terms of explicit orders linking Than Shwe to these crimes, but his failure to discipline the perpetrators, and his silence on the subject, makes him more than complicit. Indeed, it makes him responsible under international law.

One former Western ambassador raised these issues with Than Shwe when he presented his credentials to the general in 1995. "I was given very strict instructions by protocol not to touch on sensitive political matters, but I didn't take any notice of that," the former diplomat recalled. "Than Shwe appeared genial and avuncular. When I raised the issue of human rights, he was most distressed by reports of soldiers behaving badly. He said he could not believe them, because, he emphasized, 'We are Buddhists and we wouldn't hurt a fly.'" The military regime has been peddling this lie for decades, and the former ambassador admits that it is "faintly possible" that Than Shwe is "totally cocooned in cotton wool," but it would be astonishing if he was genuinely unaware of the violations taking place. "It was an early lesson that the prestige of the country is so important, that lies are justified. He could have made the same point in a less crude way, but no. There was no finesse about it."

Although some observers claim that there is a Potemkin-like situation in Burma, in which Than Shwe is not told of facts by his subordinates, it is impossible that Than Shwe could be unaware of the atrocities his troops are committing. If he were a civilian leader such as Dr. Maung Maung, who came from academia, it would be marginally more plausible to use ignorance as an excuse, but Than Shwe spent his career in the military system and would certainly have been fully exposed to its behavior. He has worked at all levels in the military and understands how it operates from top to bottom. When he was southwest regional commander, he presided over forced labor. In the conflict areas in which he served, human rights abuses were prolific. When he worked in the military's communications infrastructure, he would have seen orders being passed and reports coming back from the conflict zones documenting the military's activities. Furthermore, he has been challenged by international actors on several occasions, from ambassadors to UN officials to numerous international organizations and their reports.

The regime's media and diplomatic service have actively refuted these reports, but Than Shwe has never once launched an investigation, aside from token sham gestures on child soldiers and forced labor designed to appease his international critics. Indeed, he has actively restricted the movements of international investigators, such as the UN Special Rapporteur for Human Rights in Burma and the International Committee of the Red Cross, and completely denied access to others. By implication, this means he knows that an investigation would find the truth, and the truth would be, at the very least, inconvenient for him. In contrast, he has set up multiple inquiries into corruption, typically as a weapon against his opponents within and beyond the regime. Were he so confident that there were no human rights abuses, or if he genuinely did not know, why has he not responded to international claims by commissioning his own inquiry or permitting international human rights monitors to have unfettered access to all parts of the country?

Questions of whether Than Shwe is aware of what is happening, or whether there is evidence of his direct approval of such crimes, are easily answered if the claims of one former Burmese diplomat and military intelligence officer are true. Aung Lynn Htut, the former deputy chief of mission at the Burmese embassy in Washington DC as well as a former intelligence officer in the military regime, accuses Than Shwe of personally ordering the murder of at least eighty-one unarmed villagers in 1998.[12] A unit led by Colonel Zaw Min, now the minister for electric power and general secretary of the Union Solidarity Development Association (USDA),* landed on Christie Island in the Mergui Archipelago of southeastern Burma in May 1998 to cordon it off for military use, and discovered fifty-nine Burmese villagers living there gathering wood and bamboo in violation of regime law. General Thura Myint Aung, now the southwest regional commander, had issued an order prohibiting civilians from living on the island.[13] When contact was made with headquarters about what to do with these villagers, says Aung Lynn Htut, the order came back that they should be "eliminated." The order came just after lunch from Than Shwe's number two, General Maung Aye, who had a reputation for drinking.

The decision was made to wait because it was possible that the order was not meant to be carried out. But the word came back from headquarters that the order had come from "Aba Gyi" or "Great Father," a term used in reference to Than Shwe, that fifty-nine villagers, including women and children, were to be shot dead and buried. A few days later, a Thai fishing boat strayed close to Christie Island, and the twenty-two fishermen on board were captured, shot, and buried alongside the villagers. In Aung Lynn Htut's view, "This is a minor incident for them. Since 1997, they instructed us to kill everyone, including a woman carrying her children.... This is the official order carried out by mouth, especially when we are in the battle-field. These orders are carried out especially in Karen State, Mon State, Shan State, and Tanintharyi Division.... Mainly these killings occur because of the forced relocation from the military.... The army forces people to move by these methods.... Burmese generals ... instructed us to clear the area. They don't want anyone alive and they officially said it. These kind of actions began from 1996, 1997, and have carried on until today."[14]

David Eubank, a former officer with the US Army Rangers and Special Forces and the founder of the Free Burma Rangers, argues that not only

---

* The USDA is the regime's proxy civil society organization that was founded by Than Shwe in 1993. It is both a political organization and a militia force.

is Than Shwe aware of the regime's crimes, but that the recriminations taken by the *tatmadaw* against those that report them to the outside world indicate that he approves of them and does not want to prevent them or bring the perpetrators to justice. "Than Shwe knows about all of this—he may not know about every single person that's killed, every village burned, but he knows they're being burnt, because that's his policy. As the leader he's guilty and liable for everything that happens. The only way that he would not be is if he stood up sincerely and said stop, and then took action to punish the perpetrators, but that's never happened. So at a bare minimum, silence implies consent." In terms of basic military discipline, Eubank further emphasizes that Than Shwe cannot plead ignorance. "No army in the world operates on its own, every army has a commander. So, if they're doing something more than one or two days, or more than one or two operations at a time, it's a policy. Even the US army, if they do something wrong, they don't keep doing it five or six times. It happens once, everyone gets in trouble, [and then] that thing stops. You may have it somewhere else, but once you have a pattern, it's what the leaders want."[15]

In some of the most damning information compiled to date, the UN Special Rapporteur on Human Rights in Burma, Paolo Sérgio Pinheiro, who served from 2000 to 2008, indicated he had received information documenting numerous rights violations. Writing in the *International Herald Tribune* in May 2009, he asserted:

> Over the past 15 years, the Burmese Army has destroyed over 3,300 villages in a systematic and widespread campaign to subjugate ethnic groups. U.N. reports indicate that Burmese soldiers have frequently recruited child soldiers, used civilians as minesweepers and forced thousands of villagers into slave labor. An official policy of impunity has empowered soldiers to rape and pillage. According to one account, in December 2008 a Burmese soldier marched into an ethnic Karen village in eastern Myanmar and abducted, raped and killed a seven-year-old girl. Authorities refused to arrest the soldier; instead, officers threatened the parents with punishment if they did not accept a cash bribe to keep quiet.[16]

Shortly thereafter, a group of the world's leading judges—one each from the United States, Asia, Africa, Latin America, and Europe—reached similar conclusions in a report commissioned by the International Human Rights Clinic at Harvard Law School. The judges, who included those that have served at international criminal tribunals on Rwanda and the former Yugoslavia, as well as a former member of the Supreme Court of Mongolia, and the former president of the Inter-American Court of Human Rights, found shocking evidence that suggested the existence of crimes against humanity in *already existing* UN reports.[17] Two of the report's commissioners, Sir Geoffrey Nice, the principal prosecutor of Slobodan Milosevic in the Hague, and Pedro Nikken, the former president of the Inter-American Court of Human Rights, subsequently issued a call to action in an opinion piece in the *Washington Post*, noting: "It is incumbent on the Security Council to authorize a commission of inquiry into crimes against humanity and war crimes in Burma. In previous, similar cases—such as the situation in the former Yugoslavia, Rwanda, and Darfur—the council voted to create such a commission to investigate charges and recommend actions. So many U.N. bodies have documented severe human rights abuses that such a move on Burma is not only justified but long overdue."[18]

Health workers and epidemiologists have also studied the effects of Than Shwe's regime on civilian health. The Back Pack Health Workers Team, a group of medics that risk their lives to provide health services in conflict zones in eastern Burma, have documented sobering statistics: "... standard public health indicators such as population pyramids, infant mortality rates, child mortality rates, and maternal mortality ratios [in Burma] more closely resemble other countries facing widespread humanitarian disasters, such as Sierra Leone, the Democratic Republic of the Congo, Niger, Angola, and Cambodia shortly after the ouster of the Khmer Rouge."[19]

A joint report by the Baltimore-based Johns Hopkins Bloomberg School of Public Health and the Human Rights Center at the University of California, Berkeley stated that the Burmese military government spends under 3 percent of its national budget on healthcare, while the "standing army of over 400,000 troops, consumes 40 percent."[20] The report's authors, who included epidemiologists as well as public health physicians, also found that "rarely disciplined for their actions, military troops often kill, torture, and rape civilians found outside of relocation camps or permitted zones. Thousands of displaced villagers hide in the jungles, usually in small, fragmented communities where they are exposed to malaria and other diseases. The *tatmadaw* prohibits foreigners from accessing these communities."[21] Than Shwe's obliteration of Burma's public health programs and the resultant effects on the Burmese population is not simply debilitating, it is arguably illegal under the Rome Statute, which established the International Criminal Court in 2002. But since Burma has not acceded to the Rome Statute little can be done under international law unless the UN Security Council calls for a Commission of Inquiry to investigate Burma's crimes.[22]

Than Shwe and his regime clearly have a particularly intense hatred of ethnic and religious minorities that seek autonomy. Influenced by a fascist ideology with echoes of Hitler and the Nazis, the junta is guided by the principle of "Amyo, Batha, Thathana," which translates as "one race, one language, one religion,"[23] with the race being Burman, the language Burmese, and the religion a distorted and perverted form of Buddhism. The regime also has a phrase "Maha Bama," referring to the Burman "master race." Non-Buddhists, as Martin Smith says, "have always been regarded with great suspicion."[24] Perhaps 40 percent of the population in Burma comes from the non-Burman ethnic nationalities that inhabit perhaps as much as 60 percent of the land. Primarily located in the border areas, the ethnic groups fall into seven broad categories, although within them there are many subgroups.

The seven major ethnic nationalities are the Karen, Karenni, Shan, and Mon in eastern Burma along the border with Thailand, the Kachin along the border with China, the Chin along the border with India, and the Rakhine (Arakan) along the border with Bangladesh. The Chin, Kachin, and Karenni are majority Christian, and approximately 40 percent of the Karen people are Christian, while the Shan, Mon, and Rakhine are overwhelmingly Buddhist. Shan State also includes smaller ethnic groups such as the Wa and the Lahu, while the Pa-O are found in several parts of Burma, particularly the Karen and Shan states. The regime claims there are 135 ethnic groups, but this is a deliberate attempt to deny the prominence of the major groups. According to Bertil Lintner, this figure was reached for superstitious reasons, because the military's lucky number is supposedly nine, and one plus three plus five equals nine. The figure of 135 includes groups that amount, in Lintner's view, to little more than clans and extended families.[25]

In addition to the seven major non-Burman groups, there is an eighth that should be considered. The Rohingya, Muslims of Bengali ethnic origin, have inhabited northern Arakan State along the Bangladesh-Burma border for generations, but are denied full citizenship.[26] While there is serious debate as to whether the Rohingya represent one of Burma's historic ethnic nationalities, it is indisputable that they have lived in Burma for centuries, and are targeted for extra persecution by Than Shwe's regime. Treated as temporary residents and subjected to serious forms of discrimination and restriction, Rohingyas are often required to obtain a permit to move from one village to another, or from one town to another, and have to pay substantial bribes and wait several days to obtain permission. They are generally denied full access to education or health care, either directly or as a result of restrictions on movement. They have to obtain permission to marry, and that can take years and significant amounts of money. They are targeted for extortion and forced labor, and face religious persecution. Mosques have been destroyed, and permission to build new ones, or renovate or extend existing ones, is typically denied.[27]

While Than Shwe and his wife make an ostentatious public display of devout Buddhism when it suits them, they use Buddhism as a political tool. When Buddhist monks challenge them, as they did in the Saffron Revolution of September 2007, they do not hesitate to suppress them. They also use Buddhism to suppress religious minorities. In Chin State, Christians have traditionally built crosses on hilltops as a symbol of their faith. In recent years, the *tatmadaw* has forced Chin Christians to tear down crosses and build pagodas in their place.[28] Children from Chin Christian families have been lured into Buddhist monasteries and forced to become novice monks. Restrictions on the construction, renovation, or extension of churches are severe, and it is difficult for churches to obtain permission to hold meetings other than a Sunday service. Christians in government service are denied promotion.[29]

Than Shwe's policies against ethnic and religious minorities amount, in varying degrees, to ethnic cleansing. The term "genocide" is controversial, and it conjures up images of Rwanda or the Holocaust—large numbers of people killed in relatively short and dramatic time frames. If that is the understanding of genocide, then it is the wrong term to apply to Burma. But according to the Convention on the Prevention and Punishment of the Crime of Genocide, it does not necessarily relate so much to numbers, nor does it mean the complete destruction of a whole race. The Convention defines genocide as "any of the following acts committed with intent to destroy, in whole or in part, a national, ethnical, racial or religious group, as such: killing members of the group; causing serious bodily or mental harm to members of the group; deliberately inflicting on the group conditions of life calculated to bring about its physical destruction in whole or in part; imposing measures intended to prevent births within the group; forcibly transferring children of the group to another group." Furthermore, there are several sub-categories of genocide, namely: "conspiracy to commit genocide; direct and public incitement to commit genocide; attempt to commit genocide; complicity in genocide." When the Burma Army attacks ethnic villages, it does not simply kill those it suspects of being insurgents. Instead, it kills civilians, rapes women, takes people for forced labor, and significantly destroys houses, cooking pots, food supplies, and paddy fields, inflicting conditions of life that are often unbearable. A case of attempted genocide in Burma should at least be investigated.

While the regime has probably been careful not to leave a trail of evidence proving its intent, it is possible from available evidence to infer intent. The violations are so widespread that they cannot be dismissed as isolated incidents or pure accident. Furthermore, a few statements from high-level military officers in recent years are telling. In 1989 General Saw Maung acknowledged that the death toll in Burma's ethnic wars "would reach as high as millions."[30] Three years later, Health Minister Ket Sein reportedly boasted to a large meeting in Rangoon: "In ten years, all Karen will be dead. If you want to see a Karen, you will have to go to a museum in Rangoon."[31]

In a speech in 2007, Than Shwe himself declared that the junta would "crush, hand-in-hand with the entire people, every danger of internal and external destructive elements obstructing the stability and development of the state."[32] While Than Shwe's words are less explicitly genocidal than Ket Sein's, they are an indication of the regime's intentions towards anyone who opposes it. That is evident from the suppression of the Saffron

Revolution in 2007, to which I will return later, and from the direct attack on Aung San Suu Kyi and her supporters in Depayin in 2003.

While it is impossible that Than Shwe could be unaware of the massive human rights abuses taking place on his watch, another thing is also certain: there has been no justice for victims of his crimes. United Nations officials have repeatedly stated that abuses taking place in Burma are in all likelihood an official policy of the military regime. In 2006 a UN rapporteur stated: "[S]erious human rights violations have been widespread and systematic, suggesting that they are not simply isolated acts of individual misconduct by middle- or low-ranking officers, but rather the result of a system under which individuals and groups have been allowed to break the law and violate human rights without being called to account."[33] As if the point needed to be reiterated, in November 2008 the current UN Special Rapporteur on Human Rights in Burma, Argentinean Tomás Ojea Quintana, stated: "There is no independent and impartial judiciary system in Burma."[34]

The Rome Statute, the latest iteration of international human rights and humanitarian law, specifically addresses the matter of "command responsibility" in situations such as Burma under Than Shwe stating that "a military commander or person effectively acting as military commander shall be criminally responsible for crimes [within the jurisdiction of the court]."[35] The International Human Rights Clinic at Harvard Law School found sixteen separate acts expressly prohibited by the Rome Statute that Than Shwe's regime is likely to have committed.[36] These are worth mentioning if only to show that the Burmese junta has committed virtually every single human rights abuse on record. They include murder, enslavement, deportation or forcible transfer of populations, torture, imprisonment or other severe deprivation of physical liberty in violation of fundamental rules of international law, rape, sexual slavery, enforced prostitution, forced pregnancy, ethnic and religious persecution, enforced disappearance of persons, and other inhumane acts of a similar character intentionally causing great suffering, or serious injury to body, or to mental or physical health.

Further acts prohibited under international law include the war crimes of intentionally directing attacks against civilian populations or against individual civilians not taking direct part in hostilities; intentionally directing attacks against buildings dedicated to religion, education, art, science or charitable purposes, and to historic monuments, hospitals, and places where the sick and wounded are collected; conscripting or enlisting children under the age of fifteen years into armed forces or using them to participate actively in hostilities; ordering the displacement of the civilian population for reasons related to the conflict; and destroying or seizing the property of an adversary not imperatively demanded by the necessities of conflict.

Aung San Suu Kyi has faced human rights abuses as well. For some years, there were indications the regime wanted to find a way of assassinating her. On May 6, 2002, she was released following nineteen months of house arrest. With the regime's permission, she resumed her tours around the country. As before, she began almost immediately to draw huge crowds. Once again, Than Shwe became alarmed by her popularity, and a campaign of harassment resumed.

Several years earlier U Win Sein, the secretary of the USDA, explicitly called on his audience to "get rid of" and "exterminate" Aung San Suu Kyi in speeches he delivered in November 1996. As if to leave no one in any doubt, he spelled out what he meant. "Do you understand what it means by 'get rid of'? It means we'll have to kill her. Have you got guts to kill her?" Later, he repeated the same challenge: "Do you dare kill Daw Suu Kyi?" he said. He repeated this three times, but no one answered him. Once again, he declared: "We must exterminate her!" and asked his audience if they knew what "exterminate" meant.[37]

Arguably earlier attempts had already been made, including when her convoy was attacked by thugs armed with rocks, iron chains, iron rods, and daggers in 1996, and in 1998 when her car was forced off the road. But on May 30, 2003, Than Shwe's men came the closest to eliminating Aung San Suu Kyi when she and her supporters were attacked in Depayin. A mob of at least five thousand launched the pre-planned attack, which U Aung Htoo, general secretary of the Burma Lawyers' Council, described as a "crime against humanity," in which NLD members were killed and Aung San Suu Kyi narrowly escaped assassination.[38]

U Khin Kyaw Han, a member of parliament from the NLD who co-chaired the Ad-Hoc Commission on the Depayin Massacre to investigate the attack, said there is no way the massacre could have been carried out without coordination by the military regime. The UN

Special Rapporteur on Human Rights, Paulo Sérgio Pinheiro, agreed, saying he is "convinced that there is prima facie evidence that the Depayin incident could not have happened without the connivance of State agents."[39]

Aung Lynn Htut, who worked closely with the then chief of intelligence Khin Nyunt, says Than Shwe "absolutely" was responsible for ordering the attempted assassination of Aung San Suu Kyi. "After Depayin, Maung Aye and Khin Nyunt approached Than Shwe and asked him if he had ordered the assassination of Aung San Suu Kyi. He admitted that yes, he had ordered the attack to kill her."

These accounts are consistent with the experience of Wunna Maung, a member of the NLD's Youth Wing, who served as a security officer for Aung San Suu Kyi during her speaking tour through Depayin. In heart-wrenching testimony in the US Congress before Elton Gallegly, chairman of the Subcommittee on International Terrorism, Nonproliferation and Human Rights, Wunna Maung described the attack in detail:

> Before our journey, we heard many rumors that local officials of the military regime were training their troops with blunt weapons, including clubs, spears, and iron spikes. For this reason, Daw Suu advised us to absolutely avoid any words or behavior that might lead to confrontation with any member of the military. She told us that if we were attacked, we must not fight back. Even if we are struck or killed, she said, we should absolutely not fight back.

> On May 29th at 9:00 a.m., our cars began our daily journey. Our party arrived at Sagaing, about 12 miles outside of Mandalay, at about 10:30 a.m. Before entering Sagaing, we witnessed about 600 people holdings signs that read: "We don't want people who don't support the USDA." The USDA is the political arm of the military regime. Standing behind these people was a large crowd of people welcoming our party, yelling: "Long live Aung San Suu Kyi." We did not stop, but continued onward.

> At about 6:00 p.m., we reached the entrance to another town, Monywa. Tens of thousands of people showed up to meet Daw Suu and the NLD members,

and we could not even reach the middle of town for another three hours. Tired after a long day, we all decided to sleep for the night.

The next day, we traveled further, stopping along the way to establish NLD offices and hang up our billboards. We stopped in one town so that Daw Suu could give words of encouragement to the family of an elected member of parliament who is still imprisoned. At this point, our scout car rode ahead, but didn't return. We sent ahead motorcycles to scout out, but they also did not return.

At about 8:30, we reached a place, near Kyi Village, between Saingpyin and Tabayin, where the attacks began. I was riding in a car two positions behind Daw Suu's car. After passing Kyi Village, two Buddhist monks blocked the way stopping the vehicle in which Daw Suu was riding. One of my colleagues exited from his car, and asked why the monks were blocking the road. The two monks said, "We have been waiting for a long time for you. Ask Daw Suu to give a speech."

As my colleague tried to respond, four trucks, full of people, quickly drove toward our caravan, yelling: "Oppose those relying on external forces . . ."

When local villagers yelled in response, the USDA members began to brutally attack the villagers with iron spikes, bars, and wooden clubs they had brought with them. After a few minutes, the USDA attackers turned to our caravan. We watched helplessly, and tried to show courage.

Because we had been told to never use violence, we tried to protect Daw Suu's car by surrounding her with our bodies in two layers. As we waited, all of the cars behind us were being attacked, and the USDA members beat the NLD members mercilessly. The attackers appeared to be either on drugs or drunk.

The USDA members struck down everyone, including youths and women. They used the iron rods to strike inside the cars. I saw the attackers beat U Tin Oo and hit him on the head before they dragged him away. He had a wound on his head and was bleeding.

The attackers beat women and pulled off their blouses and sarongs. When victims, covered in blood, fell to the ground, the attackers grabbed their hair and pounded their heads on the pavement until their bodies stopped moving. The whole time, the attackers were screaming the words: "Die, die, die ..." There was so much blood. I still cannot get rid of the sight of people, covered in blood, being beaten mercilessly to death.

As the USDA members approached Daw Suu's car, we braced ourselves for the attacks. The attackers first beat the outer ring of my colleagues on the left side of Daw Suu's car, and smashed the glass windows of the car. As my colleagues fell one by one, the attackers then started beating the inner ring of security. The attackers hit my colleagues ferociously, because they knew we would not fight back. I was lucky and was not struck because I stood on the right side of the car.

I would like to stress that during the attacks, we never fought back.

After the attackers broke the windows on Daw Suu's car, the driver sped off. She escaped beating, because she did not get out of the car. If she did, the attackers would have killed her.

As Daw Suu's car left, we also ran away. People fled on motorcycle and foot. We ran as far as we could, but we grew tired. We flagged down a car and tried to drive away with 18 people crammed inside, but the USDA members were waiting for us, blocking the way and beating people who had fled earlier.

We were trapped. Since we had nowhere to go, we drove off the road and got stuck in a ditch. Fortunately, there were some woods nearby. Altogether, we counted 97 people hiding in the woods, and we all slept there overnight.

Two of those hiding with us turned out to be part of the gang that had attacked us. They told us they had been ordered to do so by the USDA. They explained, "We had never done such a thing in our life and since we could not bear to do such a thing, we came fleeing with you."

The next morning, we all slowly approached the main road at about 5:00 a.m. Shortly thereafter, we heard several gunshots. The military regime's police, from their cars, were firing at our motorcycles.

Since the police were firing at anyone who used the road, we walked across rice fields until we reached a village where local people allowed us to stay for the night. We exchanged clothes with some others the next day, and continued walking. Along the way, we met some other USDA members, who told us that they had been paid 800 kyats, and given meals and liquor in exchange for beating up a group of people. The USDA members had not realized that the people they were going to beat up were NLD members.[40]

Than Shwe's military regime denied that the attacks had taken place, and then claimed that the blame for the attacks rested not with the military regime, but with Aung San Suu Kyi herself. In a formal press conference, the regime claimed that Aung San Suu Kyi and U Tin Oo had incited unrest, causing traffic jams and instability, and suggested that five thousand people had shown up to protest against her speaking tour, causing "clashes" to break out spontaneously between her and the demonstrators.[41] For a regime that had, time and time again, used deadly violence against nonviolent democracy activists, the explanation was almost laughable.

The United Nations appeared to concur. Nearly a year later, UN Special Rapporteur Pinheiro called on the military regime to take action in light of Depayin: "In order to reverse the regression, all those who have been detained or put under house arrest since 30 May 2003 must be immediately and unconditionally released, the surviving victims and the families of those who lost their lives must receive compensation, and the offices of the National League for Democracy (NLD) must be reopened immediately."[42] The regime did not take even one of these steps.

In the weeks following the Depayin Massacre, Than Shwe essentially admitted in a letter to Asian governments that the incident had been premeditated. He accused Aung San Suu Kyi and her party of "conspiring to create an anarchic situation ... with a view to attaining power" by her birthday on June 19. He also claimed that he was faced with a "threat to national security by this militant group" and was thus "compelled to take firm measures to prevent the country from sliding down the road to anarchy and disintegration." Than Shwe further accused the democracy movement of intending to "arouse people to take to the streets . . . and create a mass movement that would result in public demonstrations and unrest."[43] He promoted Lieutenant General Soe Win to the post of prime minister—the man who was rumored to have overseen the execution of the attacks.[44]

Aung Lynn Htut, the former Burmese intelligence officer who worked at senior levels in the military hierarchy, reports that the only thing that saved Aung San Suu Kyi's life was the fact that Than Shwe and Soe Win had not anticipated that her car would be at the front of the caravan. The attacks had focused on the rear and middle of the convoy, and the quick thinking of Aung San Suu Kyi's driver probably saved her life. He used the car to break through barriers that had been created on the road, and drove to a nearby police station. The plan to kill Aung San Suu Kyi was unknown to the local police, who promptly informed military intelligence. By all accounts, the regime's intelligence chief Khin Nyunt was also unaware—and clearly shocked. He intervened, arranging for Aung San Suu Kyi's transport back to Rangoon where she was placed in Rangoon's infamous Insein Prison, before being returned to house arrest.

Razali Ismail, UN special envoy at the time, went to Burma within days of the Depayin massacre. The regime had not announced that Aung San Suu Kyi was in prison, but he demanded to see her. "I was taken in a car with darkened windows, and we changed cars along the way. Finally, we arrived at Insein Prison, and I was totally shocked," he recalls. "They had never admitted she was in jail. Khin Nyunt had simply told me he had rescued her from the mob." Remarkably, although shaken, Aung San Suu Kyi was once again willing, in Razali Ismail's words, "to turn the page" and use the situation as an opportunity for dialogue. But the special envoy was furious with the regime. "I came out very angry. I told Khin Nyunt: 'What are you doing? Do you know that if I go out and tell the world that Aung San Suu Kyi is in Insein Prison, what will happen? What are your intentions? Why are you keeping her like this? Why is she looking so bedraggled?' The next day, she was given clean clothes, better food, and within two weeks she was out [and back under house arrest]."

Like Pinheiro, another former UN Special Rapporteur for Human Rights in Burma, Yozo Yokota, believes what has been happening under Than Shwe's watch amounts to crimes against humanity. He served as UN Special Rapporteur from 1991 until 1996. "By then the world had reached agreement that such killings and such serious violations of human rights, as mass rapes and forced labor, for example, would be regarded as crimes against humanity and that kind of understanding had already been established, so it is not something that we established later and applied to that situation. At that time I felt that it was against humanity," he explains. He also believes the regime knew what it was doing was wrong. "I think that the military government felt some kind of guilty feeling. Whether [or not] they formulated them as crimes against humanity—they did not know the concept—but they felt that this should not happen, because every time I raised these issues, they never said no, we can do it. They said we would never do such terrible inhumane things. We are Buddhists, how could we do such things to our own people. They understood it was unacceptable."

Amnesty International agrees. In a report published in June 2008, the organization described specific violations in eastern Burma as "crimes against humanity."[45] Even the famously cautious International Committee of the Red Cross has denounced "major and repeated violations of international humanitarian law" against civilians.[46]

International institutions have also shown great concern about Burma's political prisoners. On November 25, 2008, the UN Working Group on Arbitrary Detention described the detention of dissidents Min Ko Naing, Ko Jimmy, Min Zayar, and Pyone Cho as "arbitrary" and in violation of at least six major articles of the Universal Declaration of Human Rights. In response, the Burma Justice Committee, a body of international lawyers, issued a statement welcoming the ruling. "Today sees the publication of one of the most important international law judgments in recent years. In a heavily argued case . . . the international legal system has ruled in the clearest possible terms that the military regime in Burma has contravened every last vestige of humanitarian law and falls to be condemned in the strongest possible way . . . The regime has been held to be operating entirely outside of the law and its violations of minimum standards of international law are described by the tribunal as 'grotesque.'"[47]

The question that, therefore, awaits the international community is, given the overwhelming prima facie evidence, will the UN Security Council initiate an official investigation into crimes against humanity in Burma or will it turn a blind eye to mass atrocities? In other countries, this move has preceded the establishment of international criminal tribunals, such as in Rwanda and Yugoslavia, and the referral of the situation in Darfur to the International Criminal Court. On June 24, 2008, the Women's League of Burma called for Than Shwe to be charged with war crimes and crimes against humanity, in accordance with UN Security Council Resolution 1820 relating to sexual violence. Will the international community have the courage to act, or will the words *never again* be exposed as empty rhetoric?

5

THE NEW EMPEROR

THE OPULENCE WAS obscene. Overdressed in an extraordinary mix of Burmese sarong and Western-style wedding train, Thandar Shwe fingered the jewelry around her neck worth tens of thousands of dollars, as she and her bridegroom Major Zaw Phyo Win sipped champagne and cut a five-tier cake. The wedding gifts the couple received, including luxury cars and houses, are said to be worth US$50 million. Some sources claim that the cost of the wedding reception, which was held in June 2006, was more than three times the state health budget.[1] It is also widely rumored among ordinary Burmese that Thandar Shwe was already pregnant, and that was the real reason for the wedding.

The scale of the luxury was perhaps an expression of the petty rivalry that exists between Burma's top generals. According to a Burma Army defector, when Maung Aye's daughter married, there was a large ceremony at Rangoon's Sedona Hotel, one of the most luxurious in the city. "When Than Shwe's daughter got married, they wanted to [out-do] Maung Aye's daughter's wedding," he says. All generals were required to spend exorbitant amounts on wedding gifts for the couple, and many ordered their battalion commanders to gather the presents for them to present. The really ambitious went even further than normally required, in order to protect their backs and win Than Shwe's favor.

A leaked video of the wedding caused outrage among Burmese and foreign observers. Aung Zaw, editor of *The Irrawaddy*, said: "Such mindless indulgence—smiling, well-fed guests wrapped in their finest clothing and most expensive jewels—is an affront to the millions of Burmese suffering under the incompetence and brutality of the country's military leadership, and the millions of Burmese migrants trying to scratch out a living on foreign soil because no proper employment is available at home. Than

Shwe was the one who accused other top leaders of corruption whenever he wanted to remove them. It's the pot calling the kettle black."[2]

According to the biographer Heidi Holland, Mugabe celebrated his eighty-third birthday in 2007 with an "enormous thickly-iced birthday cake" and a similarly extravagant feast for the ruling elite, "while ordinary Zimbabweans faced empty shelves and in some cases starvation." The party cost a million dollars.[3] Yet if the reports are even close to correct, the money spent by Than Shwe's cronies for his daughter's wedding was up to fifty times the amount Mugabe spent on his birthday. Singapore's influential and authoritarian leader Lee Kuan Yew—despite his country being an investor in Burma and a primary destination among the generals' families for shopping, education, and medical care—described Thandar Shwe as looking "like a Christmas tree" at her wedding, because she was covered in diamonds.[4]

This lavish display of abundant wealth by Burma's rulers and their cronies was in a country ranked by the United Nations as one of the poorest in the world, with the second highest child mortality rate in Asia, and the fourth highest in the world.[5] According to the World Health Organization, Burma is second only to Sierra Leone at the bottom of the league table for health care, ranking 190 out of 191 countries.[6] The regime spends forty cents per person per year on health care, compared to neighboring Thailand, which spends sixty-one dollars.[7] The average per capita income is us$220,[8] and at least three-quarters of the population live below the poverty line.

Such is the gap between Burma's people and the country's New Emperor, Than Shwe, who sees himself as a modern day version of Burmese warrior kings. If he is truly as humble and ordinary as those that knew him before he reached the top of the junta say, then he has certainly not passed on such characteristics to his family. Their grandeur stretches even beyond the country's borders. On the wall of a Buddhist pagoda in Lumbini, Nepal hangs a plaque listing as sponsors Than Shwe and Daw Kyaing Kyaing's eight children: Ko Nyaing San Shwe, Ko Tun Naing Shwe, Ma Dewa Shwe, Ma Khin Pyone Shwe, Ma Kyi Kyi Shwe, Ko Thant Zaw Shwe, Ma Aye Aye Thit Shwe, and Ma Thandar Shwe. All have arguably benefited from their father's position. One daughter is said to work in the Foreign Service. She is believed to be currently based at the Burmese embassy in Singapore and was previously in Beijing; another allegedly works in the agriculture ministry, despite having no background in agriculture.

The expenditure on the wedding was not, however, untypical for Than Shwe's children, which is perhaps one reason why in 2007 Transparency International ranked Burma, along with Somalia, as the most corrupt country in the world.[9] Than Shwe seems to turns a blind eye to the alleged corruption of those most loyal to him such as General Maung Bo, General Ye Myint, and Industry Minister Aung Thaung,[10] as well as his children. In 2008 reports emerged that one of Than Shwe's daughters visited the Aung Tharmarde gold shop on Mandalay's 22nd Street, and bought gold worth 100 million kyat (us$80,645).[11] She apparently then told the local military commander to pay the bill. A year before, an unconfirmed report claimed that Than Shwe's second daughter had made us$200 million through selling land to Chinese tycoons. The deal, between Ma Khin Pyone Shwe and Wang Xiaohua and Zeng Guang'an of Guangxi Liugong Industrial Investment Company, involved the sale of Burmese land to the Nanning Overseas Chinese Investment Zone for the formation of a China-ASEAN economic park. The agreement was made through the Union of Myanmar Federation of Chambers of Commerce and Industry, and was completed within a week.[12] Reports suggest that Than Shwe's son, Naing San Shwe, may be involved in an illegal gambling business, as well as running the construction group Classic International Company.[13]

Some extraordinarily unbelievable stories about Than Shwe's family are circulated in Burma, which are almost impossible to substantiate. They should be treated with a significant degree of skepticism, but are worth relating, so that they can be further investigated. Even if untrue, the fact that such rumors abound indicates the contempt with which Than Shwe's people regard him and his family, and the levels to which people believe Than Shwe is capable of stooping. It is claimed, for example, the family who loaned the jewels to Thandar Shwe for her wedding were murdered in 2008. They were the richest family in Moguk and owned an expensive jewelry store. Five family members were shot dead by gunmen, and a general's car was seen five times outside the house. The security cameras were cut off. All this, supposedly, was carried out because Thandar Shwe liked the jewels she had borrowed and did not want to return them.

Sometimes their greed is surprisingly petty. In 2002 when Than Shwe and his family were in Moulmein, they were reported visiting a department store, where Than Shwe apparently decided he rather liked the department store's generator. After leaving the store, he allegedly ordered the regional commander to arrange a truck to take the generator to Rangoon for him. On another occasion in Maymo, Than Shwe's family is said to have visited a supermarket that had received only few customers that year. To the owner's dismay, they took a huge amount of the stock without paying a single *kyat*. The nearby Defense Services Academy held a meeting after Than Shwe had left, and decided that the costs must be borne by the local people, so reportedly forced contributions were ordered. On another occasion, during one of his supposedly regular visits to Maymyo, Than Shwe and his family decided at midnight one evening that they wanted to eat the traditional Burmese pastries known as "husband-and-wife" cakes. These are difficult to obtain in Maymyo, but the soldiers dispatched to buy them apparently knew they could not return empty handed. Finally, at two o'clock in the morning, the senior general and his family are said to have had their cakes. Another story that has been circulated is that one time the family decided they wanted to wash with a particular brand of soap—Sun Light—and a captain was sent by motorbike to buy it. He supposedly spent an entire night searching for a shop that stocked it, and finally found one and forced it to open. It is rumored that some of the generals insist that their wives wash their clothes by hand in the traditional way using Sun Light soap, refusing to accept their laundry any other way.

Than Shwe has a grandson on whom he dotes. Nay Shwe Thway Aung, known as Poe La Pyae ("Full Moon") and sometimes as "Sein Myauk Myauk" ("the Royal Monkey"), was born on May 22, 1991, Buddha's birthday, which is the reason he is Than Shwe's favorite grandson, according to one story. An alternative, unconfirmed version suggests that Nay Shwe Thway Aung's parents had marriage problems and Than Shwe and Daw Kyaing Kyaing essentially raised the boy who is now in his late teens. As a child, he regularly accompanied his grandfather to inspect the troops, and it is said that the two of them sometimes watch their favorite football team, Manchester United, on television together. In April 2007, while accompanying his family to Maymyo, a helicopter was sent to Rangoon especially to buy roast duck for Nay Shwe Thway Aung.[14] That same year a lavish party was held for his sixteenth birthday in the Sedona Hotel in Rangoon, where Nay Shwe Thway Aung decorated the walls with pictures of football stars, including David Beckham. The wives of top generals Maung Aye and Thura Shwe Mann joined rock musician Zaw Win Htut, businessman Zaw Zaw, and other Burmese celebrities at the party. Zaw Zaw, who runs Max Myanmar Corporation, paid the bill.[15]

Nay Shwe Thway Aung, who is the son of an army doctor, Lieutenant Colonel Nay Soe Maung, and Than Shwe's daughter Kyi Kyi Shwe, reportedly studied in Singapore for a few years. Traveling on either Silk Air or Myanmar Airways International, he returned to Rangoon almost every weekend. The airlines were allegedly requested to alter their flight schedules in order to accommodate his weekend trips. But he reportedly moved back to Rangoon in 2008—some say because he failed to be awarded a place at Nanyang Technological University of Singapore, while others claim Than Shwe recalled him, believing it did his image no favors if his offspring's child was studying abroad. However, it has also been suggested that Nay Shwe Thway Aung never studied in Singapore at all, and instead was educated at the International School of Rangoon and by a private tutor. He supposedly wanted to go to Singapore, but his grandfather told him it would not help his credibility. Either way, he now studies at Rangoon's Technological University, where special privileges have been granted, including specially selected teachers, security guards, and a special class shared with just seventeen other chosen students. The road he uses to get to the university was cleared and cleaned by municipal workers who destroyed roadside stalls selling water.[16]

Nay Shwe Thway Aung's parents divorced and his father, the son of Major General Tin Sein, is widely reported by some to have come out as gay.[17] In June 2008, life became even more problematic for Nay Shwe Thway Aung, when it was alleged that he was involved in a drug scandal. Two of his close friends, Aung Zaw Ye Myint, the son of Lieutenant General Ye Myint, and Maung Waik, a former Burmese golf champion and famous business crony, were arrested in connection with drugs, and it was claimed that ecstasy pills were found on Nay Shwe Thway Aung.[18] Maung Waik was sentenced to twenty-five years for importing crystallized methamphetamines—a move probably designed to placate Than Shwe, who was furious at the embarrassment caused to his grandson.

The latest rumor in Nay Shwe Thway Aung's colorful life is that he helped a friend to kidnap a celebrity model. Nay Shwe Thway Aung and Aung Myo allegedly abducted Aung Myo's ex-girlfriend, Wut Hmone Shwe Yee. They drove her to Nay Shwe Thway Aung's home in Hlaing Thayar Township, where they held her for three days.[19] Wut Hmone Shwe Yee was apparently dating Burmese hip hop star Sai Sai Khan Hlaing, thus sparking Aung Myo's jealousy.

In a country as poor as Burma, the wealth of Than Shwe and his cronies begs the obvious question: Where does the money come from? One major source is the drugs trade, which is why Nay Shwe Thway Aung's alleged involvement in drugs, if true, would be no surprise—his grandfather's regime is knee-deep in narcotics. The catering at Thandar Shwe's wedding was provided by Burma's largest conglomerate, Asia World, owned by former drug-lord Lo Hsing Han and his son Steven Law.[20] Asia World was also involved in the construction of the new capital, Naypyidaw, and runs a terminal at Rangoon's new deepwater port at Thilawa. Asia World has been involved in the renovation of Rangoon's airport and the construction of a major highway to the China border.[21] The US Department of Treasury, announcing new sanctions on Than Shwe's cronies in 2008, said: "In addition to their support for the Burmese regime, Steven Law and Lo Hsing Han have a history of involvement in illicit activities. Lo Hsing Han, known as the "Godfather of Heroin," has been one of the world's key drug traffickers dating back to the early 1970s. Steven Law joined his father's drug empire in the 1990s and has since become one of the wealthiest individuals in Burma. Lo Hsing Han founded Asia World Co. Ltd. in 1992. His son, Steven Law, is the current managing director. Asia World has provided critical support to the Burmese regime, and has received numerous lucrative government concessions, including the construction of ports, highways, and government facilities."[22] Former US president George W. Bush named Steven Law "a regime crony also suspected of drug trafficking activities."

Some diplomats, commentators, and UN officials dismiss the idea that Than Shwe and the top leadership are involved in drugs, claiming there is no evidence. While it is true that there is nothing to suggest Than Shwe himself is directly trading in drugs, there is abundant evidence pointing to his regime's complicity. Jalal Alamgir, a professor of political science at the University of Massachusetts, claims that arms, narcotics, and the black market account for 50 percent of Burma's trade today.[23] And Bertil Lintner notes that "Burma and North Korea may be the only two Asian countries where the drug business remains a state affair."[24] In his book on the drug trade written with Michael Black, Lintner argues that "the role of the military authorities is not to buy and sell drugs but to protect the trade," which has developed significantly since ceasefires were agreed to with several ethnic groups, particularly the United Wa State Army (UWSA) and the Democratic Karen Buddhist Army (DKBA). These groups have joined forces with the *tatmadaw* to fight other ethnic groups who continue to resist the regime—both are deeply engaged in the production of drugs, particularly methamphetamines. Drug lord Lin Ming Xian was even a delegate to the regime's National Convention in the 1990s.[25]

According to Lintner and Black, a former Burma Army officer responsible for signing shipping orders inspected the freight on a truck on one occasion and found a pile of *yaba* (methamphetamine pills). He reported it to his boss, a former general, whose response was: "This is the way of life from the top down through the whole country. How do you think our Senior General Than Shwe, with [only] a monthly pay of 150,000 kyat [US$150], is able to maintain his lavish lifestyle?" Than Shwe's pay, Lintner and Black add, is now 1.2 million kyat, or US$1,000.[26]

Burma is one of the world's largest producers of drugs, second only to Afghanistan in the production of opium and a major source of methamphetamines. It is inconceivable that with a regime as bent on control as the SPDC, the drugs trade could continue without official approval and connivance. As early as March 1998, *Jane's Intelligence Review* noted,

The repatriation and laundering of narco-profits as well as the impunity enjoyed by the barons has clearly been institutionalized: a "don't-ask" policy over the source of funds used by Burma's new generation of narco-capitalists has been adopted at the highest levels of government . . . [T]he reality is a creeping criminalization of the economy: narco-capitalists and their close associates are now involved in running ports, toll roads, airlines, banks, and industries, often in joint ventures with the government. No less disturbing is the military regime's growing dependence on narco-dollars to keep a desperately floundering economy above water.[27]

As Lintner and Black conclude, "Without the protection of the government it would be impossible for companies such as Asia World ... to function and operate freely. Burma today has become a country where the drug business is an integral part of the mainstream economy and one of the country's most lucrative growth industries."[28]

Sean Turnell, an economist at Macquarie University in Australia as well as editor of Burma Economic Watch and author of *Fiery Dragons: Banks, Moneylenders and Microfinance in Burma*, argues that gas is another major revenue stream for Than Shwe's regime. In the mid-1990s, the Burmese approved construction of a natural gas pipeline from the Gulf of Martaban across Burma's southern Tenassirim Division and into Thailand. The Yadana natural gas pipeline, jointly created by the French company Total, the US corporation Unocal, Thailand's PTTEP (PTT Exploration and Production Public Company Limited), and regime-owned Myanmar Oil and Gas Enterprise, as well as other gas projects, brings the military regime over two billion dollars per year, in Turnell's assessment. Yet, as he points out, these funds do not appear to be used for the Burmese population; at least, they are not on the books.[29] Through a dual exchange rate system, the regime keeps less than 0.5 percent of the funds from the gas earnings in its official budget. The other 99.5 percent has mysteriously disappeared. Turnell points out that this is enough money to eliminate Burma's budget deficit as well as its "destructionary inflationary money printing" that the regime uses to finance its debt.[30] The International Monetary Fund confirmed these findings in a recent report obtained by the *Financial Times* that has not been released to the public. According to FT journalist Amy Kazmin, "How Burma's rulers use the revenue from natural gas exports to Thailand, through pipelines operated by Total and Petronas, is also under scrutiny. Gas revenues are added to the budget at the 30-year-old official exchange rate of Kt 6 to the dollar. The black market rate is about Kt 1,000."[31]

Burma's gas pipelines have been heavily criticized by international NGOs, as evidence emerges of increased militarization along the routes of the pipelines, as well as alleged displacement of villages and human rights violations. The pipelines benefit the regime financially and benefit Burma's neighbors by providing energy but bring little, if any, advantage and plenty of misery to the people. EarthRights International, an international non-governmental organization, reports that the Yadana pipeline was "marred by serious and widespread human rights abuses committed by pipeline security forces on behalf of the companies, including forced labor, land confiscation, forced relocation, rape, torture and murder. Many of these abuses continue today."[32] In the late 1990s, a group of villagers that claimed to have suffered such abuses sued the original American participant, Unocal Corporation, which was subsequently acquired by Chevron. The lawsuit was followed by years of legal wrangling in court in which Unocal ultimately paid an undisclosed sum of money in compensation to the villagers.

According to EarthRights International, the company subsequently tried to press for its insurers to reimburse the compensation, and when the insurers refused, Unocal sued. However, a Los Angeles judge found "evidence that Unocal knew the Burmese military was likely to commit human rights abuses on its behalf and concealed this from the insurers."[33] This point was further underlined when in 2007 the court ruled that the "pattern of pipeline abuses alleged by the victims in Doe v. Unocal amounted to 'military terrorism,' and therefore Unocal could not be reimbursed."[34] According to Richard Herz, EarthRights International's litigation coordinator, "Unocal was complicit in crimes against humanity. Then, it tried to leave its insurers holding the bag. Unocal, now Chevron, got what it deserves."[35]

An ambitious plan for the construction of a series of dams to generate electricity for sale to Thailand and China is another impending source of significant revenue that will likely result in the displacement of thousands of ethnic people and the destruction of their villages. The testimony of a young girl in a documentary produced by the Karenni Research Development Group sums up the situation for one ethnic minority group living in the area: "I come from an ancient land, Yin Ta Lai, where people co-exist with nature. Our life depends on the sacred Salween River. But my father tells me soon the Burmese government will dam our river and our way of life. If the dam was to be built, all our land will be submerged, and the Yin Ta Lai will be no more."[36]

In 1994 the Kachin Independence Organization (KIO) signed a cease-fire agreement with the regime. Soon afterwards, taking advantage of the cessation in hostilities, the regime began to militarize the area, moving in its troops and assuming control of natural resources, in what the Kachin Environmental Organization calls a "drastic expansion of army troops together with destructive development projects that have resulted in what some local leaders are calling an economic, environmental, and social crisis."[37] The *Hydropower and Dams* industry magazine points out that the Burmese regime is currently implementing twenty-nine projects throughout the country, one of which is the Myitsone dam project in Kachin State.[38] The Kachin Environmental Organization claims that the first dam to be built will be based forty kilometers north of Myitkyina. It is estimated that the power produced by the dam will be worth us$500 million per year and produce 3,600 megawatts of electricity, which will be sold to China.[39] Citizens throughout the area have written to Than Shwe to object, but the call for a more sensitive form of development has been simply ignored, despite the fact that forty-seven villages and ten thousand people will be immediately affected. Like the Yadana pipeline, the money earned from the dam is expected to go directly to the ruling military apparatus and in no way benefits the local population. Burma's ethnic groups, who live predominantly in many areas that are the focus of such natural resource exploitation, understandably feel their heritage is simply being stolen and sold off to the most convenient buyer, and as these projects show, the partners are American, European, and Asian.

One of the most significant infrastructure projects currently underway is the Shwe Project, which will create a pipeline from the Bay of Bengal, off the coast of western Burma at the city of Kyaukphyu, slinking across Burma's Arakan State, and ending in China's southwest Yunnan Province. According to Singapore's *Straits Times* and Japan's *Nikkei*, China's state-owned China National Petroleum Corporation will "hold a 50.9 per cent stake in the project, which it co-manages with the other stakeholder, Myanmar Oil & Gas Enterprise."[40] Korean conglomerate Daewoo is another major partner in the consortium. Since approximately 80 percent of China's oil imports from the Middle East currently travel through the hazardous Malacca Straits, the project could allow China to avoid the shipping lanes altogether and simply move the oil directly into China via

Burma, saving untold sums of money and time, as well as dangers associated with pirates and terrorism. Since the project is jointly owned by Myanmar Oil and Gas Enterprises, it is again expected that the Burmese people will see none of the proceeds of the shipments, which will instead exclusively fund Burma's military leadership or its cronies. EarthRights International and the Shwe Gas Movement, a grassroots network led by Arakanese activists, have already documented human rights abuses connected to the Shwe Project.

Than Shwe has a particular interest in infrastructure, and he takes great pride in what he sees as the regime's accomplishments. As former British ambassador Mark Canning sees it, Than Shwe is "very proud of having unified the country, in his view, and having made it stable, and he's very proud of all the bridges and roads and dams." There's no doubt, according to Canning, that Than Shwe and the regime "think this is a big deal." "But," as Canning further explains, "you wonder about the software. They haven't done anything there; in fact they've let it wither."

In addition to infrastructure projects and natural resource development, another funding source for the regime is foreign investment, which is channeled through military-owned conglomerates such as the Union of Myanmar Economic Holdings (UMEH) and the Myanmar Economic Corporation (MEC). According to Maung Aung Myoe, the Burmese military regime had thirty-five major "fully-owned" firms as of 2007, including major companies such as the Myanmar Ruby Enterprise, Myawaddy Bank, Myanmar Imperial Jade Co. Ltd., and Myawaddy Trading Corporation. At the same time, the military had interests in companies that included Myanmar Daewoo International, Rothmans of Pall Mall Myanmar, Myanmar Brewery Ltd., and the National Development Corporation.[41]

In 2008 the Office of Foreign Assets Control of the US Treasury imposed sanctions on businesses run by cronies of the military regime. These businesses include those of Steven Law, the drug baron, as well Tay Za's business empire that stretches as far as Singapore and includes Air Bagan, Htoo Wood Products, and Pavo Trading Pte Ltd. The latter is run under the directorship of Tay Za's key "financial front man" U Kyaw Thein. In operating the Htoo group of companies, Tay Za has also done business with Aung Thet Mann, the son of top general Thura Shwe Mann.[42]

The gem trade is yet another major moneymaker for Than Shwe's regime, earning hundreds of millions of dollars each year. In 2008 the US Congress passed a bill, the Tom Lantos Block Burmese JADE (Junta's Anti-Democratic Efforts) Act, banning the import of many Burmese gems and other commodities in an attempt to diminish the regime's income sources, as well as imposing sanctions on officials of the SPDC. According to findings made by the US Congress, the Burmese regime earned more than US$300 million from the sale of rubies and jade, over US$500 million from the sale of hardwoods, and more than US$500 million from oil and gas projects, with the regime owning "a majority stake in virtually all enterprises responsible for the extraction and trade of Burmese natural resources...." The legislation further noted: "Virtually all profits from these enterprises enrich the SPDC."[43]

Through regime and personal enrichment, Than Shwe has let the economy wither. While the regime benefits from lucrative oil and gas deals, the economy as a whole is in a dire condition. Burma produces 90 percent of the world's rubies and 80 percent of its teak and, in the first nine months of 2008, foreign investment almost doubled year on year to US$1 billion.[44] Yet Burma's people see almost none of the benefits. According to Sean Turnell, economic development today requires an economy to move from being primarily a subsistence agriculture economy to one in which industry and services assume greater importance. Turnell argues there are no exceptions to this rule—and yet, in Burma, agriculture represents a growing proportion of the country's gross domestic product. In 1962 when Ne Win took power, agriculture made up 32.1 percent of GDP. By 2000 it was 59.9 percent. The industrial sector, in 1980, accounted for 12.7 percent of GDP, but by 2000 it was just 9.1 percent. The service sector fell from 40.8 percent in 1980 to 31 percent in 2000. Between 1962 and 1988, real GDP growth was 3.1 percent. During the period 1999–2006, it was 4.8 percent, not much of an increase in real terms. "In other words," Turnell concludes, "in structural terms Burma has been going backwards under Than Shwe."[45] In 1987 Burma was granted Least Developed Nation status by the UN. Than Shwe has done nothing to change that designation.

Once he latches on to an idea, however hare-brained, Than Shwe tends to refuse to listen to advice. One of his favored schemes at the moment is the development of biofuels from the production of jatropha, commonly known as physic nuts. Farmers throughout the country have been ordered to grow these plants, regardless of whether the soil and climate is suitable. In some places, the effects have been dangerous because the nuts contain two toxins. In 2007 twenty-seven children fell ill after eating physic nuts by mistake,[46] and in February 2009 it was reported that twenty-nine school children in Thaketa Township, near Rangoon, suffered from food poisoning from physic nuts.[47]

The preoccupation with physic nuts is said to come from their Burmese name, *kyet suu*, a combination of words in Burmese that are associated with auspicious sounds assigned to different days of the week—in this case Monday and Tuesday. Aung San Suu Kyi's name is associated with Tuesday and Monday, and Than Shwe was advised by his astrologer to plant *kyet suu* throughout Burma to neutralize her powers.[48] In 2007 farmers in Pegu Division were ordered to grow whatever Than Shwe's supporters advised, in order to ensure his long stay in power—this meant sunflowers, because sunflower in Burmese is called *nay kyar*, meaning "long stay."[49]

However, the extent to which the orders come from Than Shwe or from overzealous underlings seeking to please is unclear. For example, according to a former diplomat, in one area Than Shwe was visiting, he requested sunflower oil for his salad. When it eventually came, after a desperate panic among those providing the food, Than Shwe is said to have made a casual, off-the-cuff remark: "I don't know why every farmer in this area isn't required to grow sunflowers!" The order immediately went out to farmers that the senior general required them to grow sunflowers—but Than Shwe himself may well have not intended such an extended program. Having come up through the military system and understanding how communications work within the regime, there is no chance that Than Shwe could be unaware of the impact of his statements. While the orders sometimes come directly from him, this may not always be the case.

Where the money from international business deals has gone is anyone's guess. Turnell suggests some of the funds may be held by the Myanmar Foreign Trade Bank, which is wholly owned by the military regime. Over the years rumors have surfaced of the money being held in Singaporean banks—a charge Singaporean officials have denied.[50] Burmese are reported to be among the top ten investors in real estate in

Singapore, and they include regime officials and cronies close to Than Shwe.[51] Whether Than Shwe's own funds have been channeled into Singaporean property is unknown, but a Burmese living there says, "Singapore is like an agent for the Burmese generals." While at times the Singaporean government has been outspoken on Burma, "it is hard to see where their loyalties lie," says another Singapore-based Burmese exile. "The Singaporean government has no specific principles. Their focus is pragmatism and self-interest." Still others suggest Than Shwe could have hidden away the funds in Dubai.

Despite the close association with narcotics and horrific human rights violations, various foreign lobbyists over the years have sought a piece of Burma's national wealth. In the 1980s and 1990s, Edward von Kloberg III, a Washington DC-based lobbyist proffered services to many of the world's most brutal military regimes that Mark Steyn, writing in the *Atlantic Monthly*, dubbed the "dictatorial A-list." Kloberg, a flamboyant bon vivant of sorts (he used to wear a cape at evening functions), worked for Romania's Nicolas Ceausescu, Mobutu Sese Seko of Zaire, now Democratic Republic of Congo, Saddam Hussein, Samuel Doe of Liberia, and Sani Abacha of Nigeria. Steyn added of Kloberg, "If you had enough blood on your hands, chances are you were on his books. Anyone can have an axis of evil, but von Kloberg had a full Rolodex of evil."[52]

Kloberg added the "von" to his name to insinuate flair or royalty, and was known for his phrase "shame is for sissies," when pressed about the nature of his representation of dictators.[53] Indeed this is a far cry from his earlier position as dean of admissions at American University in Washington DC.

In August 1991, Kloberg's firm, van (not von) Kloberg & Associates, registered with the Department of Justice in order to get clearance to represent the Burmese embassy in Washington DC. The ambassador at the time was U Thaung, a close associate of Than Shwe who, as noted earlier, comes from Than Shwe's hometown of Kyaukse, and as of 2009 is said to be heading up the country's efforts to obtain nuclear capabilities. *The Irrawaddy* magazine reported that U Thaung was also behind the attacks on the monks and civilian protestors in the Saffron Revolution of August and September 2007. Kloberg stated that his intention in representing the embassy would be to establish "contacts with members of Congress, the

Administration, and other pertinent government officials." He also said that one of his "main objectives" was to "counter the unrestrained negative representation of Myanmar and its embassy in Washington DC." To do so, he offered to arrange meetings between the Burmese ambassador and influential decision-makers; prepare speeches, testimony, and briefing papers; and provide coaching assistance, noting that mailings would go out every other week to key people on Capitol Hill.[54] Ken Silverstein, writing in the *Village Voice*, said that Kloberg "helped arrange meetings between Burma's ambassador U Thaung and 23 members of Congress."[55] Kloberg reported a monthly retainer of us$10,000, plus expenses.

According to Maureen Aung-Thwin, director of the Burma Project at the Open Society Institute who met Kloberg, the contract with the regime was ended after the regime refused to show him respect. Indeed, in a letter to the Department of Justice dated April 13, 1992, U Thaung stated: "At no time has this embassy or its Government ever engaged van Kloberg & Associates for any purpose whatsoever, and that, therefore, there is and was no basis in law or in fact for such registration." The ambassador instead suggested that Kloberg had been working for "a patriotic American of Burmese birth." However, U Thaung then hedged his statement, claiming: "In any event, if there ever was a constructive agreement, it ended on its own terms at the end of a three-month period."[56] *The Progressive* magazine reported that Kloberg rejected this notion, claiming that the regime failed to honor its side of the bargain: "U Thaung is a little s--t ... I worked directly with him, I saw him constantly. Sent my staff with him to meetings on the Hill. Wrote him daily, weekly, monthly reports. And then they stiffed me for about $5,000." In reality, *The Progressive* suggests, the Burmese had simply found better representation.[57]

In a bizarre ending, after over a decade of representing some of the world's most heinous leaders, Kloberg jumped to his death from a castle in Rome—apparently distraught over a romantic relationship that had soured. *The Washington Post* reported that he was survived by his companion, Darius.[58]

The new advisors hired by Than Shwe's regime had much greater access than Kloberg. Shortly after ending Kloberg's contract, U Thaung hired Lester L. Wolff, a former congressman from New York who had served as chairman of the Select Committee on Narcotics Abuses and Control in Congress, and on the Asia Pacific Affairs Committee in the House Committee on Foreign Affairs. Wolff signed a deal amounting to us$10,000 per month, plus expenses.[59] Like other ex-congressional members who consult on businesses previously before their committees, Wolff had established the International Trade and Development Agency based in Arlington, Virginia. The agreement promised the Burmese embassy "fifty hours per month of professional staff time, in direct charge of the Hon. Lester L. Wolff," as well as advice on "public relations and trade promotions."[60] At the time, Wolff also led two separate organizations, the Pacific Community Institute and the Honest Ballot Association.[61] The Pacific Community Institute arranged a minimum of five congressional delegations to Burma.[62] Bertil Lintner reported that ex-congressmen and politicians went on all-expenses-paid "fact-finding" tours of Burma under the auspices of the Honest Ballot Association and the "care and guidance of the SLORC." According to Lintner, the trips "differed little from the well-orchestrated propaganda trips which, for instance, the Soviet Union organised for Western intellectuals in the 1930s ... while thousands of political prisoners languished in jail."[63] Denis Gray, the Associated Press bureau chief in Bangkok, wrote that "several Wolff-sponsored tours last year resulted in positive remarks about Burma's military [from US Congress members]." Gray said: "Clearly the junta is pleased with the congressional guests. In a recent interview in Rangoon, Information Minister Myo Thant described what most [Congress members] had to say about his country as 'very good.'"[64]

The Progressive reported that at least three other Washington DC lobbying groups had been approached with requests to represent the SLORC but each one declined.[65] It is not clear when Wolff terminated his relationship with Than Shwe's military regime, but the end of his contract did not deter representatives of Than Shwe's regime from seeking other advisors in Washington.

In 1997 companies reported to be close to the Burmese regime sought out international support to burnish the regime's reputation. In July 1997 a prominent Burmese company hired US-based Bain and Associates, a "strategic communications firm" headed by former television reporter Jackson Bain and his wife.[66]

Many questions have been raised about whether Bain was working for
Than Shwe's military regime or its ambassador in Washington DC. While
not hired directly to represent Than Shwe's regime, Bain was enlisted to
support U Khin Shwe, the chairman and CEO of Zaykabar Company, a
Rangoon-based corporation. Bain and Associates did not report it was
working for Than Shwe's regime, which it was required to do by law, if it
were doing so. Instead, in its filing with the Department of Justice it wrote
in the section that asked if its client was a foreign government or state,
"This is not applicable."[67] Yet, subsequently, the *Washington Post* reported
that US government officials believed the company did "business deals with
members of the country's leadership," a relationship that Bain admitted
in the *Post* could be true. More damningly, the *Post* obtained documents
indicating that Bain's firm "repeatedly sent its advice directly to the Burmese ambassador in Washington, Tin Winn or his deputy, Thaung Tun ..."
The *Post* also reported higher level contacts between Bain and Than Shwe's
regime: "Progress reports on its work were sent directly to Lieutenant
Colonel Hla Min, director of the defense ministry's office of strategic
studies and the regime's chief publicist."[68]

The specifics of Bain's documents filed with the Department of Justice
show that Bain was to be paid US$21,500 per month. The nature and method
of Bain's performance included "public relations" and "media relations."[69]
Up front, Bain acknowledged that the company would "disseminate information through the US media to the US public about Myanmar." In a
statement that perhaps revealed Bain's true intentions, he wrote: "Some of
this information may encourage public support for a change in US policy
with respect to Myanmar." The "Public Relations Work Plan" submitted by
Bain said that it would undertake both "defensive" and "proactive" public
relations activities, including providing "key reporters and editors with
responses and demonstrable evidence to the most-frequently-asked questions about the *difficult issues*" [emphasis added]. Bain also said it would
organize a grassroots campaign effort to seek out "supportive individuals
in local communities in the US" and to create "communications lines to
deliver up-to-date information." Bain added that it would coordinate with
corporations and associations promoting engagement with Burma, noting
that it would work with "supportive organizations such as USA Engage
to coordinate messages and enlist assistance with proactive events, trips,

etc." At the same time, Bain outlined a plan to carry out "event-driven PR activities" to "seek opportunities for a demonstrative publicity . . ." while at the same time assisting with the creation, operation, and coordination of the Myanmar-American Business Council Administration.[70]

The Washington Post said that the documents it had found from Bain's firm "provide a window into how Washington public relations firms conduct a campaign on behalf of an unpopular client."[71] Bain said it would work closely with the Myanmar American Forum, Unocal Corporation, and the Asia Pacific Council.[72]

Interestingly, the *Washington Post* also reported that Frances Zwenig, who at one time was director of the International Center, a Washington DC-based organization focused on issues between the US and the developing world, "drew on donations from [American] corporations to help fund a trip in October [to Burma] by three former high ranking Defense Department and State Department officials . . ." The *Post* reported that Zwenig said: "The funds were not intermingled with those of the other corporations that helped underwrite the trip." However, the *Post* also said that it had obtained a letter addressed to Unocal in which Zwenig, who also worked at the Burma/Myanmar Forum for the International Group, "promoted the idea" of bringing high-level officials to Burma.[73] As with Bain, Zwenig did not formally work for Than Shwe's regime. However, the *Post* noted that Zwenig sent a draft itinerary for the trip to Thaung Tun, the Burmese ambassador's deputy in Washington DC, saying, "I would like you all to review it and help me edit it." Later, Zwenig went to work for the US-ASEAN Business Council, an organization promoting business in Southeast Asia. Officials at Unocal have served on the firm's board of directors.[74] Ken Silverstein of the *Village Voice* reported Unocal also hired Tom Korogolos, "a prominent GOP lobbyist who served as one of Bob Dole's top campaign advisers." Unocal paid the firm US$280,000 in 1996—money that Silverstein says went partially to "issues including Burma." Similarly, Unocal hired the law firm Davidoff & Malito, allegedly to help stop a New York City selective purchasing law that would have restricted the city's business with companies doing business in Burma. Silverstein also reported that the Burma/Myanmar Forum, run by Frances Zwenig, had sponsored several trips to Burma, including in February 1997 when it "covered the costs for five carefully selected Hill staffers."

Apparently Zwenig would not identify her organization's financial backers, according to Silverstein, but he reported that "a Unocal spokesman acknowledged that the company subsidizes both operations [Zwenig's outfit as well as the Asia-Pacific Exchange Foundation]."[75]

Bain, Zwenig, and Korogolos were not the only people working on Burma at the time. In February 1997, the Myanmar Resources Development, Ltd., a Burmese company, which US officials described as "close to the military leadership," hired Ann Wrobleski, then president of Jefferson Waterman International, a firm whose website in 2009 stated that its services included "combining worldwide knowledge of key people, politics, and processes to advance client interests."[76] Jefferson Waterman's activities would include meeting "with Executive and Legislative branch officials, and private sector and non-governmental representatives, as appropriate or necessary, to monitor and report to the Foreign Principal on relevant US foreign and trade policies."[77] For these services, Jefferson Waterman agreed to be paid an astonishing us$400,000, with the first payment due upon signing. Additionally, the Burmese company agreed to pay Jefferson Waterman "incidental expenses," including foreign travel up to us$25,000. Wrobleski's decision to work for the Burmese company was in some ways similar to the move by Lester Wolff, since both of them had previously dealt with Burma in an official capacity. Wrobleski had served as assistant secretary of state for narcotics control, a position seemingly at odds with the Burmese regime's collusion in the drug trade. While in her official governmental position, and not receiving money from interests in Burma, she had taken a strong line on the military regime. The *Washington Post* reported she had stated that the chances of Burma slowing the narcotics trade were slim until "a government enjoying greater credibility and support among the Burmese people than the current military regime is seated in Rangoon."[78] Yet the *Post* claimed that Wrobleski was "well known to the regime from her counter-narcotics work, which occurred when Burma was becoming the principal exporter of heroin sold on US streets." It further noted that internal State Department cables cited Jefferson Waterman as the "US-based lobbying firm" for the regime.[79]

The Burma-related activities of Bain and Associates, Inc. and Jefferson Waterman International appear to have ended soon after the *Washington*

Post exposé was published. Yet a few years later, another set of lobbyists would line up at the Burmese financial trough.

In 2002 Than Shwe's regime—in the form of then intelligence chief Khin Nyunt—contracted with DCI Associates, a firm in Washington DC that later became the DCI Group. The firm said that its intentions were to "brief members of Congress and Administration officials to improve relations between the United States and Myanmar."[80] DCI reported to the Department of Justice that its "areas of interest include trade policy, human rights, public health, HIV/AIDS, and promotion of democracy." Yet shortly after being hired, DCI moved to defend Burma's military regime from charges that it was carrying out widespread rape against Burma's ethnic minorities. After the UN Special Rapporteur Pinheiro had received information documenting hundreds of rapes, London's *Daily Telegraph* reported that a statement by DCI "described the report as a 'vicious smear campaign' designed to poison supposedly improving relations between Burma and America."[81]

Like Lester Wolff and Ann Wrobleski, who had previously dealt with the regime in an official capacity as, respectively, a member of Congress and an official at the State Department, DCI moved to hire a well-placed American who had relations with the regime. Even more sordid than the previous deals, according to the *Boston Globe*, DCI hired the former American CIA station chief in Burma who had served there in the mid-1990s. *The Boston Globe* broke the news of the hiring in an exposé in 2003, writing: "In the mid-'90s, Barry Broman was CIA station chief in Burma, also known as Myanmar, a leading producer of illegal narcotics that is governed by one of Southeast Asia's most repressive military regimes. In retirement, though, Broman switched clients: Last year, the former US intelligence officer worked on behalf of Burma as a $5,000-a-month lobbyist, trying to persuade American officials to adopt a friendlier stance toward the regime."[82]

The *Globe* also interviewed Melvin Goodman, the former chief of the CIA's Soviet Union desk, who slammed Broman publicly, stating that the move "shows a lack of any notion of what ethical behavior is. The fact that he is certainly capitalizing on his former clandestine relationships makes it even worse." Susan Rice, currently serving as President Barack Obama's ambassador to the United Nations, who at the time was out of

government, criticized the practice in general stating: "A foreign government's interests are not the same as those of the United States. To turn
around for moneymaking purposes and work for another government
is reprehensible."[83]

The *Washington Post* also covered the DCI story, and found that DCI
lobbyist Charles Francis, reportedly a long-time friend of the Bush family, "ran a sophisticated campaign to improve the regime's image—and
steer the conversation away from its rampant human rights abuses and
such."[84] This is despite President George W. Bush, and especially First
Lady Laura Bush, later becoming outspoken critics of the regime. Francis
had organized meetings with the White House National Security Council's Southeast Asia Director Karen Brooks to "tout Burma's cooperation
on anti-drug, HIV/AIDS, and anti-terrorism efforts, and in finding the
remains of US soldiers from World War II."[85] Apparently, Francis, along
with Broman, also lobbied Congress members, including Senator Chuck
Hagel (R-NE) and Representative Jim Kolbe (R-AZ), the latter of whom
was in charge of appropriating foreign aid through his chairmanship of
the Foreign Operations Subcommittee. According to the *Post*, DCI's work
for its Burmese clients ended shortly thereafter—although not before
reportedly receiving US$340,000.

The saga didn't end there. Doug Goodyear, the chief executive of DCI,
who had been chosen by John McCain's (R-AZ) campaign to organize
the summer 2008 Republican Convention, resigned after *Newsweek* re-
reported DCI's involvement in Burma.[86] McCain, like fellow Republican
Senator Mitch McConnell and Democrat Senators Richard Durbin and
Dianne Feinstein, and House Speaker Nancy Pelosi, is a long-time supporter of Aung San Suu Kyi and human rights in Burma, and apparently
would not brook support from someone like Goodyear, although a *New
York Times* blogger suggested the cause could have been broader issues—
that McCain did not want to be perceived as surrounded by lobbyists in
the midst of his presidential campaign.[87]

In building his gas and drug supported empire, Than Shwe has shown
a determination to expand the military, both in terms of numbers and in
weaponry. His defense policy draws heavily on the *tatmadaw*'s nationalistic ideology, expressed in slogans such as the "Three Main National
Causes," which refer to the non-disintegration of the Union, the non-

disintegration of national solidarity, and the perpetuation of national sovereignty. The regime has also developed twelve "national objectives." These relate to political, economic, and social themes that revolve around the same principles: stability of the state, uplifting the dynamism of "patriotic spirit," and uplifting the morale and morality of the entire nation.[88] These three national causes and twelve national objectives are encapsulated in propaganda billboards all around the country that summarize Than Shwe's mentality. Known as "The People's Desire," the billboards encourage people to:

- Oppose those relying on external elements, acting as stooges, holding negative views

- Oppose those trying to jeopardize the stability of the State and the progress of the nation

- Oppose foreign nations interfering in the internal affairs of the State

- Crush all internal and external destructive elements as the common enemy

In July 1997 Than Shwe reportedly made a secret speech to top military commanders in which he explained for the first time Burma's defense policy and mission, as he saw it. A transcript of the speech is not available, but according to Maung Aung Myoe, a national defense policy based on Than Shwe's speech was published in 1999.[89] The policy outlined a doctrine of "total people's defense" for the country, aimed at repelling threats to national unity, territorial integrity, and state security.

Than Shwe emphasizes aggressiveness in justifying the expansion of the military, while at the same time pointing to the military itself as the defining feature of Burmese politics. In 2004 he spoke to the Defense Services Medical Academy at its annual graduation parade, stating that graduates "must have the fighting spirit. You should have the ability to show your courage in accord with the motto—charge bravely, fight with valor, and crush the enemy daringly."[90]

This speech, like many others by Than Shwe and his fellow regime leaders, hails the *tatmadaw* as the singular, legitimate power capable of running the country. Those who oppose military rule are branded as "internal destructionists, under external influences craving power," or "destructive elements who are trying to jeopardize the stability of the state and slacken the impetus of national achievement."[91] Such elements, Than Shwe's propaganda argues, must be opposed and crushed.

In practical terms, these doctrinal statements translate into a massive expansion of the army, and an extensive militarization of Burma. In 1995 the regime confirmed that its aim was to have a well-armed military of five hundred thousand soldiers by the end of the century.[92] While the regime may not yet have succeeded in reaching that goal, the armed forces have grown to approximately four-hundred thousand by some estimates, though others suggest there may be as few as two hundred fifty thousand. These figures primarily refer to the army, but also include the small number of navy and air force personnel.[93]

Following the 1988 pro-democracy uprising, Burma's military regime went on a spending spree for arms. As Andrew Selth writes, "The enormous scale of the pro-democracy demonstrations . . . left the regime badly shaken. It also placed a severe strain on its military resources . . . The SLORC acted quickly to ensure that the *tatmadaw* had an adequate supply of munitions." Mortars, ammunition, 84mm rockets for M2 Carl Gustav recoilless guns, and raw materials for Burma's arms industry were shipped from Singapore, the first country, in Selth's words, "to come to the regime's rescue."[94]

Singapore's initial arms shipment to Burma occurred on October 6, 1988, within weeks of the crackdown and the reestablishment of direct military rule. It is believed that since then, Singaporean companies have acted as middlemen, providing a conduit for arms sales to Burma.[95] Later supplies of RPG2 grenade launchers and 57mm anti-tank guns were shipped by Singapore, although they originated in Israel and Belgium. In 1992 it was claimed that Portuguese-manufactured mortars were being sold via Singapore to Burma, worth US$1.5 million, in violation of the European Union's arms embargo.[96] Locally made Singaporean arms have reportedly also been sold to the regime in Burma, and Singaporean technicians have provided expertise at Burmese arms factories.[97] The Singaporean armed forces have been accused of providing training to specialist units in the Burma Army, including the *tatmadaw*'s parachute regiment team, and there are unconfirmed reports that Singapore provided Burma with its first guided missile system as well as artillery and intelligence training.[98] Although many of these reports are still unconfirmed, as William Ashton argues, "it is highly unlikely that any of these arms shipments to Burma could have been made without the knowledge and support of the Singapore Government."[99] In 1994 Singaporean prime minister Goh Chok Tong visited Burma, and received a very warm welcome from Than Shwe. The senior general said, "My expression will not be complete if I do not put on record the most constructive vision and pragmatic advice of Senior Minister Lee Kuan Yew in providing an atmosphere of mutual confidence between our two countries."[100] In March 2009, Singapore's state-run Botanic Gardens named an orchid after the junta's prime minister Thein Sein—in the face of rare protests by Singaporean activists who attempted to present Thein Sein with a bouquet of orchids for Aung San Suu Kyi.[101]

Pakistan became a major supplier of machine guns, ammunition, and mortar bombs to Burma. Ukraine, Russia, and others also supplied weaponry. India, despite initially supporting the democracy movement, became a provider of arms to the regime, including artillery shells, bullets, guns, and training.[102] But by far the most significant supplier is China. In 1989 Than Shwe, as commander in chief of the army, led a delegation of twenty-four senior Burmese defense officials to China, where they agreed to "a massive arms deal valued at $1.4 billion."[103] This included fighter aircraft, tanks, armored personnel carriers, field and anti-aircraft artillery, small arms, ammunition, and patrol boats. Since then, according to Bertil Lintner, "a seemingly never-ending stream of Chinese arms has been pouring into" Burma, including tanks, armored personnel carriers, rocket launchers, surface-to-air missiles, anti-aircraft guns, radar equipment, and us$290 million worth of light arms and ammunition.[104] In 1994 a further deal was concluded, worth us$400 million, involving military helicopters, artillery pieces, armored vehicles, military parachutes, and small arms.[105] Over the years since then, Burma has procured tanks and armored personnel carriers, fighter jets, attack aircraft, coastal patrol ships, small arms and light weapons, and logistical and transportation equipment from China and other countries. China has also provided military advisors for training and engineers for building projects. Between December 2007 and August

2008, for example, China provided four separate consignments of over 750 military trucks designed to tow artillery and transport military supplies. Eyewitnesses have seen these trucks in Karen State being used to move troops around and to deliver supplies to army camps.

Along with its arms sales, China has offered Burma protection from international moves to quell human rights abuses in the country through its veto power at the UN Security Council. In January 2007, China, along with Russia, vetoed a Security Council resolution that would have simply pressed for moves toward human rights and democracy. In explaining its veto of the resolution, China claimed that events taking place in Burma were the "internal affairs" of the Burmese people, and therefore not subject to international action by the Security Council. In 2009, as pressure on Burma mounted, Thura Shwe Mann, the number three in the regime and Than Shwe's chosen successor, reportedly made three secret visits to China within almost as many months, to shore up China's diplomatic and political support for the junta. But for Than Shwe, the relationship with China is one of pure self-interest. According to a former Burma Army officer, Than Shwe is as uncompromising in foreign relations as he is in domestic affairs, once claiming in a meeting, "There is no such thing as an eternal enemy or friend." He reportedly added: "We are not kissing China because we love China," leaving the conclusion implicit.

The cost to the Burmese people of China's arms sales, as well as political cover at the United Nations, is, however, high. In 2007 Than Shwe reportedly granted special privileges to China for exploiting Burma's natural resources, agreeing to sell to China new found gas from the Shwe gas fields for the price of US$4.28 per million British Thermal Units (BTU), amounting to 180 billion cubic meters of gas over twenty years. India had earlier offered the regime US$4.76 per million BTU but Than Shwe rejected India's offer in favor of China's—a move which cost Burma US$2.35 billion in revenue. At the time of the deal, the current market rate for natural gas was around US$7.30 per million BTU and for a long-term contract such as this one, experts estimate the regime could have negotiated for US$6 per million BTU. In real terms, this means Burma is losing out on US$8.4 billion in potential natural gas revenues.[106] Of course, given the country's dual exchange-rate system, it is highly unlikely this money would have been spent on the Burmese people. Instead, it will probably be pocketed by the leaders of the regime or stashed in overseas bank accounts. Meanwhile, Than Shwe's regime has not hesitated to dramatically increase the price of energy in Burma. In 2007 the regime suddenly and drastically introduced a five-fold increase in the price of compressed natural gas, doubling the price of oil and diesel. Many Burmese people, who live on less than a dollar per day, were reportedly struggling to pay even for their most basic energy needs. Indeed, it was the increase in energy prices that provided the context for human rights activists and Buddhist monks to launch an uprising against military rule in Burma in 2007, an event that came to be known as the Saffron Revolution.

In addition to conventional weaponry, there have been occasional reports alleging that Than Shwe's army has chemical or biological weapons.[107] For instance, in December 1994 the Burma Army started a major offensive against the Karen people and their base in Kaw Moo Rah, north of the Thai border town of Mae Sot. The Karen had held out in Kaw Moo Rah for years, despite frequent offensives, and it looked as if they would once again succeed in repelling the *tatmadaw*. The regime's troops were enduring heavy casualties and gaining no ground." Yet suddenly, on the night of February 20, the Burma Army took Kaw Moo Rah in the space of eighteen hours, without using ground assault. According to the Karen Human Rights Group (KHRG), "The Karen soldiers were forced to withdraw, complaining of SLORC shells that caused dizziness, nausea, vomiting and unconsciousness." Eyewitnesses claim to have seen "liquid" shells, which caused burning, in addition to alleged chemical shells. "These appear to be white phosphorous shells, another form of chemical weapon usually used as incendiaries," KHRG notes. "SLORC is known to frequently use these shells in offensives and to burn down villages. The effects when the phosphorous comes into contact with human flesh are horrifying."[108]

Although generally Than Shwe's regime denies possessing chemical or biological weapons, Thai general Chettha Thanajaro was quoted in a Thai newspaper as suggesting that the then Secretary-1 of the junta, Lt. General Tin Oo, confirmed the use of chemical weapons to him at a meeting soon after the attack on Kaw Moo Rah. "Concerning the Australian government's protest over SLORC's use of chemicals against the Karen," General Chettha said, "Tin Oo replied that they had to wipe out the thieves and rebels that are against the government. He said that although the use of chemicals is not right, it is necessary."[109] At the same time, the regime's newspaper, the *New Light of Myanmar*, claimed bizarrely that it was the Karen, not the *tatmadaw*, that had used chemical and biological weapons—and that it was the Karen who had attacked their own base in Kaw Moo Rah. Interestingly, the article referred specifically to potassium cyanide. The symptoms of potassium cyanide are known as "cyanosis," which includes the inability to breathe, respiratory failure and, if mixed with other elements, can cause skin burns and blistering.[110]

In addition to the Karen and Karenni, the Kachin claimed to have captured a "gas weapon" in 1992, which had been dropped from the air by Burmese fighter planes as well as several unexploded shells containing chemical warheads. They had also intercepted radio messages from Burma Army commanders to frontline troops, ordering them to withdraw three hundred meters from the frontline before the air strikes began. Similarly, the Shan have also experienced weapons, causing the same side effects described by the Karen and Karenni.[111]

In 1998 the defense publishing group, *Jane's*, concluded that: "A biological warfare capability appears to exist ... It is likely that a chemical warfare capability also exists."[112] Twelve years earlier, the US director of naval intelligence, Rear Admiral William Studeman, stated that Burma was one of a number of countries developing chemical warfare capability, and by 1991 his successor, Rear Admiral Thomas Brooks, said that Burma "probably possessed" an offensive chemical weapons capacity.[113] In 2005 the US Congressional Research Service listed Burma as a country "suspected" of possessing a chemical weapons capability.[114] If this is true, it may be that the regime is using some of its secret, heavily-guarded defense industries to produce such weaponry, perhaps those based in Sinde, just south of Pyay (Prome). A large defense industrial complex on the western bank of the Irrawaddy River near Pyay next to Burma's mint facility at Wasi houses the Htonebo, Padaung, and Nyaungchitauk factories. Another large military manufacturing complex is located in Malun, near Magwe. Some sources believe chemical weapons are produced at a fertilizer plant across the Irrawaddy from Bagan, built with assistance from the German company Fritz Werner Industrie-Ausrustungen GmbH.[115]

The evidence is still not conclusive, and experts are not yet convinced, but the amount of anecdotal evidence from all the ethnic conflict zones provides a strong indication that the Burma Army may be using some form of unconventional warfare.

There are also signs that Than Shwe is trying to develop a nuclear program. Russian and North Korean experts are in the country, and several hundred Burmese soldiers are reported to have received training in nuclear technology in Russia. At the Defense Services Academy in Maymyo, Russian military experts and language teachers have been seen.

As long ago as 1956, Burma began a nuclear research program and established the Union of Burma Atomic Energy Center in Rangoon. Surprisingly, however, Ne Win shut it down. It was only revitalized in 2001 when Than Shwe's regime reached an agreement with the Russian Atomic Energy Mission to build a ten-megawatt nuclear research reactor in Central Burma. A few months later, a Department of Atomic Energy was established, and in 2006 a new nuclear physics department was opened in Rangoon and Mandalay universities. According to Bertil Lintner, Thein Po Saw, a US-trained nuclear scientist who studied in Moscow in the 1970s, and U Thaung, the minister of science and technology and the former ambassador to the United States, are the brains behind the program.[116]

Although the agreement with Russia was signed in 2001, plans stalled until 2005 when Russia's Ministry for Atomic Energy (Minatom) confirmed that talks had resumed. A ten-megawatt reactor was to be built in the mountains northeast of Than Shwe's hometown of Kyaukse.[117] In 2007 Russia's atomic energy agency, Rosatom, confirmed the construction of a reactor, which would use low-enriched uranium, not plutonium. Burma has uranium deposits in mines near Mohnyin, Kachin State, and near Mogok in Mandalay Division. Defectors from the Burma Army have said that a ten-megawatt nuclear reactor is under construction at Myaing, north of Pakokku in Magwe Division, and another is being built at Naung Lai, south of Maymyo. Uranium refineries are located at Thabeikkyin, one hundred kilometers north of Mandalay, and near Naung Lai, close to the Myit Nge River.[118] Lintner believes that the key locations of Kyaukse, Than Shwe's hometown, Naypyidaw, the new capital, and Maymyo, a major military center, form a triangle within which the key nuclear developments are taking place. In addition to Russian experts, North Koreans are reported to be working in Maymyo, and in 2007 it was claimed that an Iranian intelligence officer had visited the site.[119] Southwest of Maymyo lies the Setkhya Mountains, where the Burma Army's "nuclear battalion" is reportedly engaged in research, according to a report by Dictator Watch. The center of this operation is near the villages of Lun Kyaw and Taung Taw, and local villagers reported hearing huge explosions at night in April, June, and September 2006.[120] Burma's Ministry of Energy lists uranium ore sources in Magwe, Taungdwingi, Kyaukphygon, Kyauksin, and Paongpyin, although the quality of the ore varies. One mine, based in Magwe, is on a significant fault line that suffered a major earthquake in 2003.[121] There have also been reports of a nuclear research facility in Kalagok Kyun Island in Mon State.[122]

The fact that a nuclear program is underway is certain; even the regime has admitted it. However, as the vice chief of military intelligence, Major-General Kyaw Win, said in 2002, in the regime's eyes, the purpose is entirely "peaceful" and designed for medical purposes. Little is known about how true that is, but the possibility that Than Shwe desires to turn it into a weapons capability should not be summarily ruled out. As Lintner says: "It may be years, if not decades, away from developing nuclear-weapons capability. But the fact that the country's military leadership is experimenting with nuclear power is a cause for concern."[123] According to Michael Green, a former US National Security Council official, and Derek Mitchell, currently a Pentagon official: "Western intelligence officials have suspected for several years that the regime had had an interest in following the model of North Korea and achieving military autarky by developing ballistic missiles and nuclear weapons." They argue Burma is a much more urgent problem for the international community than most people realize.[124]

The reactor the Russians are building in Burma is, apparently, similar to the one they built in Yongbyon, North Korea in 1965, from which the North Koreans did not hesitate to extract plutonium.[125] Than Shwe must have noticed how having a nuclear program has emboldened, and perhaps to a certain extent protected, Kim Jong-il from US aggression. In the face of harsh criticism and strong sanctions from the US, it is feasible that he would wish for similar protection.

The Pyongyang connection does not end there. In 2003 the Democratic Voice of Burma (DVB) reported that eighty Burmese military personnel might be studying nuclear atomic energy technology in North Korea. In July 2007, it was reported that a 2,900-ton North Korean cargo vessel, called MV Bong Hoafan, had sailed into a Burmese port eight months previously. While Burmese officials claimed that an inspection had found "no suspicious material or military equipment," the international community was skeptical. The South Korean news agency reported that a North Korean ship had unloaded self-propelled artillery in Burma.[126] In 2008 a Japanese broadcaster claimed North Korea had been selling the regime multiple rocket launchers with a sixty-five kilometer range,[127] and in June 2009 the US navy identified another North Korean vessel, the Kang Nam, heading to Burma and believed to be carrying missiles and other arms.[128] North Korea's national airline, Air Koryo, has been sighted landing aircraft at military airfields in central Burma.[129]

In June 2009, photographic evidence was leaked, pointing to the presence of North Korean and other foreign experts in Burma, possibly assisting the regime in the construction of a network of underground facilities and tunnels. The pictures and video footage obtained by DVB show between six hundred and eight hundred tunnels at various stages of construction. Some are reportedly large enough for heavy vehicles to drive through, with built-in ventilation facilities and power supply, as well as provision for food storage, weaponry, and space for at least six hundred personnel.

According to DVB, "Photographs of a number of tunnel sites clearly show North Korean advisers present, while some construction equipment being used on the sites displays the Korean script."[130] One photograph of a site in Pyinmanar Taung Nyo, dated May 26, 2006, shows North Koreans training Burmese soldiers and technicians in tunnel construction. It is speculated that the regime has spent "billions" on the network of tunnels, in a project code named "Tortoise Shells." DVB claims that the regime's records indicate that foreign aid and loans were used for the construction work, which began in 1996. Intelligence agencies intercepted messages from Naypyidaw in 2006 confirming the arrival of North Korean tunneling experts,[131] and in November 2008 a high-level Burmese military delegation made a week-long secret visit to North Korea. It is likely that they went to view North Korea's own extensive network of tunnels and underground military installations.[132] North Korean technicians have also been spotted at several other locations, including Monkey Point, Natmauk, and at a Defense Ministry guesthouse in a northern suburb of Rangoon.[133] According to Lintner, who also received the photographs, the tunnels are built possibly to help the junta "survive any threats from their own people as well as from outside."[134]

Many of the tunnels have been built around the new capital, Naypyidaw, although additional facilities have been constructed near Taunggyi, Shan State. Several Burmese military officials have been arrested since the leaking of the photographs, according to DVB.

Nuclear consultant John Large believes that "what you may be seeing in Burma is the laying down of the seeds of a long-term nuclear weapons program." Even if the regime claims it is for non-military use, Large argues that "if you install a nuclear reactor and all the nuclear gismos and widgets and, particularly the technicians and the way you train and educate the technicians ... you have everything you need to [create nuclear weapons components]."[135]

But Andrew Selth is not convinced. "Despite the rather breathless claims of some activist groups, Burma is not likely to acquire a nuclear weapon for decades, if at all," he writes. "Of concern to some countries, however, is the possibility that the SPDC ... will seek to acquire weapons of mass destruction (WMD) as a bargaining chip to protect itself against the US and its allies."[136] As Tai Sam Yone argues, if the regime did have a nuclear or WMD program, "it is kept under wraps." The regime, he suggests, "has most of the ingredients for such a program—materials (uranium ore, basic processing facilities), missiles, collaborators, and the motivation to develop such a capability. What they lack is top scientists and engineers to bring it all together—only so much expertise can be brought in from their friends without compromising their control over the end result."[137]

Some analysts, however, have cited what they consider to be some strong evidence. In August 2009, Desmond Ball, a regional security expert at Australian National University, and journalist Phil Thornton released a report claiming that Burma may develop a reactor capable of producing one nuclear bomb a year by 2014.[138]

Even if the evidence of a nuclear program is not as conclusive as that, it is enough to raise some concerns about Than Shwe's plans. In 2009 US secretary of state Hillary Clinton raised concerns about the nuclear program during an ASEAN regional forum.[139] Stephen Dun, a Karen activist in the US, gave evidence to a Congressional hearing, in which he said that the military build-up in Burma "is escalating" and warned that whether it is used for energy, medical, or military purposes, Burma is not ready to handle nuclear power. "Burma does not have the technological support system to safely operate a nuclear power plant," he said. "Even basic services such as a dependable electric supply do not exist. It is a nuclear disaster waiting to happen. It is cause for concern for the whole region... There is no peaceful reason why the junta should seek to go nuclear."[140]

Perhaps most alarming is that soon after the terrorist attacks on September 11, 2001, two Pakistani nuclear scientists, Dr. Suleiman Asad and Dr. Muhammad Ali Muktar, with long experience of secret nuclear installations in Pakistan, appeared in Burma. It is believed that as the war on terror began Pakistan's president at the time, Pervez Musharraf, asked Than Shwe to give them shelter. The US reportedly wanted to question them about alleged links with Osama bin Laden.[141] It is not known what influence they may have had with the junta, or what expertise they may have transferred.

Than Shwe certainly retains a far-fetched paranoia of Western powers. As Andrew Selth puts it, "They fear intervention by the United States and its allies—possibly even an invasion—to restore democracy to Burma ... these concerns have already prompted the regime to consider the acquisition of ballistic missiles." Selth believes it is, however, "highly unlikely" that Burma will acquire nuclear weapons.[142] But can we be sure? As Senator Lugar, ranking member of the US Senate Foreign Relations Committee, put it, regarding the new friendship between Burma and North Korea, "the link-up of these two pariah states can only spell trouble."[143] In the summer of 2009, Assistant Secretary of State for East Asia and the Pacific Kurt Campbell said that the United States was keeping a close watch on nuclear developments in Burma.[144]

Like many dictators, Than Shwe often justifies his rule as a response to colonialism. Opposition forces are referred to by Than Shwe's spokesmen, such Kyaw Hsan, as "neo-colonialists" who will "stab the back of the people while pretending to be good in front of the people."[145] In Burma, the military as an institution is publicly credited with winning independence from Britain, and Than Shwe makes every effort to utilize this mythology to perpetuate military rule. Since the United States began speaking out in favor of the Burmese people's desire for democracy, media outlets, official propaganda, and radio addresses by Than Shwe's regime also attempt to portray the United States as Burma's enemy: "The US and its associates are attempting to make the nation get into crisis and undermine the stability of the State . . ."[146] While the United States and others have mainly called for an end to human rights abuses in Burma and genuine national reconciliation, Than Shwe's regime claims Western ideals "pose grave dangers to the security of the people" and the stability of the Union. Another of Than Shwe's favorite terms in regard to his domestic opponents is the word "puppet," implying they are under the influence of foreign governments.

An extensive paper entitled "A Free People or Satellite Nation?" articulates the regime's mission, glorifying the military, while also criticizing the United States. The article begins with a review of British colonialism in which the author attempts to link such colonialism to current US support for Burma's democracy movement: "In addition to the protection of their homeland, they now look to spread or impose American values and democracy around the world as a political and moral absolute." The article goes on to describe ways in which the United States seeks to influence the world through the promotion of human rights.[147]

The regime and its cronies dismiss out of hand Western criticism over Than Shwe's human rights abuses, claiming the West is "creating opposition by claiming poor human rights . . . against Myanmar and other countries to serve their own interests."[148] This conveniently ignores the fact that the United States government has not primarily been documenting first-hand evidence of such abuses—research on human rights in Burma has become public because of the work of Burmese activists and human rights groups, and international organizations such as Human Rights Watch, Amnesty International, and others. At the same time, the regime ignores criticism by its own Asian neighbors, including members of parliament throughout Thailand, Singapore, the Philippines, Cambodia, Malaysia, South Korea, and Japan.

After questioning the motives of Burma's democracy movement, as well as countries promoting human rights, the regime moves on to blatantly false allegations. It has a tendency to accuse opposition members of terrorism, arguing that human rights activists are "committing terrorist acts, detonating bombs, putting pressure and inciting protests."[149] The latter two points have merit. Burma's underground student union, the country's Buddhist monks, the National League for Democracy, and many others have attempted both to pressure the regime to change as well as to organize protests. However, by linking terrorism and peaceful protest together, Than Shwe's regime has sought to discredit any dissent.

Even though the main threat to the well-being of the Burmese people is Than Shwe's military regime, Than Shwe invokes outside threats to justify his rule, including the dangers of science and technology. In a speech he delivered to graduates from the DSA, Than Shwe stated that the twenty-first century is seeing "rapid advancement and progress in science and technology ... and the fact stands witness to the global powers' dogmatism practices to dominate and manipulate the world for self-interest."[150]

Propaganda knows no bounds in the day-to-day life of the Burmese. From graduation speeches to children's programs to mass media, citizens receive daily reminders of Than Shwe's belief in the need for military involvement in politics. His regime responds to these supposed dangers and threats to Burma by invoking the unity of the *tatmadaw*, claiming it is "taking necessary measures such as preventing, questioning, holding in custody, and taking action against harming the stability of the State ... like other nations, Myanmar has to take such measures for the security of the people."[151] In other words, only the military is capable of pursuing Burma's genuine interests, a curious statist approach to sovereignty.

While using fierce propaganda at home, Than Shwe has proven adept at promoting a kinder image to the international community from time to time. In June 1998, for instance, he gave an interview to *Leaders* magazine that was extremely rare—not the tone itself, as Than Shwe often uses gentle rhetoric when interacting with international visitors, but in the fact that an interview with an international publication took place at all. According to its website in 2009, *Leaders* considers itself as "the one magazine that represents a forum of ideas and opinions on the major issues of change, and that distinguishes the special provinces of the world's leaders," defining them as "individuals who, by their position of leadership, exercise inherent influence and commanding authority over the allocation of the world's human and material resources."[152]

Whatever *Leaders* intentions, it could not have found a better fit than Than Shwe. In the *Leaders* interview, Than Shwe explained his lack of interaction with the media by stating that he lived "a very quiet life," and "so I don't push myself to talk to the press." He also told *Leaders* that he had been "misinterpreted" by the media, which was why he avoided international interviews. In a series of softball questions that followed *Leaders* suggested:

> This is a good opportunity to show the world that you are a statesman who is concerned for your nation and its future. As such, one of the things you are focusing on now is rebuilding the country; for you, politics comes later. But as you know, countries in the West are under the impression that you think it is necessary to have the security of a nation before you have democracy— that you can't have people voting if the votes are not honestly counted. Can you explain this to those in the West who seem to be anti-Myanmar?

Than Shwe, a man who had spent years crushing all resistance to military rule, responded by referring to his desire for peace:

> As you are aware, we are vigorously engaged in the national reconstruction of the country. We are working for the development and peace of our nation. At the same time, we are trying to place our country on the path of democracy, and to build a democratic system.[153]

The interview went on and on like this, with Than Shwe articulating his supposed dreams and desires, having just carried out a brutal resettlement program in Shan State that forced between two and three hundred thousand people to flee their homes. The interview with Than Shwe proceeded around the same time that two leading companies in his country, both reputed to be related to the military regime, had secured the services of two Washington DC-based public relations/lobbying firms: Bain and Associates and Jefferson Waterman. No proof of their involvement with the interview, however, has ever been offered.

Than Shwe's tactics with *Leaders* magazine, as well as the hiring of US public relations and lobbying firms, together with the claims that he wouldn't kill because he is Buddhist, seem to suggest that one of his main intentions is ending American support for Burma's democracy movement. He knows that—propaganda notwithstanding—the United States is widely admired by the Burmese people, largely because America began to take a stronger stance against the military regime in the 1990s. Essentially Than Shwe has set a trap. If he can convince journalists and visiting politicians that he seeks positive direct relations with the United States, policymakers in Washington may be convinced to drop their complaints about one of the world's worst human rights abusers and end their support for Aung San Suu Kyi and the legitimate leaders of Burma. It is for these reasons, for example, that he granted visiting US Senator Jim Webb a personal audience in 2009, even though Webb did not represent his government. For the same reasons, Than Shwe initially responded more positively than expected to overtures from President Barack Obama's administration following a policy review conducted by the US State Department. In late 2009 US assistant secretary of state Kurt Campbell visited Burma and was permitted to hold discussions with Aung San Suu Kyi as well as senior junta leaders.

Than Shwe hopes to refocus the main issues surrounding Burma from national reconciliation within the country to positive relations with other governments. As if to underline this point, he arranged to have the *Leaders* magazine article printed, in its entirety, on the front page of the *New Light of Myanmar*, the military regime's official propaganda newspaper.

Despite these international public relations efforts, Than Shwe, unlike Zimbabwe's Robert Mugabe, has not had much exposure to the international community. There is no record of him having ever traveled to a Western country, though some dissidents suggest he did travel to the West at least once.[154] Few Western politicians or diplomats have met him. He has been described as "obscure, often grimly hidden behind dark sunglasses and a military uniform decorated with medals."[155] A former Western diplomat said he was "a characteristic product of the *tatmadaw* over the past forty years—insular, very skilled in Burmese military politics which is a pretty murky world—and that is why he got where he was. He is suspicious, but pretty confident of his own position. He was certainly large. I do not think he had been stinting on the good things of life." Than Shwe was not strikingly intelligent, he added. "There were many intelligent soldiers, and he was not one of them. He was a bit of a thug."

Consistently people point to Than Shwe's understated personality, his lack of charisma and charm, a tendency to be "cold and humorless"[156] with a "plump, sullen face,"[157] although he can be "very charming and friendly when he wants to be," according to Razali Ismail.[158] Other former diplomats agree. In contrast to his public image, one former ambassador said, "Than Shwe had a more mobile cast, and was more friendly. He is not like Kim Jong-il, a wooden figure in a sinister Mao suit. There is a little bit of similarity, but Than Shwe is a more human, rounded person." Humor, however, is not "part of his personality," says one foreign diplomat who met him several times. "It is difficult to feel anything." Compromise does not appear to be in his vocabulary either. "Than Shwe is such an old fox, and a psychological warfare guy, I don't believe he will personally cave in," said Bradley Babson, a retired World Bank official. "I don't see him as a compromiser."[159] A former Burma Army officer recalls how Than Shwe, during a visit to a battalion, summed up his approach with these words: "Whether it is a battalion or a country, ruling it is like playing with a rubber band. If it is stretched too far, loosen it a bit. If it is too loose, stretch it until it is tight."

Former diplomats say Than Shwe speaks English quite well. He apparently reads *Time* magazine[160] and surfs the Internet. Those who have met him say he does not require interpretation, although he always has a translator and answers questions in Burmese. "But he talks in English too, especially when he is disappointed with us. Sometimes he corrects the translator," said one foreigner who has met him four times. A former Western ambassador claims, surprisingly, that Than Shwe's English was actually better than Khin Nyunt's. Although when the ambassador presented his credentials, Than Shwe—who was accompanied by Khin Nyunt and the then foreign minister Ohn Kyaw—relied on translation from the director-general of the Political Department, U Khin Maung Win, who later became deputy foreign minister. "He understood some English, not too bad, but he was not bright. One had the distinct impression that he was someone of limited background."

Formal meetings with Than Shwe rarely involve much dialogue. Rather, "he starts with a long monologue, and then you answer with a long monologue, and then the meeting is almost over," said one foreign negotiator. However, when Aung San Suu Kyi's name is mentioned he becomes agitated. "Why do you focus on only one individual, when there are 54 million people in my country?" he complains. And when political issues are raised, he responds with a long account of all his achievements, the number of bridges, hospitals, and roads built. Razali Ismail says the first time he met Than Shwe, "he talked 'I . . . I . . . I . . .'" It was all about him, although Than Shwe agreed on that occasion to allow the UN envoy to talk to Aung San Suu Kyi, and appointed Khin Nyunt as the contact point.

On one occasion, when Razali Ismail met Than Shwe, the senior general was clearly in a bad mood. "He was very disappointed with us about something," recalls another foreigner present in the meeting. "He didn't shout, but he was really impolite. After two or three minutes, he said he had no more time for us, he had to chair a cabinet meeting, so he would leave General Khin Nyunt to continue the meeting. We knew that he was disappointed, but we did not know exactly why."

Another former Western diplomat met Than Shwe at a credentials ceremony where he launched into a lecture on the number of bridges he had built, and then discussed British history, British education, and Big Ben. Sometimes his eccentricities get the better of him. A former US military attaché met Than Shwe at a reception, soon after the move to Naypyidaw. To his surprise, the senior general was standing alone in a corner, so the attaché went over to introduce himself. He held out his hand to the dictator, but before he could even utter his name, Than Shwe looked at him and said: "Canberra, Sydney; Washington DC, New York; The Hague, Amsterdam; Ottawa, Toronto. Many countries have an administrative capital separate from the major economic and population centers." With that, he sauntered away.

Razali Ismail recalls Than Shwe as "quite a vain guy," who dresses well, sits straight, and looks good. "One day he asked me, 'Why are you looking so fit? You don't have this,' patting his stomach. I said, 'Well, you are in charge of the country. What do I do? I just work for the UN, so I have more time to play golf and exercise.' It was a jocular answer, but he was serious."

Than Shwe is said to enjoy Chinese Shaolin martial arts movies and, of course, golf, a favorite sport of the military. Additionally, Aung Lynn

Htut, the former military intelligence officer who worked at the Burmese embassy in Washington DC, said that while he was in that diplomatic posting he was required to copy VHS tapes of boxing matches and send them back to Rangoon for Than Shwe to watch. When he took office in 1992, Than Shwe promised that the army would not hold onto power for long—a pledge long since broken.[161]

Than Shwe is known to suffer from diabetes and hypertension, and is rumored to have intestinal cancer, but shows no signs of giving up.[162] In January 2007, he spent a week in a Singapore hospital, surrounded by tight security and close family members.[163] He eats simply, preferring basic curries, fried morning glory, fish head soup, and gourd and magnolia fritters. Unlike Maung Aye, he rarely drinks alcohol and seldom expresses his emotions.

But although he is at times insular and, according to a Thai diplomat, he is uncomfortable with foreigners, Than Shwe has pursued a foreign policy that is far less isolationist than Ne Win's. It cannot be plausibly argued that Than Shwe is isolated or somehow cut-off from the world. His regime has launched tourist promotion campaigns such as the 1996 "Visit Myanmar Year," built new airports and hotels, opened new embassies, launched an English-language television channel, and welcomed foreign investment.

In 1997 Burma was admitted to the Association of Southeast Asian Nations (ASEAN), on the recommendation of Malaysia's prime minister Mahathir Mohamad. Burma first attended an ASEAN meeting, as a guest of Thailand in 1994, two years after Than Shwe became senior general. However, Than Shwe's willingness to engage with the international community is limited to the pursuit of his own interpretation of Burma's interests. It is aptly summed up by Renaud Egreteau and Larry Jagan as "isolationism without isolation."[164] According to Stephen McCarthy, a research fellow at Griffith University in Australia, "Burma's political and economic situation in the early 1990s made a partnership with ASEAN seem an attractive proposition. Facing diplomatic isolation and punitive sanctions from Western countries, Burma saw the advantages of ASEAN members having access to international funding (particularly the World Bank); a common voice in the UN; and a common posture on major policy issues and in negotiations with major powers—especially the US, the EU, India and Japan."[165]

Former Thai diplomat Surapong Jayanama agrees. "Burma has been able to benefit from the positive image and international standing of ASEAN. Burma has used ASEAN as its protective shield in its foreign relations. Put differently, the Burmese military junta has successfully transformed the conflict it is having with the international community into a conflict between ASEAN and the international community. Other ASEAN member states . . . are thus lingering in a nauseous condition derived from their inability to digest the 'Burma problem.'"[166]

However, Burma's membership in ASEAN has "at times become uncomfortable for its generals, and embarrassing for ASEAN," argues McCarthy. In the aftermath of the Depayin massacre, the EU, US, and Japan all introduced new economic sanctions. "All of this activity placed ASEAN in an awkward position with respect to its principle of non-interference . . . the SPDC's actions were an unnecessary embarrassment that impinged upon ASEAN's credibility as an organization. At their annual meeting of foreign ministers held in Phnom Penh in June [2003], ASEAN issued an unprecedented joint statement calling for Suu Kyi's release." This statement was, McCarthy says, the first time ASEAN had taken "a collective stand against one of its regional neighbors," let alone a full member, since Vietnam's occupation of Cambodia.[167]

Than Shwe responded to this by dispatching his foreign minister and deputy foreign minister on a tour of Thailand, Japan, Malaysia, Indonesia, Singapore, China, Bangladesh, Pakistan, and India with the personal letter from Than Shwe, claiming that he had been forced to act against Aung San Suu Kyi because she and the NLD were plotting an uprising and encouraging the armed ethnic groups to take part. This drew further anger from some in the region, because it was an admission from Than Shwe that the attack had been premeditated, despite the regime's simultaneous attempts to blame it on criminal mobs. Mahathir Mohamad, Malaysia's leader and the man who had promoted Burma's membership of ASEAN, threatened Burma's expulsion if Aung San Suu Kyi was not freed.[168] The threat, however, came to nothing.

Ironically at the Asia-Europe Meeting (ASEM) of foreign ministers in July 2003, Thailand's foreign minister Surakiart Sathirathai proposed the introduction of a "Road Map to Democracy," entailing the release of Aung San Suu Kyi, an investigation into the Depayin massacre, peace talks with the ethnic groups, a new constitution drawn up through an inclusive process, a transitional period leading to elections, ending with democratic elections monitored by international observers.[169] A month later Khin Nyunt announced the regime would indeed introduce a seven-stage road map to "disciplined democracy." The steps, however, were very different, and involved neither Aung San Suu Kyi's release, nor an investigation into Depayin, nor peace talks, nor a meaningful and inclusive process. Instead, it entailed the imposition of a constitution drawn up to enshrine military rule, effectively eliminating the democratic parties from the political process. Surapong Jayanama believes "subsequent actions by the Burmese military junta have indicated that the decision to hastily welcome Rangoon into ASEAN was a tragic mistake and a major political blunder. Additionally, it was a decision that severely lacked a good and transparent deliberative process. Double standards were applied." He believes Burma was not required to follow any of the requirements for ASEAN membership applied to Cambodia, such as "a gesture of democratic reform." Instead, Burma joined "without any strings attached."[170] ASEAN's policy of "constructive engagement" amounted, in Surapong's view, to "a recipe for political inaction" that involved "distorting the gravity of the political situation and tacitly consenting to the derailing of democratization in Burma." Comparisons between Asia's relations with Burma and Africa's failure to stop Mugabe's reign of terror in Zimbabwe are not completely unjustified.

In 2005 Burma was due to take the chairmanship of ASEAN. Western pressure, however, was intense, with threats of boycotts of summits with ASEAN under the junta's chairmanship. After months of wrangling, Burma announced it would give up its turn at the chairmanship, citing its preparations for a national convention as an excuse. This marked a slight shift in the dynamics in ASEAN. McCarthy concludes that the move was "reflective of a change in ASEAN's attitude toward the handling of domestic problems among its member states."[171]

While some compare Than Shwe to other dictators such as Saddam Hussein, Kim Jong-il, and Robert Mugabe, Than Shwe actually seems to be a blend of all three, although he does not see himself in that same category. He once complained to Australian foreign minister Alexander Downer that while people call him a dictator, it is a description that does not apply to himself. Curiously, "what strikes me about him," says one Westerner who met him a number of times, "is that when you meet him, you don't have the impression that you are talking to a dictator. He does not look like Castro or Saddam Hussein. He is a short fellow, a little bit fat, with not a strong voice."

A former Thai diplomat remembers him as a "stout man with glasses and teeth covered in red spots from betel nut." He was nicknamed "bespectacled man," which, the former Thai ambassador claims, "is not a compliment" in Burma. When they shook hands, he adds, "I noticed that his hands were quite rough." But like Mugabe, Than Shwe faces an organized democratic opposition that has domestic and international legitimacy—one which he loathes. Like Kim Jong-il, he is reclusive, uncharismatic, and controlling. And like Saddam Hussein, Than Shwe is intolerant of anyone within his own regime who he feels may challenge him. "While Saddam's practices of killing and torture were more visible and shocking to the international community," writes Nyo Ohn Myint, an NLD-Liberated Area spokesperson, "Than Shwe has used marginally more civilized methods when the eyes of the international community are upon him. But beyond the reach of the media and witnesses, both can be equally blamed."[172]

Than Shwe, according to Nyo Ohn Myint, "not only eliminates his opponents, but also eradicates colleagues and subordinates who express an alternative view." This was evident when Than Shwe removed Briga-dier General Zaw Htun after he had proposed an alternative economic strategy. And it was most apparent in 2004, when the prime minister and intelligence chief, Khin Nyunt, and his entire military intelligence appa-ratus were purged. Many of Khin Nyunt's subordinates were physically tortured—some, apparently, to death.

The purge came on October 18, 2004, in a simple one-sentence announcement signed by Than Shwe. The statement claimed that Khin Nyunt had been "permitted to retire on health grounds." He was replaced as prime minister by General Soe Win, a Than Shwe protégé, and the man believed to be the architect of the Depayin massacre. More than a dozen Burmese ambassadors in overseas postings were recalled, along with a further twenty other diplomats, all believed to be associated with Khin Nyunt and the military intelligence. At least eleven new ambassadors were appointed, all of whom were brigadier-generals.[173] A few days after Khin Nyunt's "retirement," Than Shwe embarked on a landmark visit to India, which some have suggested was used to thumb his nose at Khin Nyunt's nurturing of relations with China.

Than Shwe's announcement of Khin Nyunt's "retirement" was misleading, however. Khin Nyunt had, in fact, been arrested and placed "under protective custody." On July 5, 2005, he was tried for corruption in Insein Prison and sentenced to forty-four years imprisonment. He is serving his time under house arrest. His sons were sentenced to fifty-one and sixty-eight years, respectively. In the view of one former Western ambassador, Khin Nyunt was "a fascinating and complex character, a smart operator, and an intelligent man," but perhaps too intelligent for his own good. He was "a supreme tactician, but he got rather lost in the labyrinth of tactical maneuverings."

Although Khin Nyunt was from the military, he was reported to have had a deeper understanding of and interest in the rest of the world than Than Shwe, Maung Aye, and other generals. This, in the end, contributed to his downfall. Khin Nyunt came to be regarded by the international community, including China, as the next leader. The fact that he was left out of the planning for the attacks in Depayin indicates that he was already on his way out, and his efforts to put Aung San Suu Kyi back under house arrest immediately after the massacre, were perhaps a final straw for Than Shwe. One foreign observer believes, "Than Shwe thought he was in danger. An alliance between Aung San Suu Kyi and Khin Nyunt could be his own end, and so he decided to stop the process."

Khin Nyunt is regarded by some as a more flexible operator, but this is only in comparison with Than Shwe. Few would describe him as a "moderate." After all, he presided over the entire system of military intelligence, involving all the instruments of torture used against political prisoners. Khin Nyunt was, however, very ambitious and marginally more inclined to take into account alternative views. "He is someone who understands the outside world, and is more ready to listen to the outside world than the other top two generals were," said one foreigner who interacted with him on several occasions. "He wanted to improve the image of Burma, and he understood that to do so, you have to make some concessions."

Khin Nyunt's approach was different from Than Shwe's. As one former diplomat put it, "He was a more subtle operator." He took the lead
in negotiating ceasefires with seventeen armed ethnic resistance groups
and played the diplomatic game with the UN more skillfully. He also
allowed non-governmental organizations (NGOs) a greater degree of space.
NGOs noticed the difference when, after Khin Nyunt's fall, Than Shwe
introduced new guidelines for UN agencies and NGOs, which amounted
to tighter restrictions. "Many NGOs found they were unable to continue
operating as before and cancelled their projects," says McCarthy. The
International Committee of the Red Cross stopped prison visits because
they were required by the regime to be accompanied by the USDA, while
Médecins sans Frontières, France withdrew, "citing unacceptable conditions imposed by the authorities."[174]

At the same time, it is entirely possible that Khin Nyunt's projection
of worldliness was simply a result of his training as an intelligence officer.
Very few people who point to Khin Nyunt as a moderate can cite specific
examples of his moderation. Former UN Special Rapporteur Yozo Yokota
found Khin Nyunt to be more open to suggestions, though subsequent
actions seem to have indicated that this was only a ploy. On one occas-
sion, Yokota asked Khin Nyunt if copies of the Universal Declaration of
Human Rights could be distributed around the country in Burmese and
ethnic languages, and he agreed. "He knew that to reject such a modest
request is not showing the world a good image of the country," says Yokota.
However, Khin Nyunt also demonstrated his caginess when Yokota subsequently complained that his request had not been fulfilled. "He told
me that the copies of the UDHR had been placed in the library of the
National Convention, along with the constitutions of the United States,
France, and other materials, so that the delegates involved in drafting a
new constitution could use it."

Many foreigners believed that Khin Nyunt was slightly more well
disposed toward Aung San Suu Kyi than Than Shwe, and according to
some foreign sources, he was eager to see her released and a compromise reached. However, one Burmese source, who worked alongside Khin
Nyunt, said that Khin Nyunt saw Aung San Suu Kyi no more favorably
than Than Shwe; he was simply better at giving foreigners the illusion
that he sought some form of reconciliation. In 2004 after Depayin, the

seven-stage "Road Map to Democracy" was announced and the National Convention reconvened. "Khin Nyunt wanted to bring her into the process," said one foreign observer previously involved in negotiations. The implication was, while they would not offer her the presidency, she might be offered a position in government and perhaps be appointed as one of the vice presidents. Five conditions were spelled out following talks with Aung San Suu Kyi: (1) the participation of the NLD in the National Convention; (2) the acceptance of the regime's 104 principles as the basis for discussions, although there was a desire that they be reconsidered; (3) an in-depth discussion of the military's role; (4) the release of Aung San Suu Kyi; and (5) the re-opening of all NLD offices around the country. "Than Shwe refused these last two conditions," said a foreign diplomat. "Someone went to see Aung San Suu Kyi to tell her she would not be released, and she said okay, no problem, that can come later. Then she was told there was no date for her release, and the NLD offices would not be reopened. So then she asked to meet the 'uncles' [her NLD colleagues] to decide what to do. It was really so close. I was 99 percent sure there was a deal. It was there, but at the last minute Than Shwe decided to pull it."

Than Shwe may have felt insecure. Even when Aung San Suu Kyi wrote to him privately, offering to work together to improve the livelihood of the people, he was suspicious. "He looked at it as a trap. It was a very good letter, but Than Shwe thought 'why is she coming up with this now'?"

Razali Ismail believes with hindsight that "we did not understand how important Khin Nyunt was," and that was a "fatal" mistake. "We did not see the true value of this man," he argues, and blames the international community for not backing Khin Nyunt.

A Western diplomat who served in Burma when Khin Nyunt was in power ponders what might have been. "Was Khin Nyunt a reformer? Did I miss something? Was there something there we should have seen and tried to work with? The trouble is in Burma, unless you have evidence, it is difficult to say that something like that is true. My gut feeling is that there was more there than I thought there was. But there is an awful lot of intricacy that no one will ever know. Who knows where the stars will turn on any particular day?"

According to someone who knew both Aung San Suu Kyi and Khin Nyunt well, towards the end of Khin Nyunt's time, Aung San Suu Kyi recognized that he was someone she could do business with. According to this source, Suu Kyi "initially thought that Khin Nyunt was not straight with her, that he was too tricky," although there was at least some dialogue and the possibility of moving towards an agreement. In the end, however, whatever his true objectives, Khin Nyunt did not have the power to deliver. As Razali Ismail recalls, "She said he was just receiving instructions."

Khin Nyunt's demise was predictable in Yozo Yokota's view. He had no base of support within the military, coming from the despised military intelligence as he did and having never served on the frontlines. He was close to Ne Win, and it was believed he won his promotions as a result of Ne Win's favor. Yet after his mentor's death, he had no protection. Ironically Khin Nyunt's appointment as prime minister in 2003 was regarded by many as a demotion from his previous post as Secretary-1, and a sign of trouble ahead. "When he became prime minister, I was afraid that this was the start of his influence being eroded," recalls Yokota. "I was really afraid that he might be ousted." A month before Khin Nyunt was removed, his key associate, Foreign Minister U Win Aung, was sacked, and that surely set alarm bells ringing.

Razali Ismail agrees. "Khin Nyunt was on a very slippery slope because he had to interpret what the *tatmadaw* really wanted, plus also try to appease international pressure. Sometimes he got it right. The fact that he was head of intelligence, which covered everything on the ground, created the impression that he had all the information [about everyone]. He was seen as too progressive. So there came a point where Than Shwe thought he had to go. If he was not toeing the line, they certainly could not keep him there."

Aung Lynn Htut, the former embassy official who worked in Khin Nyunt's intelligence circles, pointedly dismisses the views of international diplomats who believe the international community could have somehow supported Khin Nyunt more: "What they don't understand is that Khin Nyunt never had real power—he could only do what Than Shwe allowed him. The minute he did more, he was removed. Even if the world supported Khin Nyunt, he couldn't do anything anyway. For the last few years of his time in power, he was just a figurehead. He had lost power long ago, and lost real power since 1993."

Ultimately Khin Nyunt may have been removed by Than Shwe not primarily because of policy differences, though they existed, but more because of power. As Lintner argues, it was not a power struggle between pragmatists and hardliners but rather more a concern on Than Shwe's part that Khin Nyunt had accumulated significant wealth and was building up a state within a state. "Than Shwe did not want to have any potential rivals around him; Khin Nyunt clearly had political ambitions," says Lintner.[175]

In June 2004, Khin Nyunt visited China, where he reportedly told the Chinese leadership he planned to be Burma's first president under the new constitution. He was dubbed the "Deng Xiaoping of Burma." This was quite possibly "the last straw for General Than Shwe," say Egreteau and Jagan.[176] In the words of one former ambassador: "The clash between Khin Nyunt, Maung Aye, and Than Shwe was over patronage within the system. But it is also true that every single chief of military intelligence in Burma has been disgraced. It is rather like being the drummer in Spinal Tap—you end up disappearing."[177]

FIG. 5. *Three kings statues, Naypyidaw. Photo by Benedict Rogers.*

6

THE SEAT OF KINGS

AT PRECISELY 6:37 a.m. on November 6, 2005, hundreds of government servants left Rangoon in trucks, shouting: "We are leaving! We are leaving!" or, according to some reports, "Out! Out! Out!" Five days later, on November 11, at exactly 11 a.m., a second convoy of eleven hundred military trucks carrying eleven military battalions and eleven ministries left Rangoon. Perhaps influenced by astrologers, Than Shwe had decided to move the country's capital. He had given government officials just two days' notice.[1]

Billions of dollars have been spent constructing a new capital from scratch, in a remote Malaria-ridden area in central Burma six hundred kilometers from Rangoon near the small town of Pyinmana, the site of Aung San's Japanese-backed independence army sixty years earlier.[2] Than Shwe has called his new capital Naypyidaw, meaning the "Seat of Kings."

The decision was greeted with incredulity by Burmese and the international community, alike. Foreign diplomats were informed of the move a few days later, and were given one fax number to use to reach the government. "Even for a populace accustomed to arbitrary decrees from the country's brutal military regime and its leader, Senior General Than Shwe, the sudden move from bustling Rangoon to Pyinmana has struck many as bizarre," wrote one foreign journalist.[3] "This is a very strange country, a very strange government," said a Burmese journalist. "Even the most senior civil servants are angered by the move, and they dismiss it as the work of a fanatic. Pyinmana is a small town. It cannot accommodate a capital."[4] One Western diplomat, succumbing to the urge to attribute Than Shwe's political moves to fanaticism, said: "All of this shows how irrational the regime is. There is no rhyme or reason in what they are doing. These guys are isolating themselves."[5] Even China was unhappy, and showed its irritation by publishing a critique of the new location and a statement of surprise that it had not been informed.[6]

A few people outside the regime had some indications that the capital might move, although almost no one believed that Than Shwe would relocate to such a remote place so suddenly. A former Burma Army officer, who once worked closely with Than Shwe, claims the idea for establishing a new capital of some kind was actually first considered long ago in 1998. He believes Aung San Suu Kyi was aware of the plan, and that it had been discussed in a meeting she had with Khin Nyunt and Than Shwe. However, the initial proposal had been simply to relocate the military to a new headquarters, and to retain Rangoon as the center for civilian administration. It was intended to symbolize a separation of military and civilian command, to be implemented following the conclusion of the National Convention. After the fall of Khin Nyunt, however, Than Shwe decided that the entire government, military, and administrative apparatus should move, although Maung Aye may have been unhappy with the idea.

In August 2005, just three months before the move, when the plans were still confidential, a Burmese doctor involved in the democracy movement told a Western physician that Than Shwe was building a secret city in the dry plain lands around some famous caves near Pyinmana. Than Shwe, she claimed, had been warned by his astrologers that a disaster was coming that could threaten his rule unless he moved the capital.

One former Western diplomat says for six months it was known that there was a major building project around Pyinmana, and that Defense Headquarters had been relocated to that area. However, everyone was caught by surprise when the announcement came that this was to be the new capital of Burma. The previous day a foreign visitor was with a general. "He said to me, 'You know what, tomorrow at 11:11 a.m. there will be a big convoy leaving Rangoon to a new capital.' I laughed. 'Are you crazy?' I asked. He said 'No, no, it is going to happen.' And it happened."

The speculation is that there are five possible reasons for the decision. All five may contain some elements of truth, although some are more logical and comprehensible than others. The most rational reason is that Naypyidaw is in the center of the country, making it easier to consolidate military campaigns in the ethnic states around Burma's borders. By withdrawing from Rangoon, Than Shwe and the leadership have also sheltered themselves from any popular uprising such as the Saffron Revolution, which came two years later. "Every time a demonstration broke out in Rangoon," claims one defector, "the military regime felt that they had no escape route out of the city." A series of bomb explosions in Rangoon only served to increase Than Shwe's fear of his own people.

Less likely, but no doubt a factor, is the concern in Than Shwe's mind of a US invasion. Following US action in Afghanistan and Iraq, Than Shwe has paid attention to the fact that a similar intervention could theoretically take place in Burma. Rangoon, close to the coast, was regarded as vulnerable to external attack, whereas the bunker city of Naypyidaw is less easily accessible. Speaking to an audience of twelve thousand troops on Armed Forces Day in 2006 in the new parade ground, which allegedly cost ten million dollars to build, Than Shwe announced: "In order to ward off any danger befalling the country, our military, together with our people, must be strong, efficient, patriotic and modern . . . We have conceived a plan so that our people can avoid the danger of facing a perilous solution that could lead to the country's annihilation."[7]

While the fear of invasion is in all realistic terms irrational, Andrew Selth reminds us that Burmese history is full of invasions, particularly by its three largest neighbors—China, India, and Thailand. To the generals, current American and European economic and diplomatic pressure for democratization, as well as the strong language used against the regime, may make an invasion seem like a possibility, even if a minor one. The generals observed armed interventions in Panama, Somalia, Haiti, Kosovo, East Timor, Sierra Leone, Afghanistan, and Iraq with growing concern. "Over the years, the regime's fears of armed intervention have been dismissed as the paranoid delusions of an isolated group of poorly educated and xenophobic soldiers, jealous of their privileges and afraid of being held to account for their crimes against the Burmese people," writes Selth.[8] Although this description may be true, if seen from the regime's perspective, Selth contends, "it is possible to construct a picture of a genuine threat to the military government that is both internally consistent and supported by hard evidence . . . all these developments have been seen as threatening, and interpreted as evidence of a sustained campaign to impose regime change on Burma, against which they need to prepare."[9]

This perspective may have helped to shape the regime's defense and foreign policies, as well as the decision to move the capital. In 2005 a secret *tatmadaw* document outlined various scenarios for a US invasion of Burma. Thailand was identified as Burma's "nearest enemy," due to its strong relationship with the US and regular joint military exercises. The document anticipated a possible attack by the US involving an alliance with ethnic resistance groups, civilian agitation, or a multinational coalition. The following year, another secret document was revealed, confirming the regime's fears of a US invasion, and quoted Than Shwe as instructing his commanders to "prepare for the worst and hope for the best." Than Shwe claimed that the CIA was developing a "destruction plan," and his commanders warned that in the event of an invasion, all NLD members would be killed.[10]

One should not dismiss the tradition of Burmese royalty as a factor in Than Shwe's thinking. He is certainly preoccupied with the examples of historical kings, and may see himself as their heir. Towering over Naypyidaw are giant statues of Anawrahta, Bayinnaung, and Alaungpaya, Burma's three most important kings. Some visitors are rumored to be given seats lower than his when they have an audience with Than Shwe, and his wife Kyaing Kyaing at times allegedly insists that people sit on the floor at her feet, while she is the only one provided with a chair.

King Bayinnaung, who ruled five hundred years ago, is said to be one of Than Shwe's favorites. "Big bronze statues of him, tall and imposing, with a broad-brimmed hat and a long ornamented sword, stare down impassively at passersby in airports, museums and public parks all around the country," writes Thant Myint-U. "For today's generals, and others of a more belligerent nationalist persuasion, Bayinnaung represents a glorious past, something to be missed, and a sign, however distant, that Burma was not always so lowly in the eyes of the world."[11] Bayinnaung saved his kingdom from fragmenting, reconquering Burma and "making relentless war, unleashing campaigns of great brutality and destruction until one day all of western mainland Southeast Asia acknowledged his sovereignty."[12] No wonder Than Shwe likes him. As Thant Myint-U has noted, "The Burmese army still sees itself, in a way, as fighting the same enemies and in the same places, subjugating the Shan hills or crushing Mon resistance in the south, their soldiers slugging their way through the same thick jungle, preparing to torch a town or press-gang villagers. The past closer, more comparable, a way to justify present action. His statues are there because the ordeal of welding a nation together by force is not just history."[13] Than Shwe himself has said that the military "should be worthy heirs to the traditions of the capable military established by the notable kings Anawrahta, Bayinnaung, and Alaungpaya."[14]

The final, quite far-fetched but perhaps relevant, factor in Than Shwe's thinking is astrology. "By heeding the advice of astrologers and founding the new capital, Than Shwe was honoring tradition while effectively asserting his own 'royal' legacy," writes Stephen McCarthy.[15] Than Shwe's astrologers allegedly predicted that his regime would fall if he did not establish a new capital quickly. They warned that his star was fading, and that the only way he could save himself and his regime was to move capitals.[16] However, when another soothsayer predicted Naypyidaw would crumble within two years, he was arrested, lending credence to the idea that astrology is simply another tool to be manipulated for Than Shwe's politics, rather than a prescription to be followed.[17]

Than Shwe is far from being the only head of state to seek astrological advice, neither is he unusual in having those who give unpalatable forecasts arrested. In June 2009, a popular Sri Lankan astrologer, Chandrasiri Bandara, was arrested because he predicted that Sri Lankan president Mahinda Rajapaksa would be ousted and replaced by his prime minister.[18] Indonesia's Suharto was, according to Richard Lloyd Parry, "close to visionaries and mystics" all his life. On one occasion, it is believed Suharto avoided assassination because "he had been advised by a seer, it was said, to spend that night 'at the confluence of two waters', and had taken one of his sons fishing at a place where a river joined the sea."[19] Ne Win and other Burmese rulers have studied astrology as well.

When Naypyidaw was first established, access was extremely restricted. Two journalists who took photographs of the city were jailed for three years in March 2006.[20] According to Lintner, an eyewitness has claimed that during the construction of the new city, "the area around Naypyidaw was depopulated in order to seal the huge compound off from the outside world. Entire villages disappeared from the map, their inhabitants driven off land their families had farmed for centuries. Hundreds—perhaps thousands—joined Burma's abused army of 'internally displaced persons'. Able-bodied villagers, however, were 'enlisted' to help build the new capital."[21]

Since then, however, Naypyidaw has opened up and a number of diplomats, as well as foreign journalists, have visited the city. The former British ambassador Mark Canning describes it simply as "the most awful place you have ever been to." Lacking any ambience, with very few shops or restaurants, there is "nothing to do," he says.

According to Canning, the city is situated "slap bang" in the middle of "the most geologically unstable area in the country." The Sagaing Fault literally intersects the city. Moreover, geological maps with images taken from a space shuttle show geologically stable areas in blue, and unstable areas in red. Naypyidaw is bright red. There are three parts to Naypyidaw. The first is the military compound, where the leaders live, nestled under some hills. "No one knows what's going on there," Canning says. Then there is the old Pyinmana town and then the new Naypyidaw city. The entire area covers several hundred square kilometers.

In 2009 my research involved a day trip to Naypyidaw, and my observations confirm those of others. The new Naypyidaw town is reminiscent, in Canning's view, of "a small Midwest American town." Others have described it as "an Arizona housing estate," "a Florida retirement community," or in British terms, "Milton Keynes." Thant Myint-U believes it is "a poor version" of the new Malaysian government center at Putra Jaya, outside Kuala Lumpur. Than Shwe had apparently visited Putra Jaya in 1996, and that may have planted the thought in his mind. "It's a collection of buildings scattered over scrubland," says Canning. "But they are all just dispersed, and there are two or three kilometers between each building. One can only presume it's so they don't get bombed or something to disperse the targets."

While there are six- to eight-lane highways through the city, the Ministry of Foreign Affairs has just a little dirt track leading up to it, and no parking lot. This, Canning believes, is indicative of their mindset. "Isn't it logical that your interface with the world should have a parking lot?" he asks. A diplomatic quarter has been built in "a couple of muddy fields," but no embassy has yet relocated from Rangoon, although the Kuwaitis say they will. The Ministry of Communications has a pristine sign outside, but hardly any people around.

"Authoritarian, stark, and human-less," the city is divided into zones: a golf course, a hotel zone, a park, a market, and a residential zone. In the hotel zone, there are at least six luxury hotels, including one called the "Premier Boutique Hotel," complete with swimming pools and chalet-style accommodation, all in a row, and three restaurants: a Thai, a Chinese, and a barbecue. In the residential zone, inhabited solely by government servants, each apartment is color-coded—blue for the Ministry of Health, for example, green for the Agriculture and Irrigation Ministry, and so on. There were few signs of life, according to *Time* journalist Hannah Beech. "No laundry hanging out, nothing that indicated the housing was occupied."[22] People complain that there is nothing to do at night except watch television.

The regime, in just one example of its hopes for the success of Naypyidaw, is building a new international airport at Naypyidaw, even though it has already built one, and expects ten million visitors a year. Yet its six-lane highway is virtually empty, and finding a taxi or a bus is almost impossible. "In the twenty-minute drive from the military section to the three-kings monument, we passed two cars," recalls Hannah Beech. The striking thing about Naypyidaw is that there are so few people out in the streets, except in the small market area. An artificial park designed for the pleasure of government employees is virtually empty, with just a few people taking in the joys of its water fountain displays. There are three golf courses and a golf driving range and caddies in hats and white gloves, but otherwise the place is virtually empty. "There's no recognition that human beings live in this place," says Canning. "There are bus shelters but no buses; telephone boxes but no telephones connected; no taxis." There is, however, twenty-four hour electricity, in a country where many people are fortunate to get just a few hours electricity a day and a large proportion of the population receive none at all. A zoo has been built, with a climate-controlled penguin house. A thousand-bed and a two thousand-bed public hospital are available, and a three hundred-bed private hospital is being built near Naypyidaw.[23] There are five police stations, with big signs in English saying: "May I help you?" Policemen stand in the center of the highway to direct the non-existent traffic.

Government employees living in Naypyidaw who have been asked say they hate living there. A former Western ambassador recalls flying over the new capital soon after it was built, accompanied by the deputy foreign minister and his wife. "She was not happy," the former ambassador said. "There is enormous resentment from other ministers, who are unable to leave Naypyidaw without permission. Their wives are especially resentful. Even one of Than Shwe's daughters made it known that she hated it, but took the view that if she had to be there, everyone does." Ironically, the sheer boredom of the place has driven civil servants to start listening to pro-democracy radio—the Burmese-language broadcasts of BBC and Voice of America, or Radio Free Asia and Democratic Voice of Burma—when endless karaoke and prostitution fails to entertain them. It would be interesting if, in a bizarre twist of fate, the regime begins to unravel because the minds of bored and frustrated officials, forced to leave their homes in Rangoon for the emptiness of Naypyidaw, begin to open. Even the top generals and their families prefer to spend their time elsewhere. No sooner was Naypyidaw complete than a new holiday destination was developed for the top ranks to escape to, near the old colonial hillside retreat of Maymyo. "No expense has been spared to allow the generals to live in what is basically a resort, complete with an artificial beach and a man-made stretch of water to lap onto it," *The Irrawaddy* reported.[24]

On March 9, 2009, Than Shwe and his family made offerings at a newly built replica of Rangoon's Shwedagon Pagoda. Naypyidaw's Uppatasanti ("Peace") Pagoda stands ninety-nine meters tall, just slightly higher than the Shwedagon. As Bertil Lintner points out, nine is the military's lucky number. There is now speculation that Than Shwe will move the Buddha relics and diamonds donated by his family from the Shwedagon to the Uppatasanti Pagoda. The *New Light of Myanmar* reported that the Shwedagon Pagoda's seventy-six karat diamond had been polished in a ceremony led by leading monks from the State Sangha Maha Nayaka, the country's highest state-sanctioned religious body, together with some high ranking members of the junta, including Lieutenant General Myint Swe of the Ministry of Defense, Rangoon Commander Brigadier-General Win Myint, and Rangoon Mayor Brigadier-General Aung Thein Lin.[25] Inside the Uppatasanti Pagoda, the ceiling and walls are adorned with gold from top to bottom, with four or five plaques of Buddhist scriptures in prominent position. One, headlined "Noble Truth of Cessation of Suffering," declares in almost incomprehensible English: "The reality of cessation of all the sufferings exist evidently. The absolute cessation of *tanha* (greed), renunciation, forsaking, forsaking at far-away, emancipation, free from attachment are the real essence of the Nibbana." Another, titled "Noble Truth of Suffering," declares that "Coming to be in new existences repeatedly, old age, illness, death and association with those one does not love, separation from those one loves, not to get what one desires are sufferings. In brief, the five aggregates of clinging are sufferings indeed." Than Shwe, it seems, is hardly experiencing these noble truths. Outside the pagoda in an exhibition hall are walls covered in photographs of Than Shwe, Daw Kyaing Kyaing, Maung Aye, and other junta members inspecting the site at various stages of the pagoda's construction.

Some historians claim that traditionally pagodas are built by rulers as acts of penance for the wars they conducted. The new pagoda in Naypyidaw might therefore be a sign of the regime's intentions to build "a modern nation with flourishing, disciplined democracy." But another observer has a different interpretation: "Traditionally, we Burmese say that the completion of new pagodas sponsored by kings will only lead to the destruction of the state. This actually happened in 1988 when Maha Wizaya Pagoda was completed by the late dictator Ne Win. Now we can hope that doomsday for Than Shwe's empire is coming soon."[26]

But was the new pagoda built with slave labor? Hannah Beech claims she saw fifty or sixty children working on the base of the new pagoda in 2008, "carrying huge amounts of rocks on their heads, and breaking up the rocks into smaller rocks with pick-axes."[27] The children, she believes, were no more than seven or eight years old.

No one dares question the wisdom of this new, silent city. "Than Shwe is a king, he wants his own palace," one local in Pyinmana told journalist Helen Beaton. "And although he is king, he is afraid of many things. He thinks that here he will be safe." Beaton concludes that "Than Shwe and his junta have locked themselves away in a fortress within a fortress, in a closely guarded secret quarter populated entirely by military leadership. No civilians—let alone foreigners—are allowed here. Reports say the area is a network of bunkers and luxury houses, from which the generals rarely venture, emerging downtown only to play golf or gamble in the specially built five-star hotels."[28] One man in Naypyidaw, upon pointing out the hills where Than Shwe's fortress lies, exclaimed in a statement indicative of the level of hatred people have for their top leader: "If I had a torpedo with me right now, I would fire it."

There is no strong evidence to suggest that the influence of astrology, which perhaps played a minor role in Than Shwe's decision to move the capital, plays a major part in his day-to-day decision-making. However, it does appear to be used as an auxiliary force. It is said that Than Shwe's wife Kyaing Kyaing has influenced him; she is a particularly strong believer in *nats* or traditional spirits, astrology, and *yadaya*, a ritual designed to ward off ill fortune. Earlier in his career, an astrologer told Kyaing Kyaing that her husband would one day lead the country, and ever since then Than Shwe has shown an interest in the advice of astrologers and soothsayers and the role of *yadaya*. The astrologer reportedly also told Kyaing Kyaing that Than Shwe had been a king in a previous life.[29] Than Shwe is rumored to have birthmarks on his stomach and back, and fortune tellers told him that these were signs that one day he would be a "king." When the SPDC liaison minister Aung Kyi was due to meet Aung San Suu Kyi, Than Shwe and Kyaing Kyaing allegedly deployed *yadaya* to influence the outcome.[30] According to some Burmese, Than Shwe has at least seven personal astrologers, focusing on specific areas: the future of the country, Than Shwe's rivals within the regime, and several who are instructed simply to focus on Aung San Suu Kyi.

A Buddhist nun, Daw Dhammathi, is one of Than Shwe's favored astrologers, and Kyaing Kyaing frequently visits her temple in North Okkalapa, Rangoon.[31] Another favorite soothsayer is "a tiny, hunched, deaf-mute in her mid-forties," called E Thi.[32] She is often known as "ET," referring to her resemblance to the extraterrestrial character in Steven Spielberg's movie, and is in high demand. Asian diplomats seek her services, and Thailand's former prime minister Thaksin Shinawatra is rumored to have consulted her just before he was deposed. She reportedly told him to leave Thailand in order to avoid death. Her sister functions as her diary-secretary and translator, and apparently she provides her prophecies with grunting noises, which only her sister can interpret. Charging seventy dollars for half an hour, she mixes regularly with wealthy Burmese, regime officials, and diplomats. In July 2008, she gave a party at Karawaik Restaurant on a lake in Rangoon, attended by members of the junta. A Burmese woman who once saw her as a child says that E Thi has "become very powerful.

She used to work from a little hut in Pathein, but now she is in Rangoon and is very grand."

Numerology is also used by Than Shwe's regime, but as with astrology, it doesn't appear to influence underlying decisions, instead being used to choose key dates and times. Ne Win's favorite number was nine, but apparently eleven is the new number for Than Shwe.[33] In September 2008 the regime announced it was releasing 9,002 prisoners. The reason for such a random number, experts say, is that 9,002 adds up to eleven. In November, the eleventh month, several dissidents, including prominent democracy leader Min Ko Naing, were sentenced at 11:00 a.m. to sixty-five years in prison. Why sixty-five? Six and five equal eleven. In 2009 Aung San Suu Kyi was sentenced to house arrest on August 11.

According to one astrologer, in the Burmese Buddhist tradition, there are "eleven fires"—greed, hatred, delusion, birth, aging, death, grief, lamentation, pain, sorrow, and despair.[34] Than Shwe, or perhaps Kyaing Kyaing, evidently wishes to be protected from these eleven fires.

Voodoo and black magic appear to play ancillary roles as well. When Ne Win's grandsons were arrested in 2002 for plotting a coup against Than Shwe, their family astrologer, Aung Pwint Khaung, was also detained. According to Aung Zaw, "The raid evidently uncovered a cache of voodoo-like dolls said to closely resemble the regime's top three generals—Senior General Than Shwe, General Maung Aye and General Khin Nyunt."[35]

Than Shwe and Kyaing Kyaing also make a public display of putting faith in Buddhism, albeit with various distortions. At the Shwedagon Pagoda in Rangoon, a new Buddha statue was installed made of jade that was never previously seen in public. Various UN dignitaries, including UN Secretary-General Ban Ki-moon and his envoy Ibrahim Gambari, were taken to make offerings and pray in front of the Buddha. "It may have missed the gaze of Ban and Gambari, but no one else failed to notice that the face of the statue was not so serene and Buddha-like," writes Aung Zaw. "It was, in fact, an effigy of Than Shwe."[36]

Than Shwe and other generals have built pagodas all over the country. Just outside Mandalay is one large pagoda in honor of the senior general—"a gleaming white structure swept spotless by a horde of workers."[37] In 2007 Kyaing Kyaing made a special visit to the Shit Myet Hna Pagoda in her husband's birthplace, Kyaukse, following the Saffron Revolution.

Known as the "Eight Faces" pagoda because it faces the eight points of the compass, it is deemed a symbolic place to pray for strength.[38] In July 2009, Than Shwe and Kyaing Kyaing visited the Shwedagon Pagoda in Rangoon on three successive mornings, leaving symbolic offerings of thirty-five pagoda replicas. Two months earlier, Than Shwe's family visited the Danok Pagoda near Rangoon and helped raise a *hti* or sacred umbrella on to the top of the structure. Three weeks later, the pagoda collapsed, killing several workers.[39]

Burmese monarchs traditionally built pagodas to earn merit and demonstrate their power. Than Shwe is following in their footsteps. "Today, pagoda-mad Than Shwe is acting more and more like one of those classic monarchs," writes journalist Josh Kurlantzick. "Ten years ago, Burma was an authoritarian state, but it lacked the strange personality cult of totalitarian states such as North Korea and Turkmenistan. At the time, Than Shwe was just one of three generals heading the ruling Burmese junta and, diplomats told me, he was considered the most dimwitted of the three. . . . Burma's metamorphosis into a more North Korean-esque state began in 2003."[40] Obviously, those diplomats, like countless other international observers over the years, didn't understand the true extent of Than Shwe's cunning or power.

Than Shwe's relatives reportedly refer to one another by royal titles, and the state media runs constant photographs of Than Shwe receiving blessings from monks. Government offices display portraits of Than Shwe.[41] Than Shwe's hometown of Kyaukse, not previously a center of development, is becoming an industrial zone, with new factories, shopping malls, a technological college, and a modern airport serving Mandalay. Burma's largest manufacturer of agricultural machinery is located near Kyaukse.[42]

"As Than Shwe travels the country, he stops in villages to issue so-called 'necessary instructions' to peasants and officials on such subjects as construction and oil drilling, about which he knows nothing," notes Kurlantzick. "Nightly television broadcasts are centered around Than Shwe: Than Shwe giving alms to monks; Than Shwe welcoming foreign visitors; Than Shwe blessing crops, as if he had the power to bring rain. Some observers say broadcasts feature Than Shwe with his grandson, to perpetuate the idea of a dynasty in the making."[43]

7

THE MONKS AND THE STORM

WHEN THAN SHWE and UN Secretary-General Ban Ki-moon finally met in the wake of Cyclone Nargis, Ban challenged the senior general more vigorously than many believe. Than Shwe gave as good as he got, and the pair spent two hours arguing about everything from human rights to democracy to Aung San Suu Kyi. Halfway through their debate, Than Shwe—often believed to be wooden and stern—apparently leaned across and slapped the secretary-general on the knee. "I am rather enjoying this," he reportedly said. "I have never had a conversation like this before."

Undoubtedly people tiptoe around Than Shwe, but since he has served at all levels of the military apparatus and understands how information becomes filtered on its way to the top, there is no chance that he does not understand how serious things have become in the country. However, some diplomats don't necessarily agree with that proposition: "If he doesn't it is shocking and he should," says Canning. "But when you look at how things are arranged for ministerial visits, the way everyone is standing by the end of their bed, you wonder what sort of world he must operate in." Unlike Mahathir, whose country was, in any case, more open to the world and who used to drop in to visit an industry or a project unexpectedly, for Than Shwe everything is choreographed.

On occasions, however, the tiptoeing stops, the choreography fails, and the people at large do not behave according to plan. On August 15, 2007, a few small protests began in various parts of the country against the regime's sudden and dramatic increases in fuel prices. The protests were mostly organized by 88 Generation pro-democracy activists. The authorities reacted as they had at times in the past, allowing the demonstrations to develop in order to draw out the full extent of the opposition, using only civilian mobs from pro-junta militias such as the USDA and Swan

Arr Shin to attack the protestors instead of sending in the army. Some activists were arrested in an attempt to remove the core leadership, and for a few days it looked as if the movement might not get off the ground. But on August 28, monks in Sittwe, Arakan State breathed new life into the faltering campaign, and took to the streets. A turning point then came on September 5, when the regime made its first mistake. Despite his ostentatious parading of the regime's Buddhist credentials, Than Shwe unleashed a brutal and violent attack on the monks. At least one monk was tied to a lamppost and severely beaten with rifle butts. It was rumored that a monk was killed, and three were arrested. In response, monks from Maha Visutarama Monastery in Pakokku took between ten and twenty officials hostage, and set fire to their vehicles, and did not release them until six hours later.[1]

On September 9, the All Burma Monks Alliance was formed. This underground movement of monks issued four demands to the regime: to apologize publicly for the brutal attack on the peaceful protests led by monks in Pakokku; to reduce commodity and fuel prices immediately; to release all political prisoners including Aung San Suu Kyi; and to enter into a process of meaningful dialogue with the democracy movement. The monks imposed a deadline of September 17 for the regime to meet these four demands, and warned the generals that if their demands were not met, monks throughout Burma would launch a boycott of religious activities and would refuse to accept alms from anyone associated with the regime. In Buddhism, such a threat is severe, akin to excommunication.

The regime sought to impose its control over monasteries throughout the country, and ordered senior abbots under its authority to stop the monks from pursuing this action. Remarkably, despite having tentacles that stretch into every part of Burmese society, including the monasteries, the junta was unable to prevent from unfolding what became known as the Saffron Revolution. The SPDC attempted to bribe senior monks from Pakokku with 30,000 kyat, but their offer was rejected. On September 14, the monks announced that the regime had not responded to its four demands, and therefore the boycott would begin three days later. In a desperate attempt to deflect the monks' influence, the state media ran stories showing the generals making offerings at monasteries.[2] But by now it was too late.

On the first day of the boycott, thousands of monks marched in Rangoon, Mandalay, Pegu, Sittwe, Kale, and Pakokku, as well as many other cities throughout the country. The generals' excommunication was announced, complete with a refusal to accept alms. In a symbolic rejection of the regime, monks carried their alms bowls upturned. The generals were described as "violent, mean, cruel, ruthless, pitiless kings" and "great thieves who live by stealing from the national treasury."[3]

For a week, the monks continued their protests, and their numbers swelled. Civilians turned out, initially as bystanders offering applause and water to the monks, who had urged them not to take part because they knew that the army would not hesitate to fire on civilians. In some cases civilians formed a human chain around the monks, to protect them from the regime's thugs. A few days later, however, civilians and monks marched together. On September 24, at least one hundred thousand people were on the streets of Rangoon. Several hundred thousand marched in other cities as well. The NLD, which had been cautious, joined in and the democracy movement's symbol, the fighting peacock, was displayed by protestors. Two days earlier monks miraculously marched through the roadblocks at the end of University Avenue, right past Aung San Suu Kyi's house. She emerged from her gate briefly to greet the monks and hear their prayers. One observer said her eyes were "full of tears," and that the moment was so emotional that even one army officer wept. "The world saw her again due to our protest," the observer said, "and it gave moral support to the Burmese people."[4]

By this time Than Shwe had had enough and the warnings came thick and fast. Order 2/88 was imposed, banning gatherings of more than five people and threatening to jail anyone guilty of "unlawful assembly." The move to brand the monks as lawbreakers was nothing new for Than Shwe. Yet again, he followed the pattern of ex-dictator Ne Win, who had claimed shortly after forcefully closing several monasteries in 1965 that he was only opposing monks who were misusing religion.[5]

On September 25, the monks and lay people turned out again in the tens of thousands, and a curfew was imposed. The atmosphere changed completely, as Than Shwe unleashed the brutal crackdown, which many had expected but had hoped could be averted. On September 26, security forces began to beat the monks.

"They beat any part of the body as much as they could," said one eyewitness. "Some monks were beaten until they fell to the ground or became unconscious. I myself witnessed at least eight people, including monks, who were beaten and kicked." Another recalled: "The monks were beaten badly on their heads. It seemed that the riot police were deliberately targeting the monks' heads. There was so much blood coming from some of them that it was hard to find where they were bleeding from."[6]

At the Shwedagon Pagoda, at least three monks were killed. On Maha Bandoola Road, soldiers opened fire without any warning on unarmed protestors. At Thakin Mya Park, protestors found themselves trapped between advancing troops and a roadblock. Two groups of soldiers fired upon them, killing at least one person. Near the Sule Pagoda, the troops "fired at everything they saw," according to one witness.[7]

Despite this carnage, protests continued the following day, although the numbers were smaller. Monasteries had been raided throughout the previous night, and hundreds of monks arrested. The shooting continued, and many more people died. The exact death toll is still unknown. A fourteen-year-old boy was hit in the chest, while others were shot in the back of their heads.[8]

Rangoon streets were stained with blood and covered with abandoned flip-flops, as people kicked off their footwear in order to run. One of those who died was a Japanese photojournalist, Kenji Nagai. A picture of his murder went around the world within hours. The regime tried to claim he was hit by a stray bullet, but the photograph clearly says it all. The journalist prostrate on his back, his camera held above his head, a soldier standing over him with his rifle pointed straight at him. Kenji Nagai was shot at point-blank range in broad daylight. If Than Shwe's army can do that to a foreign journalist, it provides an indication of how much worse it treats its own people.

The regime was desperate to hide the evidence. Bloodstained streets were washed clean, and corpses were gathered quickly. It is not known what happened to the dead, but it is widely believed that many bodies were secretly cremated. Apparently, as this was going on, Than Shwe—secluded in Naypyidaw—sunk into a deep depression and barely ate. His staff kept trying to persuade him to eat, but the only dish he could summon up a desire for was chicken rice soup. He refused to speak to anyone.

Unconfirmed reports suggest that his wife and family members fled the country on September 26, the day troops opened fire on the monks. It was rumored that they went to Dubai, and checked in at one of the tallest hotels in the world, the seven-star Dubai Burj Al Arab. An *Al-Jazeera* reporter who tried to visit room no. 709 of the hotel, where a delegation of Burmese had checked in, apparently found his path blocked by hotel staff.[9] Although the family reportedly owns a luxury condominium in Singapore, it was believed that they would be too easily identifiable by Burmese exiles there—so Dubai seemed safer.

While the numbers were significantly reduced, protests continued on September 28, but by the end of the month the Saffron Revolution had been crushed. Not satisfied, however, with ending the demonstrations, Than Shwe pursued his opponents with a ruthlessness and vindictiveness surpassed by few other rulers in the world. Monasteries and homes were raided, monks and activists went into hiding, and dozens escaped to neighboring countries. Soldiers looted and smashed monasteries with a complete absence of respect for Buddhism. By the first week of October, it was estimated that the regime had arrested at least six thousand people, including fourteen hundred monks.[10] Not only were demonstrators arrested, the authorities went through photographs and video footage to identify people who had watched the protests, smiled, clapped, or handed a protestor a bottle of water. They were then hunted down. No one who had been anywhere near a protest was safe.

The Saffron Revolution was the largest and most widespread uprising in Burma since 1988, and the most significant threat to Than Shwe's rule since he took power fifteen years earlier. Yet there was one difference between 2007 and 1988, which made the Saffron Revolution even more dangerous for the regime. In 1988 the crackdown largely escaped the international community's notice until after it had occurred. In 2007, however, the world received virtual real-time coverage of events. Brave Burmese took photographs on cameras and mobile telephones, and then e-mailed the images along with reports out of the country. The dramatic footage hit the headlines of most major newspapers and television networks, and drew strong condemnation from most countries. The US president George W. Bush described it as "inexcusable," and British prime minister Gordon Brown called for an urgent discussion at the UN Security Council. UN

Secretary-General Ban Ki-moon described it as "abhorrent and unacceptable." ASEAN was also surprisingly blunt. The organization, usually known for its weak policies stemming from its principles of "non-interference" and corporatist constructive engagement, expressed "revulsion" at the reports of the crackdown.[11] The prime minister of Singapore wrote to Than Shwe on September 29, "strongly urging" him to exercise "utmost restraint" and calling for a peaceful transition to democracy. "We are most disturbed by reports of the violent means that the authorities in Myanmar have deployed against the demonstrators, which have resulted in injuries and deaths," he wrote.[12]

On October 2, UN Special Envoy Ibrahim Gambari arrived in Burma, a visit reportedly brokered by China. In a move designed to look like a concession without actually conceding anything, Than Shwe met Gambari and on October 4 announced that he would be willing to meet with Aung San Suu Kyi with certain conditions, namely that she abandon what he ironically called her confrontational approach and drop calls for economic sanctions.[13] Four days later, the regime appointed Major-General Aung Kyi as a liaison minister to hold talks with Aung San Suu Kyi, and Gambari read out a statement in Singapore on her behalf. She reiterated her willingness to hold "a meaningful and time-bound dialogue" with the generals "as early as possible," and expressed her hope of a dialogue would include "the interests and opinions of as broad a range of political organizations and forces as possible, in particular those of ethnic nationality races."[14]

It is known that Than Shwe holds an intense dislike for Aung San Suu Kyi and so, even the slightest indication that he might meet her, for some, was seen as progress. However, Than Shwe has demonstrated time and again his skill at offering just enough of a concession to hold the international community at bay whenever pressure intensifies. In each instance without fail, he promises only the most minimal of token steps to satisfy the international community, which are nevertheless welcomed. And then, each time the pressure eases Than Shwe quietly abandons his promises.

Despite Aung San Suu Kyi's willingness to meet, Than Shwe has stuck rigidly to the status quo. After five meetings with the liaison minister, Aung San Suu Kyi complained that the regime was playing games and that its promises of dialogue without providing any time frame gave "false hope."[15] Although Gambari made several more visits to the country, each time he was shunned by Than Shwe. The two have not met since October 2007. Following Gambari's first meeting with Than Shwe in May 2006, then UN Secretary-General Kofi Annan appealed to Than Shwe to release Aung San Suu Kyi. A day later her detention was extended for another year. Comparing Than Shwe's handling of Gambari to the experiences of Captain Michael Symes, the British envoy to the court of King Bodawpaya in the late eighteenth century, journalist Neil Lawrence concludes that like Bodawpaya, Than Shwe has been successful in "repelling diplomatic attempts to restrain his behavior." He has done this "by forcing a long line of envoys to either give up in disgust or . . . to portray their efforts as a success rather than concede defeat." The historian D. G. E. Hall describes Captain Symes' reception by the Burmese monarch as "a strange mixture of friendly hospitality and studied rudeness," not unlike Than Shwe's response to Gambari. The greatest threat to Burma today, Lawrence argues, is Than Shwe's belief "that he can rule as he pleases, without regard for world opinion."[16] That became particularly apparent when, despite conceding to meet Gambari, the regime expelled the UN's resident coordinator Charles Petrie for expressing some mild remarks about the humanitarian situation and the crackdown on the demonstrators.

According to another foreigner who was with Petrie in Naypyidaw when he was informed of his expulsion, the manner in which the regime communicated the decision was what uninformed observers might call eccentric. Although it was, in fact, consistent with the method Than Shwe is said to have used to engineer the removal of his predecessor Saw Maung. A routine meeting with regime officials was held, with no indication of what was to come. At one point an official took exception to Petrie's suggestion that one third of the population was malnourished, rebuking him and informing him that his figures were completely wrong, and that the correct statistic was 31 percent (a difference of 2 percent). At the end of the meeting, regime officials and the foreign delegation agreed that they should talk more regularly. Tea was served and the foreign delegation actually got out their diaries and agreed to a date for another meeting. Bidding the regime hosts goodbye, they were seen out to a coach waiting to take them to the airport. Each delegation member was then presented with an envelope. Assuming it contained protocol pleasantries or the like, it was a while before anyone opened theirs. As the coach got closer to Naypyidaw Airport, one of the delegation members decided to open his envelope—only to find an announcement of Charles Petrie's expulsion. Petrie was informed in the same way as everyone else, reading the document on the way to the airport.

Than Shwe turned his attentions from the international community to internal matters of his regime. Five generals and more than four hundred soldiers were reportedly detained for refusing to shoot monks and protestors in Rangoon. Ye Min Tun, a foreign ministry official, resigned from the Burmese embassy in London in early October over the "horrible" treatment of the monks, and then on October 12, Prime Minister Soe Win died of cancer. Not long after, Than Shwe carried out a portfolio reshuffle. Lieutenant-General Thein Sein became prime minister and his position as Secretary-1 was filled by Lieutenant-General Thiha Thura Tin Aung Myint Oo. A further reshuffle in June 2008 resulted in changes of personnel among seven regional commanders, five senior regime officials, two ministers, two hundred army officers, and the navy's commander in chief. Than Shwe's strategy, it seems, is to replace high-ranking officials with younger officers to ensure a military presence in future governments, and to place his loyalists in strategic command positions. Eighty-three new battalions were deployed in Karen State, bringing the military presence there to a total of 187 battalions.[17] The offensive against Karen civilians consequently intensified.

Than Shwe pressed ahead with his constitution drafting process, and put the final version to a referendum in May 2008. The constitution was drafted by 1,088 delegates at the National Convention, and took fourteen years to complete. The delegates were entirely handpicked. The legitimate representatives elected in 1990 were in effect excluded, and most major ethnic representatives were sidelined. During the National Convention the delegates were forbidden to contact their families, or to discuss the constitution outside the National Convention. Some delegates have described how pointless the whole initiative was, complaining that there was no opportunity for discussion or for proposals to be considered. When asked what he got out of it, one former delegate said: "I learned to play golf." The process was dismissed as "meaningless and undemocratic" by the then UN Special Rapporteur Paulo Sérgio Pinheiro. "I don't understand the purpose of this surrealistic exercise," Pinheiro said. "If you pursue this path, you will not be successful. It will not work . . . This way of political transition will not work; will not work on the moon, will not work on Mars!"[18] Nevertheless, Than Shwe pressed on.

The referendum was held with Order 5/96 hanging over it. This particular law imposed a twenty-year prison sentence on anyone criticizing the National Convention. As Pinheiro said, "Everything is forbidden under this law." A free and fair referendum campaign was impossible.

Just before the referendum was due to be held, the worst natural disaster in Burma's recent history hit its shores. During the evening of May 2, Cyclone Nargis struck, causing widespread devastation to the Irrawaddy Delta region of the country. The regime had received numerous warnings from the Indian meteorological authorities of the impending disaster, but did nothing to alert or prepare people. After the cyclone struck, in an extraordinary act of inhumane callousness, the junta initially rejected offers of international aid. It subsequently relented and agreed to accept aid but refused to allow foreign aid workers into the country to distribute supplies and to monitor the relief effort. Only as a result of intense diplomatic and political pressure from the UN secretary-general, ASEAN, and China, combined with the looming presence of French, British, and American naval vessels loaded with supplies and moored off Burma's coast, did Than Shwe finally and grudgingly concede, although even then not without restrictions. On May 23, Ban Ki-moon met Than Shwe, who had previously refused to take his calls. In a statement to the world media in the Sedona Hotel in Rangoon after the meeting, the UN secretary-general announced: "I am happy to report that we have made progress . . . This morning, I had a good meeting with Senior General Than Shwe. He agreed to allow international aid workers into the affected areas, regardless of nationality. He has taken quite a flexible position." Flexibility is not an adjective normally ascribed to Than Shwe, and as soon as Ban Ki-moon had left the country, the good news seemed not quite as good as it had first appeared. Prime Minister Thein Sein declared that the regime would "consider" allowing foreign aid workers in, "if they wish to engage in rehabilitation and reconstruction work."[19] Later in the year, the SPDC's Secretary-1 Lieutenant General Thiha Thura Tin Aung Myint Oo, stated that "co-operation with the United Nations is the cornerstone of Myanmar's foreign policy" and that the country was "honored" by Ban Ki-moon's visit.[20] Yet there was little evidence of that in practice.

In yet more extraordinary statements compounding the callousness, the regime announced with a straight face that Cyclone Nargis had killed 665,271 ducks, 56,163 cows, and 1,614,502 chickens. It appeared to ignore the fact that thousands of human corpses were rotting in the floodwaters, floating next to the dead ducks and chickens, or hanging from trees. One regime official told foreign aid workers: "What you westerners don't seem to understand is that people in the delta are used to having no water to drink and nothing to eat."[21] In another step along the parameters of absurdity, the state media then declared that farmers did not need food aid, because they could "go out with lamps at night and catch plump frogs,"[22] and that they did not need "chocolate" from foreign countries.

In the midst of this madness, thirty-six prisoners were shot dead for trying to get out of their cells to avoid being crushed by a collapsing roof and debris, and Aung San Suu Kyi's period of house arrest was extended for another year, even though she had served the maximum time allowable under the State Protection Act. The regime had earlier declared that she deserved to be "flogged." The US secretary of defense Robert Gates accused the junta of "criminal neglect," and French foreign minister Bernard Kouchner called for the "responsibility to protect" mechanism to be invoked. Earlier, however, Thailand's prime minister Samak Sundaravej declared that "killings and suppression are normal," and that Than Shwe was a "good Buddhist" who prayed and meditated every day.[23]

On May 10, just eight days after the cyclone, the referendum went ahead as planned. Than Shwe rejected international appeals to delay the vote in light of the disaster, and pressed on. Only the worst affected areas were exempt from voting on May 10, and their ballots were cast on May 22. The result, however, was declared in the meantime. Even though millions were homeless and thousands dead, the regime claimed that turnout was nearly 100 percent.[24]

It is estimated that in total, at least one hundred forty thousand people died as a result of Cyclone Nargis, and over 2.5 million were left homeless. Many of these suffered or died not directly as a result of the storm, but due to the regime's deliberate neglect—its rejection and subsequent restriction, manipulation, and diversion of humanitarian aid. One source reported that Burma's state bank was taxing all aid money at a rate of 10 percent, and that the UN had lost at least ten million dollars due to the regime's manipulation of currency conversions.[25]

An enterprising journalist at the United Nations, Matthew Russell Lee of *Inner City Press*, followed the story of the stolen aid money closely, writing numerous articles and identifying a leaked UN document, which showed that as early as June 26, just weeks after the cyclone hit, the UN knew of a "very serious 20% loss on foreign exchange . . . changing US dollars to Foreign Exchange Certificates [FEC] then to the local currency, kyats." Lee pressed the United Nations humanitarian chief John Holmes about the money the regime was allegedly stealing from the cyclone aid, and Holmes acknowledged that US$10 million had indeed disappeared. Holmes claimed that the UN had been "a bit slow to recognize" the problem, but Lee pointed out that UN operations were already losing an astonishing 15 percent to currency exchange manipulations by the junta "prior to the cyclone."[26] Lee further questioned why the UN continued to appeal for aid money from the international community while such a substantial portion was being siphoned off by the Burmese regime. Yet the UN never provided the full documentation that Lee requested. According to Lee, there were indications that the UN Development Programme, prior to Cyclone Nargis, had "provided larger cuts to Myanmar's Than Shwe government than the 25 percent now admitted by the UN's humanitarian operations." Holmes subsequently raised the issue with the Burmese regime and a solution was supposedly developed, but using exchange analysis Lee showed that the solution did not work. In concluding his story, Lee pointedly asked: "Even at its best, is a 17% loss of aid funds to the Myanmar government acceptable to donors? Why were these losses never disclosed while funds were being raised, including in UN appeals for $200 million and then, earlier this month, $300 million more?"[27]

Two weeks after the cyclone, Than Shwe—who had not appeared in public following the disaster—finally emerged and toured temporary camps set up for those who had lost their homes in the Irrawaddy Delta. The question on most people's minds was "what took him so long?" Was he genuinely unaware of the scale of the disaster due to misinformation or was his neglect willful and his eventual appearance reluctant? It would be extraordinary if he had truly not grasped the severity of the situation, and it seems he only decided to put on a show of compassion when he saw the public response of the Chinese leadership to a large earthquake that hit Sichuan a few days earlier. "Still, it seems particularly inhuman—even by Than Shwe's standards—that he would willfully prevent humanitarian aid from reaching the cyclone," wrote Aung Zaw in the June 2008 issue of *The Irrawaddy* magazine.[28]

One theory is that Than Shwe's lack of response to the crisis was, in part, influenced by the fact that the population in the delta contains many Karen. A cynic might even think that he welcomed the storm for eliminating some of the non-Burman ethnic peoples. Others suggest that even if the Karen's ethnicity was not much of a factor, Than Shwe remembered the delta as an area of insurgency and a recruiting ground for Karen rebels. "Many cyclone survivors will also recall it was Than Shwe who led efforts to root out Karen rebels in Bogalay in 1991 during a campaign ironically named 'Operation Storm,'" Aung Zaw reminded readers. "Helicopters, jet fighters and naval vessels were brought in to reinforce the ground forces and to hunt down suspected Karen rebels who were, for the most part, just ordinary villagers." The regime admits that 275 Karen combatants were killed, thirteen arrested and three surrendered—and most analysts believe these are underestimates. Hundreds of Karen villagers were jailed and tortured. "In the wake of Cyclone Nargis, it is a painful irony for villagers in Bogalay, Laputta and the rest of the delta region that Than Shwe is again at the helm," concluded Aung Zaw. "Ironically, this time he is preventing helicopters, ships and personnel carriers from being deployed, thwarting efforts to aid the cyclone survivors. In a way, the brutal face of Operation Storm has reappeared, albeit belatedly. Yet again, Than Shwe has placed military and political interests ahead of humanitarian concerns."[29]

In spite of the horrors left in the wake of these two events just eight months apart—the Saffron Revolution and Cyclone Nargis—the Burmese people retain their determination to continue their struggle for freedom. Despite facing severe oppression and being under constant watch, several activists who founded a group called Generation Wave continued small-scale activities aimed at expressing their opposition to the regime. A4 paper size posters in Rangoon were displayed with Than Shwe's picture and the words: "Dictator General Than Shwe wanted by the new generation youths for being responsible for the deteriorating economic, social, health and education conditions in people's life."[30]

A group of exiled Burmese women in Thailand, calling themselves Lanna Action for Burma, launched a campaign Than Shwe may never have anticipated: Panty Power. In one aspect of Burmese tradition, men cannot touch a woman's underwear, and they believe that if they do, they will lose their power. The women, therefore, mobilized people around the world to post ladies' underwear to Burmese embassies, adopting the slogan "Panties for Peace." A website was established, which included a computer game that entailed trying to place a pair of panties on Than Shwe's head. The campaign was expanded to a "Sarong Revolution," in which women were asked to lift their sarongs at Burmese embassies around the world. The Lanna Action for Burma website warns: "Than Shwe and the SPDC—we are here to tell you that not one of your tricks nor a single one of your lies has fooled us for a second. You're not dealing with the UN now . . . you are dealing with us . . . the angry women of Burma and the rest of the world. Panties were just the beginning, Than Shwe."[31]

FIG. 6. Top: *Poster of Aung San Suu Kyi at the India-Burma border.*
Bottom: Her house in Rangoon. Photos by Benedict Rogers.

8

THE RIVALS, THE HEIRS, THE CRONIES, AND THE FUTURE

IN MARCH 2007, a British member of parliament, Andrew Mitchell, went to Rangoon to meet members of the regime and the democracy movement. He was traveling as his party's spokesman on international development and as a member of the Shadow Cabinet. While the regime had attempted to orchestrate a choreographed visit, when Mitchell refused to meet the leader of the Union Solidarity Development Association, the SPDC, in retaliation, cancelled all his other appointments with government ministers, except one. Mitchell was left with the deputy foreign minister, and spent the rest of his visit with 88 Generation Students, NLD leaders, foreign diplomats, UN agencies, and NGOs.

In his meeting with the deputy foreign minister, whom he describes as "educated, polite, and wary," Mitchell asked if he could visit Aung San Suu Kyi under house arrest. He explained that he had met Michael Aris before he died, and that he had some gifts for her—chocolates and soap. "He told me that only one man could give permission to visit her," Mitchell recalls. "So I said, 'Well, call him up.'" Such an idea brought fear to the deputy foreign minister's face. "I cannot disturb him," he told the visiting politician.

The discussion continued. "We had a full and frank exchange of views," says Mitchell. "I asked him how he felt as a representative of a pariah regime, which was both wicked and illegitimate. I asked how he could look himself in the mirror, in the knowledge that he represented a government that had brought his country to its knees and that was an obscenity. He said simply that his religion prepared him for such difficulties."

Two things, recalls Mitchell, were clear from this exchange. "First was that he was not used to a [foreign] politician coming in and giving him both barrels. Second, that one man was in charge."

Long before Khin Nyunt's demise, it was clear to some observers that Than Shwe was the dominant general. Although a few analysts speculated that Khin Nyunt was the real power in the regime, one foreigner who observed the interactions between them said that it was always obvious that Khin Nyunt was "subordinate." Prior to one meeting with UN Special Envoy Razali Ismail, it was apparent that Than Shwe had threatened Khin Nyunt. "When he was sitting together with Than Shwe in the meeting, Khin Nyunt was like a school boy," recalls one observer. "He was very shy, totally different from when he was alone." On one occasion, when the UN special envoy raised a particular point, Khin Nyunt became nervous. It was clear it was a step too far. "If you insist on this, Mr. Razali, you will never come back to my country," Khin Nyunt told the envoy. In the view of one observer, this was not the tone Khin Nyunt normally took with UN officials. "So it showed that Than Shwe is the big boss."

Since the overthrow of Khin Nyunt, Than Shwe's dominance in the regime has become unquestioned. The days when decisions were taken collectively by the SPDC were gone long ago, but now almost everyone in the international community agrees that Than Shwe is *the* leader of Burma. Than Shwe enjoys "unquestioned authority."[1] No decisions can be made without his agreement, and he makes all major decisions alone. How has he sustained this position? Why has no one made a move against him, in the same way that he has purged others? As Thai parliamentarian Kraisak Choonhavan asks: "The guy is mad. But how is he so powerful? It is a mystery. He is so crazy and paranoid—how could he have carried out purges and succeeded? Maung Aye and Khin Nyunt are smarter. Why did they not dump Than Shwe? Than Shwe has surprised all of us." But a former Western diplomat cautions against such a reductionist analysis of Than Shwe. "He is not mad, he is rational according to the information he has and his cultural upbringing," she argues.

The answers to these questions lie partially in the explanation provided by another former Western diplomat. Than Shwe "controls the levers of power in the army," he argues. "If you control promotion, it is a standard technique—you have your group of generals and you can do what you like. Ultimately, the *tatmadaw* sticks together, or it falls apart together, and they choose to stick together." In 1997, after renaming the SLORC the State Peace and Development Council (SPDC), Than Shwe axed all the top generals, except Maung Aye, Khin Nyunt, and Tin Oo (yet another Tin Oo—not the Tin Oo who had served as chief of staff in the 1970s nor the "MI" Tin Oo who had served as intelligence chief under Ne Win). Than Shwe brought in a different group of generals, who were not necessarily prepared for government but would be beholden to Than Shwe since he had effectively made their careers—just as Ne Win had before him often sacked underlings in favor of younger officers. Over the years, Than Shwe shuffled and reshuffled SLORC and then SPDC, but in all likelihood this was not as a result of threats to his power from within the military. In 2001 and 2002, Than Shwe again moved to shuffle some of the leadership within the military apparatus.

Ne Win held a ninetieth birthday party in 2001 at the Sedona Hotel in Rangoon. Shortly thereafter some of his grandchildren began approaching military officials asking them to take part in a coup to overthrow Than Shwe and establish them as the rulers of Burma. They approached the air force chief, police chief, and commander of the triangle region command, as well as others. The military officials met with Ne Win's grandchildren, whom they may have assumed were working at the behest of Ne Win's daughter Sandar Win. Sandar Win had previously been influential when Ne Win was in power, and was particularly close to Khin Nyunt, whose career she had helped to advance in the 1980s. However, she was never close to Than Shwe, since Than Shwe had apparently been an acolyte of Aye Ko, and not Ne Win directly. Unlike Khin Nyunt and Saw Maung, Than Shwe did not owe his career directly to Ne Win. Indeed, in the mid-1990s Than Shwe had even removed military protection from Ne Win after one of the military bodyguards assigned to protect him had become embroiled in a fight between Ne Win's relatives.

Hearing of the coup plot, Than Shwe promptly arrested three of Ne Win's grandchildren, and placed Sandar Win under house arrest. Ne Win himself was also, in a sense, under house arrest, since he lived on the same compound as Sandar Win. While the media reported that Ne Win had been placed under house arrest, the real intention had been to teach Sandar Win a lesson. For the senior general to get into a position where he places the former dictator Ne Win and his family under arrest, says a former Western ambassador, "is a pretty powerful statement of intent."

Than Shwe fired all of the military officials who had been approached by Ne Win's grandchildren—not because the coup attempt was a serious or dangerous plot, but because they had laughed off the attempt and not reported it to Than Shwe himself. As if to give the former dictator a final insult, when Ne Win died in December 2002, Than Shwe ordered all military officials to boycott the funeral. Well-placed sources state that when one ex-military official, former navy chief Thaung Tin, attended the funeral, Than Shwe fired Thaung Tin's relatives who were still serving in the military, including his son and son-in-law.

According to Timo Kivimaki and Morten Pedersen, "Than Shwe has stacked the top levels of the defense ministry with handpicked subordinates" who are "fiercely loyal to their leader," making an internal coup unlikely.[2] Furthermore, ever since Ne Win's coup in 1962—and perhaps even before then—the Burma Army has been, in Lintner's words, "a state within a state." Lintner notes that between 1962 and 1974, there were sixty-four military takeovers throughout the world, most of them involving the overthrow of civilian governments. Only two of these remain today: Colonel Qaddafi's Libya and the junta in Burma. What makes the military regime in Burma stand out, Lintner argues, is its control over enough economic institutions that as a result, not only are military personnel bought off through dependency, but so too are their families. Soldiers and their families, argues Lintner, "enjoy a position far more privileged than their counterparts ever had in, for instance, Thailand and Indonesia." There are special schools and hospitals for the military and their dependents, housing is provided for them and they can shop for goods normally unavailable in ordinary stores. "An army pass assures the holder of a seat on a train or an airplane, and a policeman would never dare to report him or her for violating traffic rules," he explains.[3]

Timo Kivimaki and Morten Pedersen agree. "The military as an institution has grown accustomed to dominating all other power structures in the country and having full decision-making and budgetary autonomy in the pursuit of its goals," they conclude. "The upper echelons of the military have come to constitute a privileged upper class in Burmese society with superior access to everything from consumer products to education and health care. These privileges have been further extended since 1988, which has seen a great increase in economic opportunities for those who control new state-linked direct foreign investments and the expansion of state control in the border areas with their rich natural resources."[4] Senior officers who have been involved in carrying out serious human rights violations may fear punishment or retribution with a regime change, although the National League for Democracy has gone out of its way to calm these fears by calling for national reconciliation instead of retribution.

That said, there have reportedly been thousands of desertions in recent years. Maung Aung Myoe claims to have received a confidential report from the regime stating that between May and August 2006, a total of 9,467 desertions were reported, while 7,761 desertions were reported between January and April 2000. Some estimates suggest that at least 1,600 soldiers desert each month.[5] Deserters and defectors that have made it to Burma's borders, where they are able to speak more easily, claim morale in the military is at an all-time low. "There is no doubt that many in the army are extremely unhappy with the way things are going, and are concerned about what will happen to them after the elections," said Byo Nein, the son of a former government minister. "But they are army officers and will continue to obey their orders unquestioningly."[6]

Again, Kivimaki and Pedersen agree. "There are officers who appreciate the intimate links between national security, economic development and participatory government, and who are more restrained in their fear of internal and external subversion. Some military officials in private indicate a certain empathy with Aung San Suu Kyi and even express support for a power sharing arrangement," they suggest. "Yet by and large, in a system that places extreme value on unity and conformity, the most powerful leaders—and often the most hard-line views—set the standard. Others play along with the illusion for strategic purposes, or simply to survive."[7]

That is the key point. There is a culture among some in Burma of not challenging superiors, although it is empirically unclear whether this is any stronger than in other military structures. As one foreign analyst puts it: "They don't challenge, they don't contest. It was like this under the kings, under Ne Win, and now under Than Shwe." In private, the analyst claims, 90 percent of the generals state that they disagree with Than Shwe's policies. "When they are together in an informal gathering, they all criticize him. So there is only one question: Why don't they do anything? If he is so bad, if his policy is so negative for the country, why do they keep him? Then you have a big silence. Nobody can answer. It is really strange."

At the same time, cultural deference to authority shouldn't be overemphasized. One needs only point to the demonstrations, protests, sit-ins, religious boycotts, and countless acts of individual defiance over the years to understand that the Burmese people are no shrinking violets. If they were so intimidated by authority, none of this would have happened, not to mention the hundreds of candidates who risked their lives to run for election in 1990 and the millions of voters who resoundingly rejected military rule. At the same time, the Burmese history of resistance, whether it be Aung San Suu Kyi, Saya San, or many others, is an example to all those seeking human rights.

Some diplomats believe that cultural issues related to deference and gender influence Than Shwe's antipathy towards Aung San Suu Kyi. However, these same diplomats state that the greater influence seems to be that Aung San Suu Kyi presents a credible alternative to military rule: "There is something deeply personal about the generals' view of her," believes one Western diplomat. "She is a woman, her path is one of nonviolence, which is diametrically opposite to theirs, and she reminds them—because of her father—of the path that they have chosen and the mistakes they have made. [The fact] that there was an alternative path that involved the military in a different role is a serious challenge to their narrative of Burmese history. They resent her education, the fact that she has traveled, her network of international friends. She represents everything that they are not, and that is very hard for them to deal with." Some say the generals' wives loathe her even more. "She is very rational, she has a very logical way of arguing, which is not theirs, and that would have wound them up even more."

A foreigner who met the top generals and Aung San Suu Kyi many times believes Than Shwe has a very patriarchal view of her. "He considers that he is the father, she is the daughter, and so she should listen to him, not make any remarks, not criticize. She should just accept what he says." This meant that on the two occasions when Than Shwe met Aung San Suu Kyi, the conversation went nowhere. The same foreigner alleges, "After ten minutes, they had nothing to discuss. She could serve the tea and talk about the weather. This has hampered any possible dialogue."

Razali Ismail says he tried to play up to this attitude in the hope that it might cause a breakthrough in the relationship. "On one occasion, I had lunch with Than Shwe, Maung Aye, and Khin Nyunt, when Aung San Suu Kyi was about to be released," the former UN special envoy recalls. "I told Than Shwe that it was very nice that he had freed her, and that it means a lot to try to bring people together. I said, 'She has certain ideas that you may not like, but you should treat her as your younger sister.' The other generals did not say one word. I carried on: 'You should try to impress her, and explain why you should work together. Tell her about the progress you have made and what the army has stood for. If you don't talk with her, it will not work.' He did not say very much."

On another occasion, the envoy tried a similar approach. "We met over breakfast in Langkawi, for about an hour. He spoke in English. He said: 'I would like to have strong leadership in Myanmar when we have democracy, like here in Malaysia with Dr. Mahathir. He gets a lot of things done.' He was very confident and expansive. So I suggested to him that he should use Aung San Suu Kyi on behalf of his country, because she can do a lot of things. 'If you do not use her, you are wasting an opportunity,' I told him. 'She is a true patriot, like her father'. 'Oh yes,' he replied. 'Good idea.' But nothing happened."

At yet another occasion, a dinner was brokered by intermediaries and attended by all the top brass of both the SPDC and the NLD. According to custom, Than Shwe, due to his seniority, should have taken the floor first, welcoming the guests, opening the discussion. It would have been culturally difficult for Aung San Suu Kyi to make the first move on such an occasion. According to one foreigner, who spoke to Aung San Suu Kyi afterwards, Than Shwe made no effort at all to break the ice. "All you could hear was the noise of forks and spoons on the plates," he recalls. Interestingly, the only general who made an attempt to talk to Aung San Suu Kyi on this occasion was Maung Aye. He talked about deforestation.

During her periods of release from house arrest Aung San Suu Kyi, according to Razali Ismail, "frightened the hell out of the military" and soon she was detained again. "They were very uncomfortable. Aung San Suu Kyi was too clever by half," recalls the former special envoy. On one occasion, Khin Nyunt offered to take her to see development projects in northern Shan State, and Razali Ismail went with them. But Aung San

Suu Kyi was shocked by what she saw. "There was no real development," says Razali Ismail. "They hid away the opium cultivation, they attempted to bring the highland people to the lowlands, and the place was full of casinos, prostitution, and karaoke, using Chinese language and Chinese currency. I sang karaoke and played backgammon with Chinese money. Why did the military encourage Aung San Suu Kyi to see all this? They treated her like royalty, and showed her their bridges and roads, and they thought she would be impressed—but they were bridges and roads that went nowhere. She saw something different and she was really frightened." As she talked with local people she realized just how little investment in education and health care there was, and what challenges this posed for the future.

On another occasion, Aung San Suu Kyi was touring Taunggyi and asked if Razali Ismail could meet her there. "At first, Khin Nyunt gave me permission," said the UN special envoy. The next morning, however, I was called in by Than Shwe who was in a foul mood, and he said, 'No you cannot go, this will play into her hands, she is going to open a new NLD office and it will be used for propaganda.' I told him that I thought everything was agreed, a government plane was ready, and I pointed to Khin Nyunt. 'I don't agree. You cannot go,' Than Shwe replied, and then told me he did not want to talk anymore, he had other things to do. He walked away. This was the beginning of his dislike for me."

For all his authoritarianism, Than Shwe is known for two other characteristics. First, some have claimed he has difficulty making decisions quickly, which others have interpreted as purposefully allowing situations to develop so he can fully think through an appropriate response. But as one observer in Rangoon put it, "His decisions are always belated, never timely. He has no confidence." Secondly, when he does make a decision, some believe he has had a tendency to overreact to a situation.

When the Saffron Revolution first started in September 2007, Than Shwe could have stomped on it immediately. He could have taken action to prevent it growing at all, and had he done so, few people would have ever known. Many argue that if Khin Nyunt and his military intelligence apparatus had still been around, they would have immediately prevented the situation from escalating, through brutal arrests and torture but without as much bloodshed. But Than Shwe waited. When Buddhist monks marched to University Avenue and were heading to Aung San Suu Kyi's home, they were stopped at a junction. The soldiers on duty reportedly telephoned Naypyidaw for orders, since they had to be given by Than Shwe—but no reply came. Nobody dared act, and so the monks passed through and Aung San Suu Kyi emerged from her gate to wave, a scene that emboldened the demonstrators. When Than Shwe finally decided to crush the movement, he ordered the bloodiest response, perhaps showing his pattern of indecisiveness followed by overreaction. At the same time, it must be reiterated, many Burmese believe that Than Shwe purposefully allows protests and demonstrations to develop, so that he can "draw out" the opposition and more effectively clamp down on opposition.

Following the purge of Khin Nyunt, rumors spread of major infighting within the regime. In January 2005, it was claimed that a row between some of the top generals led to a gun battle, and resulted in the death of Maung Aye's personal assistant, Lieutenant Colonel Bo Win Tun. Persistent stories spread of a power struggle between Than Shwe and Maung Aye, known to some as the "John Wayne of Burma." Maung Aye, according to *The Irrawaddy*, is known to be a quick-thinking combat commander, while Than Shwe is "a chess player and schemer, thus making Maung Aye stand out like a sore thumb and maybe likely to be axed." Even high-ranking officers, *The Irrawaddy* further claims, "are not sure where they stand at the moment—if they are found to be linked to Khin Nyunt, they will be fired and face trial."[8] Than Shwe, one commentator said, "has all the cards, and he can push the button to remove his rivals anytime he wants."[9]

That Than Shwe is ruthless is undeniable. But while Than Shwe and Maung Aye may have a mutual suspicion, even a dislike, of one another, stories of an impending power struggle are farfetched. Maung Aye was said to be angry after the Depayin massacre, the brutal crackdown on the Buddhist monks in the Saffron Revolution, and the failure to provide help to the victims of Cyclone Nargis, but one Western diplomat is skeptical. "You often hear rumors of conflict. [Sometimes] businessmen close to one of the top men will periodically search you out to say that their patron, Maung Aye, for example, is very upset by what he sees, he's such an enlightened individual, all this pains him greatly. I have to say, the longer I was there the less I believed it, because my answer to them obviously was 'why doesn't he do something about it?' I am not quite sure what those sort of overtures are about." Certainly the image of Maung Aye as "enlightened" sits uncomfortably with his reported hatred of the ethnic groups. In 1997 troops under his command won a crushing victory over part of the Karen resistance. Upon accepting their surrender, instead of acting magnanimously as he could certainly have afforded to do, Maung Aye walked across the Karen flag that had been laid before him, ground it underneath his boots and ordered the Karen captain to kneel down and apologize.[10]

Former British ambassador Mark Canning believes Maung Aye, a heavy drinker who is regarded as lazy, lacks ambition. Unlike some other generals, Maung Aye apparently does not have expensive tastes apart from suits. On a flight to Bangkok, Maung Aye and his assistant were overheard talking about how much they were looking forward to having Kentucky Fried Chicken when they reached Bangkok—and how they were particularly fond of coleslaw. "He is the number two. Like all 'number twos,' he would like to be 'number one' one day, but he clearly hasn't got ambition of a degree that would push him towards making it happen. He's a soldier's soldier—enjoys drinking, is good in the field. He seems to be quite happy where he is." If Maung Aye wanted to make a move against the ailing Than Shwe, Canning asks, "What's stopping him?" The answer: comfort. "You can imagine, you're in the number two position, it's quite a big decision to go for it. He's comfortable, he's got his twenty-seven inch flat screen television, the kids—does he really want to risk being slammed up in Insein Jail for the rest of his life? His attitude is 'let's just see how things play out.'" Other observers believe that Maung Aye is unlikely to make a move against Than Shwe since he, too, is indebted to the senior general. When he was plucked from his position as head of the Eastern Regional Command to join the original SLORC, he was the second youngest among the regional commanders. Like many before him, Maung Aye would have originally felt some loyalty to Than Shwe for promoting him.

Most people agree that if Than Shwe were to die tomorrow, Maung Aye would succeed him automatically, because of his position in the hierarchy. But if Than Shwe can transfer power to a person and in a manner and timing of his choice, his successor is more likely to be General Thura Shwe Mann. *The Irrawaddy* reported in July 2009 that Than Shwe told Shwe Mann at a cabinet meeting in Naypyidaw: "You are going to be president."[11]

Those who know Shwe Mann personally describe him as polite and diplomatic, and "a good listener." He would, said one source inside Burma, be "far better than Than Shwe." However, it should be remembered that he would not be Than Shwe's favorite, if he were not ultimately a hardliner.

In his early sixties and one of the youngest of the top generals, Shwe Mann is "a military man down to his shiny black shoes."[12] He earned his honorific title "Thura" in battle, when he commanded operations against the Karen in 1989.[13] Rumors abound that he himself is a Karen Buddhist, and if this is true, he could be the first from that ethnic group to reach the top since General Smith Dun. However, he has shown no sympathy for his own people if he is Karen, and would be regarded by many Karen as a traitor. He serves as chief of staff of all three armed services, and is known for his loyalty and opportunism. "Observers say he shies away from public appearances and there is no record of his views on Suu Kyi, or what backroom role he had in the bloody suppression of protesting students in Rangoon in 1988,"[14] writes Graham Lees.

Promoted to full general only in 2003, Shwe Mann graduated from the Defense Services Academy in 1969, and served with Light Infantry Division 11 near Rangoon, under the Rangoon Command and the 10th Light Infantry Battalion. In 1997, a year after becoming a brigadier-general, he was appointed commander of the southwest region, based in Pathein—a post Than Shwe himself had previously held when it was know as Bassein. According to a source inside Burma, on the rare occasions that Than Shwe delegates any decisions, it is to Shwe Mann. "Shwe Mann is like a son to Than Shwe. The history of their relationship is not very long, and there are several people closer to Than Shwe personally, but he is certainly Than Shwe's chosen successor," said the source. Since 2007 Shwe Mann's position has been significantly strengthened. Most of the regiments providing security around Naypyidaw are commanded by people handpicked by Shwe Mann, and according to several sources, he now has day-to-day command of the armed forces and the country's internal affairs.[15] This is all part of Than Shwe's plan for the succession. A Thai foreign ministry official who follows the maneuverings closely believes Thura Shwe Mann is "the only possible successor" from the military.

Than Shwe's other protégés are Myint Swe, who became the Rangoon regional commander in 2002, and Minister of Industry-1 Aung Thaung, regarded as one of the masterminds of the Depayin massacre and, some-one who comes from Than Shwe's hometown of Kyaukse. His family runs various companies involved in oil, gas, and agricultural products, as well as timber, rice trading, and the importation of computers and other elec-tronic goods.[16] Aung Thaung is also very influential within the USDA.

Others loyal to Than Shwe but less likely to succeed him include the current prime minister Thein Sein, who chaired the National Convention and was promoted after the death of Soe Win. Regarded as a "mystery man," Thein Sein has risen quietly under Than Shwe's patronage, to whom he has shown "total loyalty."[17] He is allegedly involved in gold mining in Kachin State, which has resulted in the seizure of hundreds of acres of villagers' land.[18] In 2009 Thein Sein reportedly told UN Special Envoy Ibrahim Gambari that if the UN wanted to see stability in Burma, it should remove economic sanctions.[19]

A significant power base for Than Shwe has been the USDA and other pro-junta militias, such as the Swan Arr Shin or the "Masters of Force." Founded in 1993, the USDA is Than Shwe's equivalent of Adolf Hitler's Brown Shirts or Mae Zedong's Red Guards, and is set to become "the new face of the military dictatorship," claims a 2006 report published by the Network for Democracy and Development (NDD).[20] Numbering 24 million, the USDA poses as "purely a social welfare organization," an NGO—or more accurately, a government-organized NGO (GONGO). As the report states, the USDA frequently presents itself as the benevolent benefactor of the people and in place of a genuine civil society it "has gradually taken over the role played by independent NGOs." But in reality, the organization is a mass movement, with its sights trained on elimi-nating the democracy movement. The mob that attacked Aung San Suu Kyi's convoy in Depayin consisted of USDA members, and that was by no means the first occasion they had attacked her. On the first anniversary of the death of former prime minister U Nu in 1996, USDA members wear-ing red armbands infiltrated the crowd and, under orders from military intelligence, threw tomatoes at Aung San Suu Kyi as she began a speech. Later the same year, USDA members were sent to attack her during a visit to a temple in Pegu—but she failed to show up. In April 1996, the road to her house was blocked, and USDA thugs threatened to beat up any NLD members attempting to visit her. Her motorcade was attacked the same year by USDA members carrying iron bars and bricks.

There are certainly not 24 million willing members of the USDA. The USDA recruits by force, pressuring university students and government officials to join. "Joining the USDA is presented to the students as compulsory . . . The same holds true for civil servants," according to NDD's report. "The teachers told me that it was compulsory to join the USDA, and that I would be expelled from the school or I would have to take exams outside the school if I didn't join," one student claimed. Some people are signed up without their knowledge. "I have not received any evidence that I was an official member, and I never filled out a membership form," said one civil servant. The USDA now controls the process of awarding business licenses, a function previously conducted by the military intelligence, and many local businesses are USDA-run. USDA members find their ability to travel without harassment is significantly increased, and have campaigned to force international agencies operating in Burma to work through the USDA.

Along with its involvement in the violent harassment of the democracy movement, the USDA has engaged in a sustained campaign to intimidate people into resigning from and denouncing the NLD, and has called for its dissolution. In April 2006, the regime claimed almost one hundred thirty NLD members had resigned, but the NLD had only received four resignations. USDA activists went house to house in Mandalay in 2005, demanding that people leave the NLD. A secret document from the USDA, obtained in 2004, included the stated objective of "narrowing and eliminating the activities of opposition forces." The USDA is regularly used by the regime to hold mass rallies to show support for the SPDC's policies and to denounce the opposition, particularly during the National Convention. In just one of many examples, a Burmese told me he was asked to join a rally to denounce the NLD, the ILO, Western countries, and the report commissioned by Václav Havel and Desmond Tutu, which called on the UN Security Council to address the crisis in Burma. Another said: "In most of the events, we have to attend as the audience, clapping after each speaker. But, I had to perform once as a speaker, just reading out a readymade paper."

The USDA has increasingly played a part in harassing religious minorities, particularly Christians and Muslims, and has sometimes been used to deliberately spark religious conflict between Buddhists and Muslims to give the regime "an excuse to retain power as they ostensibly can restore stability in the country," says the NDD report.

There is evidence that the USDA and other mass movement organizations have been given military training and used as civilian armed militia, consistent with Than Shwe's proposal for a total people's defense. Since the year 2000, USDA members, along with members of the fire brigade and the National Red Cross, have been provided military training and arms. In 2003, for example, the *tatmadaw* provided basic military training to the USDA in Mon State. General Maung Aye described the USDA as an "auxiliary national defense force" in 1997, and in the *Manual for Application of People's War Strategy*, published on Than Shwe's instructions, readers were told that in the case of foreign intervention, USDA members were to be "trained and organized as people's militias." Than Shwe himself said on Myanmar Television in 1994, soon after the USDA was created, that the USDA was formed "specifically with the objective to fill the role of strengthening national unity." What that meant in practice, he indicated, was that the USDA would target "those who echo foreign claims about a lack of democracy and human rights violations in Myanmar." The USDA was formed, he continued, in light of "acts of anarchy" in 1988, and would "prevent similar events in the future, and to promote the observance of law and order among the general public." Those receiving military training constitute, according to Than Shwe, "the hard core force of the USDA, but also the sole national force that will always join hands with the *tatmadaw* to serve national and public interests. They should be morally and physically strong with sharp national defense qualities. The trainees will be taught military parade, military tactics and the use of weapons."[21] Coming from the senior general himself, the purpose of the USDA could not be clearer.

Now, however, there is speculation that Than Shwe is turning the USDA into a political party ahead of the 2010 elections. The USDA's general secretary, Htay Oo, suggested at a press conference in 2005 that the USDA might become a political party. Under the new constitution, 25 percent of the parliamentary seats at the national level and 33 percent at the state level will be reserved directly for the military. If the USDA contests the elections, with its 24 million members, it is likely—through rigging and harassment—to win many if not most of the remaining seats, thereby cementing the regime's total political control. As the NDD report suggests, if this happens it is possible that Than Shwe's rule will simply continue, but he will swap his military uniform for a civilian suit and "Senior General Than Shwe will transition to U Than Shwe, from patron of the USDA into party chairman." It would bring Burma full circle, in a remarkable repeat of Ne Win's transition from the Revolutionary Council to the Burma Socialist Program Party.

But the USDA is merely the largest in a number of civil society facades Than Shwe and the regime have created. Some are subtler than others. Swan Arr Shin is the most blatantly thuggish, consisting mainly of common criminals released from prison and paid, and perhaps drugged, to rough up democracy activists. Perhaps more deceptive are organizations such as the Myanmar Maternal and Child Welfare Association, the Myanmar Women's Affairs Federation, and the Myanmar Red Cross Society, all of which are controlled or manipulated by the generals in some way, and act as a fronts for regime activities.

Business entrepreneurs have also been labeled as Than Shwe's allies. Known as the "cronies," they include Tay Za, Tun Myint Naing or Steven Law, Aung Ko Win, Serge Pun, Maung Weik, Htay Myint, Khin Shwe, Zaw Zaw, Eike Htun, and Chit Khaing.[22] Of these, Tay Za, president of the Htoo Trading Company, is the best known and probably the most influential. He is rumored to have helped fund Thandar Shwe's opulent wedding, paid for or carried out much of the construction of Naypyidaw, and helped Than Shwe with arms deals. According to a defector from the Burma Army, Than Shwe is known to consult Tay Za alone over some key decisions.

Tay Za founded Myanmar Avia Export, which acts as the sole representative in Burma for Russia's aircraft manufacturer Mapo and helicopter firm Rostvertol.[23] It is claimed that he was instrumental in securing for the regime the sale from Russia of ten MiG-29 jet fighters, for 130 million dollars.[24] With property in Singapore and a mansion in Rangoon, Tay Za also owns a football club and several expensive cars, including a Lamborghini, a Cadillac, a Ferrari, two Humvees, as well as a Bentley, and reportedly drives a different one each day. His children were educated at the expensive United World College of South East Asia (UWCSEA) in Singapore, an international school with twenty-nine hundred students representing sixty-five different nationalities. When a visit was made to the college as part of the research for this book, a teacher confirmed that several influential and wealthy Burmese send their children to UWCSEA because the education system inside Burma is so poor. "Many of them want to see change in Burma, but they are afraid," the teacher claimed. "We certainly do not compromise on what we say. We have discussions on global concerns, including Burma, and a range of views are expressed."

Tay Za's party-going son Htet Tay Za has hit the headlines, however, having been photographed with bikini-clad Caucasian girls around him, drinking and smoking. His expensive UWCSEA education has not, it appears, broadened his mind, because soon after the brutal suppression of the Saffron Revolution in 2007, an e-mail allegedly from Htet Tay Za to friends in Singapore was circulated following the imposition of new US sanctions. The sanctions hit his father's business, but Htet Tay Za appeared unconcerned, reportededly claiming that although "the US bans us, we're still f--g cool in Singapore." He continued: "We're sitting on the whole Burmese GDP. We've got timber, gems and gas to be sold to other countries like Singapore, China, India and Russia. My brother is rocking on his red brand new Lamborghini with hot sexy Western chicks . . . and I need another Ferrari to rock on."[25]

Htet Tay Za is on Facebook, the Internet social networking site, and several attempts were made to contact him as part of the research for this book. He did not reply. Similarly, an attempt was made to visit the Singapore office of Tay Za's company, the Htoo Group, in Shenton Way, but the office was no longer at the listed address. A telephone call made to the published Htoo Group phone number was answered by a nervous-sounding Singaporean receptionist, who claimed that the entire company had left Singapore and gone back to Burma. When questioned, she said the move was "permanent" but she did not know when they left or why.

Than Shwe reportedly first met Tay Za when he visited a coastal resort immediately after the Depayin massacre. He escaped to a luxury retreat when UN envoy Razali Ismail arrived in the country. Tay Za was running a hotel in addition to his timber export business, and Than Shwe was impressed. It is also rumored that Tay Za helped facilitate one of Than Shwe's visits to Singapore for medical treatment, and that is when their relationship first started. Than Shwe has also allegedly recruited Singaporean doctors to come to Naypyidaw when he needs medical care, and Tay Za may well have brokered that arrangement.

Tay Za started out in life as a recruit of the Defense Services Academy, but was apparently expelled from military training. He did not come from a wealthy family, but married the daughter of Daw Htoo, an affluent businesswoman involved in the teak business.

According to Mark Canning, Tay Za has invested in various "vanity" projects including Air Bagan and Orient Hotels, which provide the regime with an ornate image, while making his real money in arms deals, and timber and jade concessions. Tay Za's involvement in building Naypyidaw was a way of ingratiating himself with Than Shwe. "The basic business model seems to be 'build me a capital and I'll give you all the jade and timber you can use,'" suggests Canning. The relationship is similar to the associations Indonesia's dictator Suharto and Malaysia's Mahathir had with their cronies, but the difference, in Canning's view, is that in Indonesia and Malaysia the cronies "actually delivered a product." In contrast, the standard of construction in Naypyidaw is "shocking" and the cronies "haven't actually produced any serious investment in the country at all, except substandard infrastructure."

Tay Za has played his cards well, remaining close to Than Shwe while developing a relationship with Shwe Mann's son Aung Thet Mann, thereby ensuring his continued influence and access in a post-Than Shwe era. Aung Thet Mann's company, Ayer Shwe Wah, is now related to Tay Za's Htoo Trading Company, and Aung Thet Mann has reaped significant financial benefits from the deal.[26] When Aung Thet Mann said he wanted a car, Tay Za bought him one of the latest models without hesitation. He retains his connection to Than Shwe's family, however, having bought a Hummer, the civilian equivalent of a Humvee, for the senior general's son Kyaing San Shwe.[27]

In addition to Tay Za, who denies his involvement in arms deals, Than Shwe's other arms broker is Dr. Thar Yin Myat, who was born into one of the wealthiest families in Burma. The son of an air force general, Thar Yin Myat served as an army medical doctor and through his father's contacts he began to assist in the purchase of air force jets from China and arms from other countries. "Since then, he has become Than Shwe's handyman," says a defector. Tay Za and Thar Yin Myat have also helped Than Shwe's wife Kyaing Kyaing undertake shopping trips to Singapore, and have allegedly transferred funds from her Singaporean bank account to a new account in Dubai.

Many of the tycoons are personally connected to the generals, as well as politically and financially. Khin Shwe's daughter is married to Shwe Mann's son, while Maung Weik is married to General Myint Swe's niece but is believed to have sought the affections of Than Shwe's middle daughter.[28]

Khin Shwe, a real estate tycoon and president of Zaykabar Corporation, is involved in politics too. In 1997 he is the one to have reportedly hired the American public relations firm Bain and Company to enhance Burma's image internationally. As Aung Zaw concludes, "The fact is that business and politics are inseparable in Burma."[29] Some Burmese exiles have suggested that the decision to change the name from the Orwellian-sounding SLORC to the more benign-sounding SPDC was on Bain's advice, though I have been unable to confirm this or find any evidence to suggest it is true. Aung Lynn Htut believes Bain had nothing to do with it. He says Than Shwe had disliked the name SLORC for quite some time and had been waiting for an opportune moment to make the change.

Serge Pun runs SPA Myanmar, a conglomerate of forty businesses that are involved in financial services, real estate, manufacturing, technology, construction, automotives, and healthcare. He and his brother Martin have thrown some bones in the direction of charity, committing some time and money to charitable causes through the SPA Foundation, which provides assistance for Burmese undergraduate and postgraduate education, and the Business Coalition Against AIDS.[30]

Some have suggested that, apart from the other generals and business cronies, Than Shwe's children could be set to play an important role in the future of the country. This may or may not be true, but one thing is certain—Than Shwe's children and sons-in-law are well placed within the Burmese establishment to provide important intelligence on military matters and foreign affairs. Additionally, virtually all of his children feed off the trough of government largesse.

Among his daughters, at least four of the five have at some time served in the Burmese foreign ministry or related positions. Khin Pyone Shwe, who married now Brigadier General Thein Naing, lives near the Mingaladon air base where her husband serves as chief of the base. Many former *tatmadaw* officials expect that he is being groomed to assume control of the entire air force (and perhaps, therefore, help Than Shwe avoid the problem that took place in 1988 when elements of the air force joined demonstrators marching on the streets calling for freedom and democracy). An official with knowledge of Khin Pyone Shwe's earlier career reports that she worked at the Burmese embassy in Geneva that is tasked with, among other things, responding to UN reports and investigations of human rights abuses committed by Than Shwe's regime. The same official noted that Khin Pyone Shwe, like most of Than Shwe's children, has developed a reputation as a spoiled brat and that even the Burmese ambassador to Geneva was petrified about upsetting her sensibilities. According to this official, Khin Pyone Shwe insisted on renting a stunning apartment in Geneva, but proceeded to furnish it with a single chair, thereby forcing the ambassador to sit on the ground in front of her when he visited her residence.

Two of Than Shwe's other daughters, Kyi Kyi Thit Shwe and Aye Aye Thit Shwe, are both rumored to work at the Burmese embassy in Singapore, where they serve as low-ranking officials. Kyi Kyi Shwe is the mother of Than Shwe's favored grandson, Nay Shwe Thway Aung.

Thandar Shwe, Than Shwe's daughter who was feted at the infamous wedding ceremony in 2006, previously worked at the Burmese embassy in China and studied there as well. According to well-placed sources, she used to date a Chinese national who had earlier worked at the Chinese embassy in Rangoon. Burmese military intelligence was so concerned about the relationship that it created the position of a liaison officer to watch her moves carefully. Nevertheless, she married a Burmese soldier Zaw Phyo Win, who the Myanmar News Association reports now serves as head of the Burmese consulate in the Chinese city of Kunming, where he recently helped to arrange a recent visit to China by Maung Aye.

To ensure the military's continued rule, albeit with a civilian face, Than Shwe pushed through the so-called "Road Map to Democracy" initially devised by his old intelligence chief Khin Nyunt in the immediate aftermath of the Depayin massacre. But while it was presented by Khin Nyunt, some observers believe Than Shwe was always behind the idea. One Burmese says that the National Convention and the USDA are "twins," both devised by Than Shwe. "They are the children of Than Shwe. But he never speaks of them himself, he uses others to talk. So although Khin Nyunt announced the seven-stage road map, it was not necessarily his idea." In 1995 former Singaporean leader Lee Kuan Yew met Than Shwe. "I suggested that he visit Indonesia," he recalls in his memoirs, "to learn how it changed from a military leadership, with General Suharto in charge, to an elected presidency."[31] This was, of course, prior to the fall of Suharto, and may have sparked in Than Shwe's mind the idea of the military remaining in power, but as pseudo-politicians with a veneer of respectability.

Nevertheless, it is not by any means an original idea. Not only was it planted in Than Shwe's mind by Lee Kuan Yew and inspired by Suharto's Indonesia, it was, in fact, a simple rehash of Ne Win's tactics. Under Than Shwe, Burma has come full circle to the BSPP-era—a period when the military retained control behind the scenes, but stepped out of their uniforms in government. Just as Ne Win developed the Burma Socialist Program Party, which was "the main means for mobilisation of support for the state,"[32] in Robert Taylor's words, so Than Shwe has developed the USDA. And just as Ne Win decided to have a constitution-drafting process that began in 1971 with guidelines drawn up by the BSPP, so too has Than Shwe embarked on an identical process of guidelines and drafting. Ne Win's new constitution was put to a referendum in 1974, in which over 95 percent of those eligible to vote turned out, and 90.19 percent voted in favor.[33] The only difference under Than Shwe was that his 2008 constitution apparently received slightly higher support and a larger percentage of the population voting. It is fair to say that with his legacy, as with his rule, Than Shwe has been extraordinarily unoriginal. He is simply aping, with even less subtlety and an absence of charisma and color, the example of Ne Win. Even the model of the SLORC and SPDC, while not initiated by Than Shwe, is a replica of Ne Win's Revolutionary Council. It is extraordinary how history is repeating itself.

Than Shwe's constitution, drafted by handpicked delegates, bars Aung San Suu Kyi from contesting elections and preserves at least a quarter of the national parliamentary seats for the military. The constitution requires a 75 percent majority for most amendments, and yet the military will hold a quarter of the seats, so they possess an in-built veto. It is, in the words of one Burmese activist, "a marriage proposal from a rapist, designed so that they can continue to carry out rape, legitimately and within the institution of marriage." A former Japanese ambassador concludes, "In a nutshell, it can be described as a continuation of military rule in another form." The commander in chief will retain the power to overthrow a civilian government when he chooses.

The constitution was rammed through in a sham referendum in the wake of Cyclone Nargis, approved by 92.48 percent of the electorate with a 99 percent turnout, according to official accounts. Law 5/96, promulgated by Than Shwe in 1996, made it illegal for anyone to criticize the National Convention and therefore the draft constitution, making a genuine referendum campaign impossible. Anyone convicted of campaigning against the draft constitution faced a possible prison sentence of between five and twenty years.

Elections planned for 2010 will doubtless provide the result Than Shwe desires—the regime will not make the mistakes it made in 1990. "Our *tatmadaw* is making relentless and dedicated efforts during its tenure of shouldering state responsibility, with the sincere aim of developing the country without any craving for power," he told troops on Armed Forces Day in 2008.[34] In 2008 in a speech to the USDA, Than Shwe lashed out at the democracy movement, claiming that "subversive elements resorted to a variety of ways and means to disrupt the National Convention. . . . Moreover, after the National Convention had been convened successfully, anti-government groups at home and abroad committed destructive acts variously with the intention of preventing the State Constitution from being approved . . . However much they were disruptive, more than 26.77 million of 27.28 million eligible voters cast votes at the referendum. Of them, over 24.76 million voters cast 'yes' votes, accounting for 92.48 per cent of all voters. In other words, the people expressed their voices, regarding the drive for building a new nation."[35] The following year Than Shwe told troops: "Democracy in Myanmar today is at a fledgling stage and still requires patient care and attention. As a Myanmar proverb puts it, 'a recently dug well cannot be expected to have water immediately'—understanding the process of gradual maturity is crucial."[36]

Few people believe him. At least 2,128 political prisoners languish in jail, with over 432 arrested and sentenced in 2008 alone.[37] The day after the country's most prominent comedian Zarganar was sentenced to forty-five years in jail, Than Shwe wrote an article on the front page of the *New Light of Myanmar* in which he said it was every citizen's duty to support the political process. "The state's seven-step road map is being implemented to build a peaceful, modern and developed new democratic nation with flourishing discipline," claimed the senior general. "The entire population is duty-bound to actively participate with united spirit and national fervour in the drive to see the seven-step road map."[38] Disciplined democracy, it would seem, means everyone can vote—as long as they vote the right way.

The pursuit of his planned "disciplined democracy"—the continued rule of the military, albeit dressed in business suits—resulted in perhaps Than Shwe's most astonishing trick yet in May 2009. With Aung San Suu Kyi's period of house arrest about to expire, and her continued detention clearly in violation of both domestic Burmese and international law, the regime had to think of a ruse to keep her behind bars. On May 1, an appeal for her release was rejected by the prime minister's office, and five days later, in a scene worthy of a trashy novel, a fifty-three-year-old diabetic overweight American Mormon, John William Yettaw, was arrested. The regime claimed he had swum across Inya Lake two days previously to Aung San Suu Kyi's home on University Avenue, and spent two nights in her compound. The next day, Aung San Suu Kyi's home was raided by twenty police officers, and her doctor was detained and denied access to her. One week later, Aung San Suu Kyi herself was moved from house arrest to the notorious Insein Prison, charged with breaking the terms of her house arrest, and put on trial.

This episode must rank as one of the most bizarre in Burma's recent history. Many observers believe it is unlikely that John Yettaw could have swum across the lake unhindered. Physically, it would have been demanding; but with Burma's secret police, it surely could not have been carried out without detection. Indeed, Yettaw admitted that a military official shook his hand as he entered her house. Furthermore, to charge her with violating the terms of her house arrest, when, in fact, Yettaw had turned up uninvited, and she had requested him to leave, is reminiscent of *Alice in Wonderland*. It all gives rise to the theory that it was a set-up by the regime, to give them an excuse to detain Aung San Suu Kyi until after the elections in 2010. As Mark Canning told the media during the trial, "It is difficult to see anything but a guilty verdict . . . these trials tend to be pre-scripted. All decisions of any significance in Burma are made by the ubiquitous 'higher authority.'"[39] After several delays, she was sentenced on August 11 to three years in prison with hard labor, reduced to eighteen months under house arrest.

Into this drama stepped Ban Ki-moon once again. Following his visit in the aftermath of Cyclone Nargis, the UN secretary-general came under intense international pressure to make another visit to Burma to discuss the political and human rights situation. Activists urged him to make the release of political prisoners, including Aung San Suu Kyi, his priority. In July 2009, he traveled to Naypyidaw and held two meetings with Than Shwe. At the first meeting he requested permission to visit Aung San Suu Kyi. At the second meeting Than Shwe told him "no."

In response to Than Shwe's refusal to allow him to meet the Nobel laureate and democracy leader, Ban Ki-moon did not hide his anger. "When I met General Than Shwe yesterday and today, I asked to visit Ms. Suu Kyi. I am deeply disappointed that he refused," he told an audience of five hundred diplomats, state officials, non-governmental organizations, and opposition politicians in Rangoon. "I believe the government of Myanmar has lost a unique opportunity to show its commitment to a new era of political openness. Allowing a visit to Daw Aung San Suu Kyi would have been an important symbol of the government's willingness to embark on the kind of meaningful engagement that will be essential if the elections in 2010 are to be seen to be credible." He said that Burma's human rights record was of "grave concern," warned the regime of "costly isolation" if it continued on its current path, and concluded with a challenge: "The question today is this: How much longer can [Burma] afford to wait for national reconciliation, democratic transition and full respect for human rights? The cost of delay will be counted in wasted lives, lost opportunities and prolonged isolation from the international community."[40] The fact that he delivered such remarks while still in Burma indicates just how far Than Shwe had tested the secretary-general's patience.

What will have irked Than Shwe even more was the personal note Ban struck. "I am Asia's second secretary-general. The first was Myanmar's U Thant. I revere his memory. I also recall his wise words. U Thant said: 'The worth of the individual human being is the most unique and precious of all our assets and must be the beginning and end of all our efforts. Governments, systems, ideologies and institutions come and go, but humanity remains.' This is why I have returned."[41] To quote U Thant would have been particularly insulting to the Burmese regime.

In his private discussions with Than Shwe, Ban says that he told him Aung San Suu Kyi should be released, the regime should initiate "a substantive and time-bound dialogue" with her, and criteria for free and fair elections should be fulfilled. "My visit has enabled me to convey the concerns of the international community very frankly and directly to Senior General Than Shwe," Ban said in a speech in Bangkok. "I told Senior General Than Shwe that the international community wants to help Myanmar to achieve democracy, national reconciliation, durable peace and sustainable development. And I emphasized that neither peace nor development can thrive without democracy and respect for human rights."[42]

In forcing Than Shwe to show his cards, *The Irrawaddy* argues, Ban has left no one in any doubt "as to what degree of flexibility the regime might be prepared to go—none . . . Ban should have earned the respect of the international community for confronting the junta and for speaking the truth. Now the gloves are off."[43]

A month before Ban Ki-moon's visit, Than Shwe received another visitor whom he would have expected to be friendlier, but he received a nasty surprise. Former Singaporean prime minister Goh Chok Tong told Than Shwe bluntly that Aung San Suu Kyi's trial had "an international dimension to the matter, which Myanmar should not ignore."[44] Goh's strong words, coming from a country as friendly to the regime as Singapore, were difficult to ignore. NLD-Liberated Area spokesman Nyo Ohn Myint said: "It would be very difficult for Senior General Than Shwe to reject his suggestion. They might not respond immediately, but when even their close friend does not agree with what they do, I think they will consider it."[45] Time will tell. Than Shwe is a master of intransigence.

The senior general's power building skills are impressive. Carefully developing several bases—the USDA, the cronies, the new capital—and playing his rivals off each other, Than Shwe has not only held onto power, but also tightened his grip in a way few would have predicted. He surrounds himself with loyalists, including his bodyguards Colonel Soe Shin and General Ne Win (not the former dictator), as well as General Kyaw Win, who he consults along with his protégés Myint Swe and U Aung Thaung. For someone as seemingly colorless and uncharismatic as Than Shwe, he has been remarkably successful. But his dull character is deceptive, and that is part of his success. "He is small, not threatening in an obvious sense, outwardly quite pleasant and friendly," says Canning. "He doesn't fit the stereotype of a sinister figure. He is a very colorless figure. He is not the 'Mr. Evil' that we might like to think in terms of persona. He doesn't lead by dint of brilliance or by dint of obvious fear, although it's obviously there. In a way you feel that he's got there by accident—the cards have fallen for him in the right way. He has got very simple tastes. He is a village boy, a peasant who has got to the top."

But the description of him as uneducated, stupid, or even mad is a caricature that does not give the full picture. Than Shwe may be uninspiring, but he is decidedly cunning and manipulative. "He leaves a lot of stuff unsaid. He is man of few words," says Canning. "He often will not make a decision, he just leaves things hanging in the air. He is pretty skilled at manipulating his regional commanders and people around him, achieving the various balances he wants to achieve." This fits with what one Burma Army defector that once worked for Than Shwe, says. "Than Shwe doesn't take responsibility. He likes picking other people's brains. He is unpredictable at times, and plays his cards close to his chest." He is also resistant to any meaningful reform. "The generals don't have a reverse gear," says Canning.

While Than Shwe is still in total control, there are also signs that he is gradually nearing the end of his reign, and preparing to move into the background. For the second time in three years, Than Shwe failed to appear at a state dinner for the diplomatic corps on January 4, 2009, marking Burma's Independence Day. The function was instead hosted by Maung Aye, with no official reason given. "He is increasingly disconnected from government," claims Canning. "He is not in his office for a lot of the time now, he is not really on top of the decisions; but it is still the case that any decision of any serious nature is still made by him. Anything relating to 'The Lady.' Anything relating to the 'Road Map to Democracy.' Down to some absurdly small details." This causes a paralysis in government. "You've got the worst of all worlds at the moment: he is slightly disconnected from things, and yet nothing happens unless he signs off on it."

Than Shwe's Burma is ranked by Médecins Sans Frontières as one of the top ten humanitarian crises in the world, and is listed at 138 out of 182 countries in the 2009 United Nations Development Programme's Human Development Index. It is one of the very few countries on which the International Committee of the Red Cross (ICRC) has spoken out. The ICRC typically retains a strictly neutral stance, but in June 2007 its president Jakob Kellenberger said Than Shwe's regime was causing "immense suffering." The regime stopped ICRC visits to prisons in December 2005, and in October 2006 its field offices in five locations were ordered to close. They were subsequently permitted to reopen, but many of their activities were curtailed. The junta's "increasingly severe restrictions" on the ICRC's operations in the country were making it impossible for the organization to operate freely, and its policies of forced portering amounted to "a major violation . . . of international humanitarian law." The "continuing deadlock" and the regime's consistent refusal "to enter into a serious discussion of these abuses with a view to putting a stop to them," led the ICRC to take "the exceptional step of making its concerns public,"[46] in what was the harshest public criticism of a regime by the organization since the Rwandan genocide.[47]

In response, Than Shwe, known sometimes as "Bulldog,"[48] rails against the West. "The neo-colonialists, instead of using much obvious colonization and coercion resorting to force, [sic] are trying to encroach on and dominate others through the media, with social, economic, human rights and narcotic drug excuses," he said in the The Myanmar Times on National Day 2005. "We all need to guard the nation against their perpetration with national awareness that originated in patriotism and Union Spirit."[49]

In an address to the opening session of the World Buddhist Summit in Rangoon in 2004, Than Shwe reminded delegates that "the timeless teaching of Lord Buddha is very relevant and essential to save humanity [from] craving, desire and suffering." The world, he continued, "is witnessing numerous conflicts and crimes. All those evils result from greed, anger and delusion. We should rid the world of the roots of all evils and sow the seeds of goodwill, tolerance, kindness and altruism for the sake of peace and prosperity." He exhorted delegates to follow the four Buddhist principles of loving kindness, compassion, joy, and equanimity as the best path for humanity to "peace and harmony."[50]

A lifelong psychological warrior, the irony didn't bother him. Motivated by power and a determination to hold onto it and protect his ill-gotten gains, Than Shwe will use any tool necessary, from detention, torture, and violence against his opponents, to lies, deceit, delay, and false promises to the international community, or the manipulation of astrology and religion to convince his own people. Without serious international pressure he will be unwilling to compromise, and is convinced that the military alone can keep his country together. The truth is, it is the military under his rule that has destroyed Burma's economy and wrought extraordinarily inhumane suffering on its people. Than Shwe ranks among the worst dictators in the world, and stands accused of crimes against humanity.

NOTES

INTRODUCTION

1. See http://www.barnesandnoble.com (browse books under "Dictators and Fascists: Political Biography").

2. See respectively, Thailand Burma Border Consortium, "Displaced Villages, 1996–2008;" United States Holocaust Memorial Museum, "Crisis in Darfur (2009 Update);" Shan Women's Action Network, "License to Rape;" Human Rights Watch, "Burma, World's Highest Number of Child Soldiers."

3. Genocide Prevention Project, "Mass Atrocity Crimes Watch List 2008–09."

4. Minority Rights Group, "Peoples Under Threat 2009;" Foreign Policy, "Failed States Index 2009."

5. Heritage Foundation, "2009 Index of Economic Freedom;" U.S. Department of State, 2009 *International Religious Freedom Report*, see Burma under "East Asia and Pacific."

6. Reporters Without Borders, "Press Freedom Index, 2009."

7. Committee to Protect Journalists, "10 Worst Countries to be a Blogger," April 30, 2009; Idem., "CPJ's 2008 Prison Census: Online and in Jail," December 4, 2008.

8. Dulyapak Preecharushh, *Naypyidaw*, xv.

9. "India Says It Warned Burma About Cyclone," *The Times*, May 6, 2008.

10. "Burma Gives 'Cronies' Slice of Storm Relief," *Washington Post*, June 13, 2008.

11. "Outrage Sparked by 'Wedding of the Year' Video," *The Nation*, November 2, 2006.

12. See Beyrer, et al., "Emerging Infectious Diseases in Burma."

13. Reuters, "Myanmar's Generals Can't Survive: Singapore's Lee," October 9, 2007.

14. Quoted in Holland, *Dinner with Mugabe*, 109, 125.

15. Quoted in Ibid., 186.

16. Holland, *Dinner with Mugabe*, 186, 195.

17. Ibid., 140.

18. Ibid., xv.

19. "Changes by Myanmar Hearten US Officials," *Washington Post*, May 21, 1992.

20. Selth, "Modern Burma Studies," 30.

1 FROM POSTMAN TO TYRANT

1. Informal translation of two-page official curriculum vitae of Than Shwe, provided to the authors by an academic source in Burma that is not part of the military government. The cv is undated but covers the period 1933 to 1992; hereinafter "Official Than Shwe cv."

2. See, e.g., Wikipedia, http://en.wikipedia.org/wiki/Kyaukse.

3. Ministry of Information, *Chronicle of National Development*, 247.

4. Bird, *Wanderings in Burma*, 388.

5. Charney, *History of Modern Burma*, 14.

6. Ibid.

7. Thant Myint-U, *River of Lost Footsteps*, 209–15.

8. Ibid., 215.

9. Wakeman and San San Tin, *No Time for Dreams*, 10–11.

10. "Official Than Shwe cv."

11. Ibid.

12. A brief overview of Theravada Buddhism is provided by Wikipedia at http://en.wikipedia.org/wiki/Theravada.

13. Democratic Voice of Burma, "Official Urges Action Against 'Bogus Monks'," news report, June 24, 2009.

14. *Burma VJ*, a film directed by Anders Østergaard (produced by Lise-Lense Møller and WG Film / Mediamente / Kamoli Films, International Sales by First Hand Films, 2008).

15. Aung Zaw, "Burma Watches Thai Politics," *The Irrawaddy* online news, September 11, 2008.

16. Min Lwin, "Than Shwe and Family Make Offerings at Shwedagon Pagoda," *The Irrawaddy* online news, July 15, 2009.

17. "Official Than Shwe cv."

18. Aung Zaw, "History of Burma's Nuclear Ambitions," *Bangkok Post*, August 9, 2009.

19. "Senior General Than Shwe Inspects Industries in Kyaukse," *New Light of Myanmar*, December 3, 2002.

20. Levin, "Remembering 1988," *Burma Debate* online.

21. Aung Moe Htet, *To Stand and Be Counted*, 132.

22. Ibid., 136.

23. Thant Myint-U, *River of Lost Footsteps*, 231.

24. Slim, *Defeat into Victory*, 473

25. Ibid., 79.

26. Jones, "Withdrawal from Burma," *Ex-CBI Roundup* online.

27. Ibid.

28. Webster, *Burma Road*, 15.

29. Slim, *Defeat into Victory*, 473–75.

30. Pilger, "In a Land of Fear."

31. Quoted in Rogers, *Land Without Evil*, 74.

32. Ibid., 69.

33. Ibid.

34. Callahan, *Making Enemies*, 58–59.

35. Slim, *Defeat into Victory*, 484.

36. Webster, *Burma Road*, 51–56.

37. Ibid., 148

38. Ibid., 6.

39. Some sources use the term "Burma Communist Party" (BCP). However, Bertil Lintner argues that all the official documents from the Communist Party refer to itself as the "Communist Party of Burma" (CPB).

40. Smith, *Burma: Insurgency and Politics*, 139.

41. Charney, *History of Modern Burma*, 57.

42. Fink, *Living Silence*, 21.

43. Silverstein, *Burmese Politics*, 99.

44. Ibid., 103.

45. Ibid., 200.

46. For further details about the Karen, see Rogers, *Land Without Evil*, 63–91.

47. Silverstein, *Burmese Politics*, 108.

48. Ibid., 114.

49. Thant Myint-U, *River of Lost Footsteps*, 253.

50. Wakeman and San San Tin, *No Time for Dreams*, 3.

51. Thant Myint-U, *River of Lost Footsteps*, 254.

52. Lintner, *Burma in Revolt*, 1–6.

53. Ibid., 35.

54. Ibid., 6.

55. Callahan, *Making Enemies*, 114.

56. Tinker, *Union of Burma*, 39.

57. Lintner, *Burma in Revolt*, 9.

58. Ibid., 10.

59. Callahan, *Making Enemies*, 119–23.

60. Ibid., 36.

61. Tinker, *Union of Burma*, 41–46.

62. Callahan, *Making Enemies*, 60.

63. Ibid., 166.

64. Silverstein, *Burmese Politics*, 222.

65. Callahan, *Making Enemies*, 160.

66. Ibid., 161.

67. Ibid., 166.

68. Maung Aung Myoe, "Building the Tatmadaw: Organizational Development," 16.

69. Ibid., 17.

70. Mya Win, "Brief History of Tatmadaw Leadership," *Working People's Daily*, February 1, 1991.

71. "Official Than Shwe CV."

72. Callahan, *Making Enemies*, 166–67.

73. Tinker, *Union of Burma*, 54–56.

74. Callahan, *Making Enemies*, 147.

75. Ibid., 155.

76. Christensen and Sann Kyaw, *Pa-O*.

77. Mya Win, "Brief History of Tatmadaw Leadership." *Working People's Daily*, February 1, 1991.

78. Family relative of Tin Htoon in conversation with the author, June 2009.

79. Callahan, *Making Enemies*, 182.

80. Chit Hlaing, "Short Note," 8. Chit Hlaing also wrote under the pen name Ko Ko Maung.

81. Ibid., 107.

82. Maung Aung Myoe, *Building the Tatmadaw: Myanmar Armed Forces*, 138. Myoe cites as his source Lieutenant Colonel Thaung Htike, *The American Staff College at Ft. Leavenworth* (Yangon: Bawathetkathi, 1987).

83. Mya Win, "Brief History of Tatmadaw Leadership," *Working People's Daily*, February 1, 1991.

84. Ibid.

85. Zoellner, "Myanmar Literature Project," see preface.

86. Chit Hlaing, "Short Note," 109.

87. Callahan, *Making Enemies*, 183.

88. Ibid.

89. Chit Hlaing, "Short Note," 116, 110.

90. Ibid. 116.

91. Human Rights Watch, "Burma: World's Highest Number of Child Soldiers," news release, October 15, 2002.

2 THE LAND OF GREEN AND ORANGE

1. Lloyd Parry, "Burma Activists Sentenced to 65 Years Each in Draconian Crackdown," *The Times*, November 12, 2008.

2. Charney, *History of Modern Burma*, 108.

3. Thant Myint-U, *River of Lost Footsteps*, 290.

4. Chit Hlaing, "Short Note," 122.

5. Ibid., 291.

6. Revolutionary Council, "Burmese Way to Socialism."

7. Chit Hlaing, "Short Note," 133.

8. Ibid., 134.

9. Smith, *Burma: Insurgency and Politics*, 124.

10. See, e.g., the "Basic Principles" of the new constitution adopted by the military regime in 2008.

11. Chit Hlaing, "Short Note," 142.

12. Silverstein, *Burma: Military Rule and Politics*, 104.

13. Ibid.

14. Maung Aung Myoe, *Building the Tatmadaw: Myanmar Armed Forces*, 105.

15. Egreteau and Jagan, "Back to the Old Habits," 15.

16. Ibid., 16.

17. Thant Myint-U, *River of Lost Footsteps*, 291–92.

18. Ibid., 293.

19. Mya Win, "Brief History of Tatmadaw Leadership," *Working People's Daily,* February 1, 1991.

20. Smith, *Burma: Insurgency and Politics*, 258–68.

21. Ibid.

22. See, e.g., Shan Women's Action Network, "License to Rape;" Apple and Martin, "No Safe Place."

23. Lintner, *Burma in Revolt*, 205.

24. Ibid.

25. Mya Win, "Brief History of Tatmadaw Leadership," *Working People's Daily*, February 1, 1991.

26. Smith, *Burma: Insurgency and Politics*, 260.

27. Lintner, *Burma in Revolt*, 219–20.

28. Mya Win, "Brief History of Tatmadaw Leadership," *Working People's Daily*, February 1, 1991.

29. Lintner, *Burma in Revolt*, 239–72.

30. See, e.g., Network for Democracy and Development, "NDD Weekly Inside News."

31. "Thakin Kodaw Hmaing (1876–1974)," *The Irrawaddy* magazine, March 2000.

32. Smith, *Burma: Insurgency and Politics*, 305.

33. "US Envoy Denied Asylum to Suspect," *New York Times*, August 23, 1976.

34. Kamm, "With China's Help, Rebels in Burma Keep Fighting," *New York Times*, August 7, 1980.

35. Smith, *Burma: Insurgency and Politics*, 307.

36. Ibid., 312.

37. Kamm, "With China's Help, Rebels in Burma Keep Fighting," *New York Times*, August 7, 1980.

38. Lintner, *Communist Party of Burma*, 30.

39. Beech, "Heavy Toll Reported in Burma War with Communists," *Los Angeles Times*, August 10, 1980.

40. Kamm, "With China's Help, Rebels in Burma Keep Fighting," *New York Times*, August 7, 1980.

41. Lloyd Parry, *In the Time of Madness*, 122.

42. "Agriculture and Livestock Multiplier Courses," *Working People's Daily*, November 10, 1983.

43. "Party Regional Committee Chairman Visits Farms," *Working People's Daily*, December 7, 1983.

44. "Timber Production Work Inspected," *Working People's Daily*, January 11, 1984.

45. "Co-ordination Meeting on Cultivation," *Working People's Daily*, April 28, 1984.

46. "Measures for Implementing Policy," *Working People's Daily*, November 28, 1983.

47. For further details on the military's control of journalism by a former government-regulated journalist, see Wakeman and San San Tin, *No Time for Dreams*.

48. "Division and Township Judges Committees," *Working People's Daily*, September 21, 1983.

49. "Independence Day and Constitution Day Hailed," *Working People's Daily*, December 30, 1983.

50. U.S. Department of Labor, *2000 Report on Labor Practices in Burma*.

51. International Labour Organization, "Forced Labour in Myanmar."

52. "Irrawaddy Division Celebrates Total Victory," *Working People's Daily*, December 24, 1983.

53. Ibid.

54. Denby, "Burmese Junta Claims 92 Per Cent Victory in Referendum," *The Times*, May 16, 2008.

55. Arkar Moe, "Experts Challenge Than Shwe's Rice Production Claims," *The Irrawaddy* online news, May 6, 2009.

56. Ibid.

57. Ibid.

58. Aung Moe Htet, *To Stand and Be Counted*, 67–68.

59. Reuters, "Newsmaker: Senior General Than Shwe, the 'Old Man' of Myanmar," May 23, 2008.

3 THE DEMOCRATIC CHALLENGE

1. Charney, *History of Modern Burma*, 146.

2. Ibid., 149.

3. Steinberg, *Burma: State of Myanmar*, 8.

4. Ibid., 2.

5. "Than Shwe," *New Internationalist*, September 2005.

6. Steinberg, *Burma: State of Myanmar*, 9.

7. Quoted in Charney, *History of Modern Burma*, 152.

8. Ibid., 153.

9. Steinberg, *Burma: State of Myanmar*, 2.

10. Lintner, *Aung San Suu Kyi*, 20.

11. Ibid., 13.

12. Levin, "Remembering 1988," *Burma Debate* online.

13. Charney, *History of Modern Burma*, 154.

14. Aung San Suu Kyi, *Voice of Hope*, 2.

15. Ibid., 2–4.

16. Lintner, *Outrage*, 168.

17. Maung Maung, *1988 Uprising*, 191.

18. Maung Aung Myoe, "Historical Overview," 14.

19. Lintner, "Burma's Warrior Kings," 72.

20. Maung Aung Myoe, "Historical Overview," 14.

21. Ibid.

22. Lintner, *Outrage*, 22.

23. Aung San Suu Kyi, *Voice of Hope*, 25.

24. Ibid.

25. Mitton, "Skewed Realities: Few See Eye-to-Eye in Myanmar," *Asiaweek*, November 6, 1988.

26. Ibid.

27. Lintner, *Outrage*, 28.

28. Ibid., 29.

29. Charney, *History of Modern Burma*, 177.

30. Ibid.

31. "Burmese Strongman Suffers Breakdown," *The Times*, December 20, 1991.

32. Casey, "Nobel Prisoner of Rangoon," *The Daily Telegraph*, 1991.

33. "Illness Forces Resignation of Burma's Junta Leader," *The Times,* April 24, 1992.

34. Ibid.

35. Aung Zaw, "Than Shwe—Man in the Iron Mask," *The Irrawaddy* magazine, February 2005.

36. Burma Action Group (UK), *Burma News*, May 1992.

37. Aung Shwe, et al., *Letters to a Dictator*, 5.

38. Ibid., 11.

39. Ibid., 13, 14.

40. Ibid., 22–23.

41. Levin, "Remembering 1988," *Burma Debate* online.

42. Ibid., 4.

4 THAN SHWE'S CRIMES AGAINST HUMANITY

1. Christian Solidarity Worldwide, "CSW Visit to the Karen and Mon Peoples," February 2007.

2. Ibid.

3. Ibid.

4. Free Burma Rangers. "A Brutal Reign of Terror," news report, June 22, 2002.

5. Shan Women's Action Network, "10,000 Shans Uprooted," press release, August 2009.

6. Lintner, *Burma In Revolt*, 398.

7. "Than Shwe," *New Internationalist*, September 2005.

8. Dictator of the Month, "Than Shwe: Dictator of the Month," January 2004.

9. Lintner, *Burma In Revolt*, 399.

10. Oberdorfer, "Changes by Myanmar Hearten US Officials," *Washington Post*, May 21, 1992.

11. Christian Solidarity Worldwide, "Over 11,000 Displaced Civilians Killed," news article, April 26, 2006.

12. Lloyd Parry, "Burma: Than Shwe 'Ordered Troops to Execute Villagers'," *The Times*, June 7, 2008.

13. Voice of America, "Interview with Aung Lynn Htut."

14. Ibid.

15. David Eubank in conversation with the author, February 2009.

16. Pinheiro, "End Burma's System of Impunity," *International Herald Tribune*, May 28, 2009.

17. International Human Rights Clinic, Harvard Law School, "Crimes in Burma."

18. Nikken and Nice, "What the U.N. Can't Ignore in Burma," *Washington Post*, June 2, 2009.

19. Back Pack Health Worker Team, "Chronic Emergency," 9.

20. Stover, et al., "The Gathering Storm," 1.

21. Ibid., 20.

22. The UN Security Council has the power to refer a country that has not ratified the Rome Statute to the International Criminal Court (ICC) if it presents a threat to international peace and security (as it did in the case of Sudan). While various human rights organizations have called for a Commission of Inquiry to investigate Burma's international crimes, no such UN mandated commission has been formed to date.

23. Rogers, "Carrying the Cross," 3.

24. Smith, *Burma: Insurgency and Politics*, 37.

25. Lintner in conversation with the author, March 2009.

26. See Amnesty International, "*Myanmar: The Rohingya Minority*."

27. Christian Solidarity Worldwide, "CSW Visit to the Bangladesh-Burma Border," August 26–31, 2008.

28. Salai Za Uk Ling and Salai Bawi Lian Mang, "Religious Persecution."

29. See Rogers, "Carrying the Cross."

30. Popham, "The Man Who Uncovered the Truth," *The Independent*, June 24, 2005.

31. Rogers, *Land Without Evil*, 40.

32. "Burma Protest Swells as 100,000 Join March," *Daily Telegraph*, September 25, 2007.

33. Pinheiro, "Report of the Special Rapporteur."

34. Solomon, "UN Rights Envoy Says Burma's Judiciary System Flawed," *Mizzima News*, November 13, 2008.

35. Rome Statute of the International Criminal Court, Article 28.

36. International Human Rights Clinic, Harvard Law School, "Crimes in Burma," 101.

37. Aung Shwe, et al., *Letters to a Dictator*, 130–32.

38. See U Aung Htoo, "The Depayin Massacre."

39. Pinheiro, "Question of the Violation of Human Rights," 8.

40. Statement of Wunna Maung, U.S. Cong., *Human Rights in Burma*.

41. Ad hoc Commission on Depayin Massacre, "Preliminary Report."

42. Pinheiro, "Question of the Violation of Human Rights," see under "Summary."

43. Kazmin, "Junta Says Suu Kyi Planned Uprising," *Financial Times*, July 10, 2003.

44. ALTSEAN-Burma, "SPDC Who's Who."

45. See Amnesty International, "Crimes Against Humanity."

46. International Committee of the Red Cross, "Myanmar: ICRC Denounces Major and Repeated Violations of International Humanitarian Law," news release, June 29, 2007.

47. Burma Justice Committee, "International Court Condemns Burma Junta," press release, March 24, 2009.

5 THE NEW EMPEROR

1. Watts, "Burmese Outraged at Lavish Junta Wedding," *The Guardian*, November 2, 2006.

2. Quoted in Ibid.

3. Holland, *Dinner with Mugabe*, xxi.

4. Reuters, "Myanmar's Generals Can't Survive: Singapore's Lee Kuan Yew," October 9, 2007.

5. UNICEF, *The State of the World's Children 2009: Maternal and New Born Health*.

6. World Health Organization, *World Health Report 2000*.

7. World Health Organization, "National Health Accounts: Myanmar," September 13, 2007.

8. World Food Programme, "Myanmar."

9. Transparency International, "Corruption Perceptions Index," 2007.

10. Aung Zaw, "Than Shwe—Man in the Iron Mask," *The Irrawaddy* magazine, February 2005.

11. Min Lwin, "Than Shwe's Daughter Goes Shopping," *The Irrawaddy* online news, October 30, 2008.

12. "Myanmar (Burma): The Biggest Corruption in Burma History," *Blogger News Network*, March 23, 2007.

13. Aung Zaw, "Than Shwe—Man in the Iron Mask," *The Irrawaddy* magazine, February 2005.

14. Saw Yan Naing, "University Privileges Granted to Than Shwe's Grandson," *The Irrawaddy* online news, January 9, 2008.

15. "Grandson's Lavish Party Foretells Future of Than Shwe," *The Irrawaddy* online news, June 22, 2007.

16. Saw Yan Naing, "University Privileges Granted to Than Shwe's Grandson," *The Irrawaddy* online news, January 9, 2008.

17. Thu Ye Kaung, "Than Shwe Family Member to USA," Weblog. *Jegsburma*, February 23, 2009.

18. Wai Moe, "Than Shwe's Grandson in Drug Scandal," *The Irrawaddy* online news, June 23, 2008.

19. Wai Moe, "Did Than Shwe's Grandson Kidnap Model?" *The Irrawaddy* online news, January 8, 2009.

20. Lintner and Black, *Merchants of Madness*, 98.

21. Ibid., 131.

22. U.S. Department of Treasury, "Treasury Sanctions Additional Financial Operatives of the Burmese Regime," press release, February 25, 2008.

23. Alamgir, "Myanmar's Foreign Trade," 977–96.

24. Lintner, *Great Leader, Dear Leader*, 146.

25. Lintner and Black, *Merchants of Madness*, 96, 78.

26. Ibid., 97.

27. Quoted in Ibid., 128.

28. Ibid., 131.

29. Turnell, "The Rape of Burma: Where Did the Wealth Go?" *Japan Times*, May 2, 2008.

30. Ibid.

31. Kazmin, "Burma's Economic Prospects 'Bleak'," *Financial Times*, May 11, 2009.

32. EarthRights International, "The Yadana Pipeline."

33. Manzella, "Judge Finds Evidence Unocal Used Burmese Military," EarthRights International press release, June 14, 2006.

34. EarthRights International, "US Court Calls Abuses Committed in Construction of Chevron's Pipeline 'Military Terrorism,'" press release, October 19, 2007.

35. Ibid.

36. Han Manman, "Young Activist Seeks Voice for Myanmar Minority," *Beijing Today*, July 3, 2009.

37. Kachin Environmental Organization, "Damming the Irrawaddy," 4.

38. Aye and Finch, "Legal Aspects of Hydropower Projects in Myanmar," 62–70.

39. Kachin Environmental Organization, "Damming the Irrawaddy," 1.

40. "China to Myanmar Pipelines," *The Straits Times*, November 20, 2008.

41. Maung Aung Myoe, *Building the Tatmadaw: Myanmar Armed Forces*, 235–37.

42. The Htoo group of companies includes Myanmar Treasure Resorts, Myanmar Avia Export Company, and Aureum Palace Hotels and Resorts. See U.S. Department of Treasury, "Tay Zaw Financial Network."

43. *Tom Lantos Block Burmese JADE Act of 2008*, H.R. 3890, 110th Cong., 2nd sess.

44. Beech, "The New Great Game," *Time Magazine*, March 30, 2009.

45. Sean Turnell in e-mail correspondence with the author, March 17, 2009.

46. Than Htike Oo, "Twenty Seven Children Poisoned by Physic Nuts," *Mizzima News*, August 29, 2008.

47. Phanida, "29 Children Suffer From Physic Nut Poisoning," *Mizzima News*, February 2, 2009.

48. Wai Moe, "Than Shwe Finds Burma's Fate in the Stars," *The Irrawaddy* online news, November 23, 2007.

49. "Asia's Rich and Powerful Turn to ET for Advice," *The Daily Telegraph*, August 4, 2007.

50. Reuters, "Singapore Denies Money Laundering Myanmar Leaders," October 5, 2007.

51. "Where is Tay Za?" Burma Watch, *The Nation* Weblog, September 30, 2007.

52. Steyn, "The Pariah Guy," *Atlantic Monthly*, September 2005.

53. Ibid.

54. U.S. Department of Justice, Foreign Agents Registration Unit, copy of contract between van Kloberg & Associates, Ltd. and the Government of the Union of Myanmar.

55. Silverstein, "Local Lobbyists and Unocal Shill for Burma's Military Junta," *Village Voice*, April 17, 1997.

56. U.S. Department of Justice, Foreign Agents Registration Unit, copy of letter from Burmese Ambassador to United States to Joseph E. Clarkson, Chief of Registration Unit.

57. Vest, "From Greenbay to Rangoon: US Flacks Spread Goodwill for Burma's Junta," *The Progressive*, November 1996.

58. Bernstein, "Tyrants' Lobbyist, Flamboyant to the End," *Washington Post*, May 3, 2005.

59. U.S. Department of Justice, Foreign Agents Registration Unit, copy of letter from Lester R. Wolff to U Thaung, Burmese ambassador to the United States.

60. Ibid.

61. Vest, "From Greenbay to Rangoon: US Flacks Spread Goodwill for Burma's Junta," *The Progressive*, November 1996.

62. Ibid.

63. Lintner, *Burma in Revolt*, 333–34.

64. Gray, [untitled], February 17, 1994.

65. Vest, "From Greenbay to Rangoon: US Flacks Spread Goodwill for Burma's Junta," *The Progressive*, November 1996.

66. See Bain and Associates website at http:// www.bainpr.com/. The firm closed its doors in 2007 but maintained this URL address as of November 2009.

67. U.S. Department of Justice, Foreign Agents Registration Unit, copy of Bain and Associates' filing with Foreign Agents Registration Unit.

68. Smith, "Burma's Image Problem is a Moneymaker for U.S. Lobbyists," *Washington Post*, February 4, 1998.

69. U.S. Department of Justice, Foreign Agents Registration Unit, copy of Bain and Associates' filing with Foreign Agents Registration Unit.

70. Ibid.

71. Smith, "Burma's Image Problem is a Moneymaker for U.S. Lobbyists," *Washington Post*, February 4, 1998.

72. U.S. Department of Justice, Foreign Agents Registration Unit, copy of Bain and Associates' filing with Foreign Agents Registration Unit.

73. Smith, "Burma's Image Problem is a Moneymaker for U.S. Lobbyists," *Washington Post*, February 4, 1998.

74. See US-ASEAN Business Council's webpage at http://www. usasean.org/Aboutus/board_of_directors.asp.

75. Silverstein, "Local Lobbyists and Unocal Shill for Burma's Military Junta," *Village Voice*, April 17, 1997.

76. Smith, "Burma's Image Problem is a Moneymaker for U.S. Lobbyists," *Washington Post*, February 4, 1998.

77. U.S. Department of Justice, Foreign Agents Registration Unit, copy of Jefferson Waterman's filing with Foreign Agents Registration Unit.

78. Smith, "Burma's Image Problem is a Moneymaker for U.S. Lobbyists," *Washington Post*, February 4, 1998.

79. Ibid.

80. U.S. Department of Justice, Foreign Agents Registration Unit, copy of DCI Associates' filing with Foreign Agents Registration Unit.

81. Spillius, "Burma Dismisses Allegations of Mass Rape," *Daily Telegraph*, July 12, 2002.

82. Thompson, "Ethics Conflict as ex-CIA Officials Turn to Lobbying," *Boston Globe*, May 13, 2003.

83. Ibid.

84. Kamen, "DCI, Burma and D.C.," *Washington Post*, February 28, 2003.

85. Ibid.

86. Isikoff, "A Convention Quandary," *Newsweek*, May 19, 2008.

87. Cooper, "McCain Convention Coordinator Resigns," The Caucus Blog, *NYTimes.com*, May 10, 2008.

88. Selth, *Burma's Armed Forces*, 30.

89. Maung Aung Myoe, "Military Doctine and Strategy," 18.

90. Than Shwe, address delivered at 7th Intake of the Defence Services Medical Academy, December 29, 2004.

91. Kyaw Hsan, address delivered at press conference of the Information Committee, November 2, 2006.

92. Selth, *Burma's Armed Forces*, 79.

93. Ibid.

94. Selth, "Burma's Arms Procurement Programme," 1, 4.

95. Lintner, "Myanmar's Chinese Connection."

96. Selth, "Burma's Arms Procurement Programme," 1.

97. Lintner, "Myanmar's Chinese Connection."

98. Ashton, "Burma Receives Advances from Its Silent Suitors in Singapore."

99. Ibid.

100. Lintner, "Myanmar's Chinese Connection."

101. "Singapore Urges Myanmar to Look West," *The Sun Daily*, March 18, 2009.

102. ALTSEAN-Burma, "Saffron Revolution A Year Later: It's Not Over."

103. Selth, "Burma's Arms Procurement Programme," 5.

104. Lintner, "Myanmar's Chinese Connection."

105. Selth, "Burma's Arms Procurement Programme," 6

106. See Turnell, "Burma's Insatiable State," 958–76.

107. See, e.g., Christian Solidarity Worldwide, "CSW Visit to the Thai-Burmese Border," April 9–15, 2005.

108. Karen Human Rights Group, "Chemical Shells at Kaw Moo Rah."

109. Karen Human Rights Group, "Chemical Shells At Kaw Moo Rah: Supplementary."

110. Ibid.

111. Selth, *Burma's Armed Forces*, 235–36.

112. Quoted in Ibid., 233.

113. Selth, *Burma's Armed Forces*, 234.

114. Squassoni, "Nuclear, Biological and Chemical Weapons," CRS Report for Congress.

115. See Selth, "Burma and Weapons of Mass Destruction."

116. Lintner, "Burma's Nuclear Temptation," *Yale Global Online*, December 3, 2008.

117. Hunter, "Burma's Nuclear Ambitions?" *Mizzima News*, October 26, 2005.

118. Bertil Lintner in e-mail correspondence with the author, July 20, 2009.

119. Ibid.

120. Watson, "Nuclear Proliferation and Burma," online article posted by Dictator Watch, November 7, 2006.

121. Kemp, "Burma Goes Ballistic," Weblog, *Webdiary*, July 2009.

122. U Ne Oo, "Burma Nuclear Program," *The Barossa*, May 28, 2004.

123. Lintner, "Burma's Nuclear Temptation," *Yale Global Online*, December 3, 2008.

124. Green and Mitchell, "Asia's Forgotten Crisis."

125. Ibid.

126. Ibid.

127. ALTSEAN-Burma, "Saffron Revolution A Year Later: It's Not Over."

128. Democratic Voice of Burma, "North Korean Ship Headed to Burma," news report, June 22, 2009.

129. Lintner and Crispin, "Burma: Dangerous Bedfellows," *Far Eastern Economic Review*, November 20, 2003.

130. Democratic Voice of Burma, "Burma's Military Regime: Digging the Tunnels," news report, June 24, 2009.

131. Ibid.

132. "Myanmar's 'Secret Tunnels' Revealed," *Al Jazeera*, June 25, 2009.

133. Lintner, "Myanmar and North Korea Share A Tunnel Vision," *Asia Times*, July 19, 2006.

134. Lintner, "Tunnels, Guns and Kimchi—Part 1," *Yale Global Online*, June 9, 2009.

135. Quoted in Hunter, "Burma's Nuclear Ambitions: Progression or Threat?" *Mizzima News*, October 26, 2005.

136. Selth, "Burma and the Threat of Invasion," 29.

137. Tai Sam Yone, "Nuclear Burma," *Burma Digest*, March 19, 2007.

138. "Defectors Detail Myanmar's Nuclear Ambitions: Report," *Taipei Times*, August 3, 2009, citing Hamish McDonald, "Revealed: Burma's Nuclear Bombshell," *Sydney Morning Herald*, August 1, 2009.

139. "Defectors Detail Myanmar's Nuclear Ambitions: Report," *Taipei Times*, August 3, 2009.

140. Statement of Stephen Dun, U.S. Cong., *Human Rights in Burma*.

141. Selth, "Burma and Nuclear Proliferation," 9.

142. Ibid., 1.

143. Quoted in Ibid., 18.

144. Cited in Kim So-hyun, "U.S. Eyeing N.K.-Myanmar Nuke Ties," *Korea Herald*, July 14, 2009.

145. Kyaw Hsan, address delivered at press conference of the Information Committee, November 2, 2006.

146. Ibid.

147. Zaw Bo, "A Free People or a Satellite Nation?"

148. Ibid.

149. Kyaw Hsan, address delivered at press conference of the Information Committee, November 2, 2006.

150. "Building of Industrialized Nation," *New Light of Myanmar*, December 25, 2004.

151. Kyaw Hsan, address delivered at press conference of the Information Committee, November 2, 2006.

152. See *Leaders* magazine website at http://www.leadersmag.com/about/about.html.

153. The *Leaders* interview was reprinted in its entirety in the *New Light of Myanmar*, the government's official media outlet, on June 14, 1998 under the title "Report on Exclusive Than Shwe Interview," as reported by Voice of America correspondent Gary Thomas.

154. Aung Zaw, "Than Shwe: Man in the Iron Mask," *The Irrawaddy* magazine, February 2005.

155. Ehrlich and Crispin, "Man Behind the Myanmar Madness," *Asia Times*, September 28, 2007.

156. Reuters, "Newsmaker: Senior General Than Shwe, the 'Old Man' of Myanmar," May 23, 2008.

157. Ehrlich and Crispin, "Man Behind the Myanmar Madness," *Asia Times*, September 28, 2007.

158. Cropley, "Newsmaker: Than Shwe, Myanmar Junta's 'Old Fox,'" Reuters, October 3, 2007.

159. Ibid.

160. Aung Zaw, "Than Shwe: Burma's Strongman?" *The Irrawaddy* magazine, January 2003.

161. Aung Zaw, "Than Shwe: Man in the Iron Mask," *The Irrawaddy* magazine, February 2005.

162. Broughton, "Army Strongmen Who Call the Shots in Burma," *The First Post*, September 26, 2007.

163. Lees, "Leader's Rumored Sickness Provides Some Small Hope," *World Politics Review*, January 23, 2007.

164. Egreteau and Jagan, "Back to the Old Habits," 8.

165. McCarthy, "Burma and ASEAN: Estranged Bedfellows," 917.

166. "Thailand, ASEAN and the 'Burma Problem'," *Mizzima News*, June 4, 2005.

167. McCarthy, "Burma and ASEAN: Estranged Bedfellows," 920.

168. Ibid.

169. Corben, "Thailand Suggests Road Map for Burma," VOA *News*, July 20, 2003.

170. "Thailand, ASEAN and the 'Burma Problem'," *Mizzima News*, June 4, 2005.

171. McCarthy, "Burma and ASEAN: Estranged Bedfellows," 911.

172. Nyo Ohn Myint, "Burma's Saddam: General Than Shwe."

173. McCarthy, "Burma and ASEAN: Estranged Bedfellows," 922.

174. Ibid., 929.

175. Lintner, "Staying Power of the Burmese Military Regime," 19.

176. Egreteau and Jagan, "Back to the Old Habits," 35.

177. Spinal Tap is a fictional heavy metal/hard rock band known for its succession of drummers, all of whom are said to have died in strange circumstances. See http:// en.wikipedia.org/wiki/Spinal_Tap_(band).

6 THE SEAT OF KINGS

1. Paddock, "Abrupt Relocation of Burma Capital Linked to Astrology," *Los Angeles Times*, January 1, 2006.

2. Charney, *History of Modern Burma*, 193.

3. Paddock, "Abrupt Relocation of Burma Capital Linked to Astrology," *Los Angeles Times*, January 1, 2006.

4. Quoted in Ibid.

5. Quoted in Ibid.

6. "Chinese Diplomats Criticize Myanmar's New Capital," *New York Times*, May 23, 2007.

7. "Than Shwe's Road to Ruin," *The Irrawaddy* online news, March 28, 2008.

8. Selth, "Burma and the Threat of Invasion," 4.

9. Ibid., 17.

10. Ibid., 19.

11. Thant Myint-U, *River of Lost Footsteps*, 63.

12. Ibid., 69.

13. Ibid.

14. "Than Shwe's Road to Ruin," *The Irrawaddy* online news, March 28, 2008.

15. McCarthy, "Burma and ASEAN: Estranged Bedfellows," 926.

16. Paddock, "Abrupt Relocation of Burma Capital Linked to Astrology," *Los Angles Times*, January 1, 2006.

17. "Asia's Rich and Powerful Turn to ET for Advice," *Daily Telegraph*, August 4, 2007.

18. "Sri Lankan Astrologer Arrested After Predicting President Rajapaksa's Exit," *The Times*, June 27, 2009.

19. Lloyd Parry, *In the Time of Madness*, 119.

20. Reporters San Frontières, "Predators of Press Freedom: Than Shwe—Burma."

21. Lintner, "Staying Power of the Burmese Military Regime."

22. Beech, "The New Great Game," *Time Magazine*, March 30, 2009.

23. "First Private Special Treatment Hospital in Myanmar New Capital Under Construction," *China View*, March 6, 2009.

24. Quoted in Lintner, "The Generals Who Would Be Kings," *Washington Post*, September 30, 2007.

25. Cited in "Naypyidaw's Version of Shwedagon Pagoda," *The Irrawaddy* online news, March 6, 2009.

26. Quoted in Ibid.

27. Beech, "The New Great Game," *Time Magazine*, March 30, 2009.

28. Beaton, "Penguins and Golf in Burma's Hidden Capital," *The Independent*, September 19, 2008.

29. Wai Moe, "Than Shwe Finds Burma's Fate in the Stars," *The Irrawaddy* online news, November 23, 2007.

30. ASEAN-Burma, "SPDC Who's Who."

31. Wai Moe, "Than Shwe Finds Burma's Fate in the Stars," *The Irrawaddy* online news, November 23, 2007.

32. "Asia's Rich and Powerful Turn to ET for Advice," *The Daily Telegraph*, August 4, 2007.

33. Aung Zaw, "Than Shwe, Voodoo and the Number 11," *The Irrawaddy* online news, December 25, 2008.

34. Ibid.

35. Ibid.

36. Ibid.

37. Kurlantzick, "Burma's Dear Leader," *The Washington Post*, April 23, 2006.

38. Wai Moe, "Than Shwe Finds Burma's Fate in the Stars," *The Irrawaddy* online news, November 23, 2007.

39. Min Lwin, "Than Shwe and Family Make Offerings at Shwedagon Pagoda," *The Irrawaddy* online news, July 15, 2009.

40. Kurlantzick, "Burma's Dear Leader," *The Washington Post*, April 23, 2006.

41. Houtman, *Mental Culture in Burmese Crisis Politics*, quoted in Selth, "Modern Burma Studies."

42. Aung Zaw, "Than Shwe: Burma's Strongman?" *The Irrawaddy* magazine, January 2003.

43. Kurlantzick, "Burma's Dear Leader," *The Washington Post*, April 23, 2006.

7 THE MONKS AND THE STORM

1. National Coalition Government, Union of Burma, "Bullets in the Alms Bowl," 40.

2. Ibid., 42–43.

3. Ibid.

4. Ibid., 46.

5. Silverstein, *Burma: Military Rule and Politics*, 98.

6. National Coalition Government, Union of Burma, "Bullets in the Alms Bowl," 50–51.

7. Ibid., 53–57.

8. Ibid., 60.

9. "Did Than Shwe's Wife Flee to Dubai?" *The Irrawaddy* online news, September 30, 2007.

10. National Coalition Government, Union of Burma, "Bullets in the Alms Bowl," 93.

11. Selth, "Burma's 'Saffron Revolution,'" 285.

12. "Letter from Prime Minister Lee Hsien Loong," press release by the Ministry of Foreign Affairs Singapore, September 29, 2007.

13. Berger, "Burmese Democracy Leader Offered Meeting," *The Daily Telegraph*, October 4, 2007.

14. ASEAN-Burma, "Saffron Revolution A Year Later: It's Not Over."

15. Ibid.

16. Lawrence, "The Despot and the Diplomat," *The Irrawaddy* magazine, September 2008.

17. ASEAN-Burma, "Saffron Revolution A Year Later: It's Not Over."

18. Quoted in Larkin, "Pinheiro: National Convention a 'Surrealistic Exercise,'" *The Irrawaddy* online news, June 2, 2004.

19. Rogers, "Tea with a Dictator," *The Guardian*, May 31, 2008.

20. "Co-operation with United Nations Cornerstone of Myanmar's Foreign Policy," *New Light of Myanmar*, October 24, 2008.

21. Ibid.

22. "Let Them Eat Frogs," *Washington Post*, May 30, 2008.

23. Cho, "ASEAN Chief Warns Thai PM about Burma," *The Irrawaddy* online news, March 19, 2008.

24. Denby, "Burmese Junta Claims 92 Per Cent Victory in Referendum," *The Times*, May 16, 2008.

25. National Coalition Government, Union of Burma, "Burma's Aid Woes," press release, October 3, 2008.

26. Lee, "UN Admits $10M Exchange Loss in Myanmar," *Inner City Press*, July 28, 2008.

27. Lee, "Leaked Minutes Show UN Knew of 20% Loss," *Inner City Press*, July 28, 2008.

28. Aung Zaw, "Operation Delta," *The Irrawaddy* magazine, June 2008.

29. Ibid.

30. Khin Ohmar, "Saffron Anniversary," Weblog, *Burma Partnership*, September 22, 2008.

31. See http://lannaactionforburma.blogspot.com/.

8 THE RIVALS, THE HEIRS, THE CRONIES, AND THE FUTURE

1. Kivimaki and Pedersen, "Burma: Mapping the Challenges and Opportunities," 40.

2. Ibid., 97.

3. Lintner, "Staying Power of the Burmese Military Regime," 2.

4. Kivimaki and Pedersen, "Burma: Mapping the Challenges and Opportunities," 51.

5. Min Lwin, "Burmese Armed Forces Day," *The Irrawaddy* online news, March 27, 2009.

6. Quoted in Jagan, "Officers Fear a Coup on Road to Vote," *The National*, March 29, 2009.

7. Kivimaki and Pedersen, "Burma: Mapping the Challenges and Opportunities," 50.

8. Aung Zaw, "Than Shwe—Man in the Iron Mask," *The Irrawaddy* magazine, February 2005.

9. Ibid.

10. Horn, "Two to Tangle," *Time Magazine,* Asia Edition, December 18, 2000.

11. "Will Shwe Mann Become Mr. President?" *The Irrawaddy* online news, July 16, 2009.

12. Lees, "Leader's Rumored Sickness Provides Some Small Hope," *World Politics Review*, January 23, 2007.

13. Broughton, "Army Strongmen Who Call the Shots in Burma," *The First Post*, September 11, 2008.

14. Lees, "Leader's Rumored Sickness Provides Some Small Hope," *World Politics Review*, January 23, 2007.

15. "Gen. Thura Shwe Mann," *The Irrawaddy* online news, October 19, 2007.

16. Wai Moe, "Burma's post-2010 Presidency," *The Irrawaddy* online news, October 15, 2008.

17. Broughton, "Army Strongmen Who Call the Shots in Burma," *The First Post*, September 11, 2008.

18. "Burmese PM in Fresh Land Scam," *Kachin News Group*, April 15, 2009.

19. Mungpi, "If UN Wants Political Stability, Drop Sanctions," *Mizzima News*, February 4, 2009.

20. The discussion of the USDA that follows draws directly from the report "The White Shirts: How the USDA Will Become the New Face of Burma's Dictatorship," published by the Network for Democracy and Development (Thailand), May 2006.

21. Ibid.

22. Aung Zaw, "Tycoon Turf," *The Irrawaddy* magazine, September 2005.

23. Ibid.

24. Beaumont and Smith, "Drugs and Astrology: How 'Bulldog' Wields Power," *The Guardian*, October 7, 2007..

25. "Shocking E-mail Sent by Son of Burma's Wealthiest Tycoon," *The First Post*, October 29, 2007.

26. Ibid.

27. Aung Zaw, "Tycoon Turf," *The Irrawaddy* magazine, September 2005.

28. Ibid.

29. Ibid.

30. Ibid.

31. Lee Kuan Yew, *From Third World to First*, 323.

32. Taylor, *State of Myanmar*, 316.

33. Ibid., 310.

34. Denby, "Than Shwe Lays Out Plans to Tighten Grip," *The Times*, March 28, 2008.

35. "Senior General Than Shwe Speech at USDA Annual General Meeting," *New Light of Myanmar*, November 29, 2008.

36. Quoted in Associated Press, "Than Shwe Sets Guidelines for 2010 Polls," *The Irrawaddy* online news, March 27, 2009.

37. ASEAN-Burma, "Burma is Still ASEAN's Shame."

38. Quoted in AFP, "Myanmar Calls for 'Duty' to Democracy After Jailing 150 Protestors," November 22, 2008.

39. Canning, "The Verdict on Aung San Suu Kyi Has Already Been Decided," *The Guardian*, May 28, 2008.

40. "U.N. Chief Outlines Vision for Myanmar," *Wall Street Journal*, July 4, 2009.

41. Ibid.

42. "Ban Ki-moon's Speech in Bangkok," *The Irrawaddy* online news, July 6, 2009.

43. "Ban—Empty-handed But Wiser," *The Irrawaddy* online news, July 6, 2009.

44. Wai Moe, "Goh's Comments Significant," *The Irrawaddy* online news, June 10, 2009.

45. Salai Pi Pi, "Observers Appreciate Goh's Blunt Suggestions," *Mizzima News*, June 11, 2009.

46. Democratic Voice of Burma, "ICRC Condemns Burmese Military," news report, June 29, 2007.

47. "Red Cross Condemns Burma 'Abuses,'" BBC News, June 29, 2007.

48. Beaumont and Smith, "Drugs and Astrology: How 'Bulldog' Wields Power," *The Guardian*, October 7, 2007.

49. Thet Khaing, "SPDC Chairman Warns of Threats from Neo-Colonialists," *The Myanmar Times*, December 5–11, 2005.

50. Kyaw Zwa Moe, "Than Shwe Shuns Politics in Speech to Buddhist Summit," *The Irrawaddy* online news, December 10, 2004.

BIBLIOGRAPHY

Ad hoc Commission on Depayin Massacre. "Preliminary Report of the Ad hoc Commission on Depayin Massacre (Burma), July 4, 2003." Bangkok, 2004.

Alamgir, Jalal. "Myanmar's Foreign Trade and Its Political Consequences." *Asian Survey* 48, no. 6 (2008): 977–96.

ALTSEAN-Burma. "Burma is Still ASEAN's Shame," Bangkok, February 17, 2008.

——. "Saffron Revolution A Year Later: It's Not Over," Bangkok, September 22, 2008.

——. "SPDC Who's Who." http:// www.altsean.org/Research.php.

Amnesty International. "Crimes Against Humanity in Eastern Myanmar." Index No. ASA 16/011/2008, June 5, 2008.

——. "Myanmar: The Rohingya Minority: Fundamental Rights Denied." Index No. ASA 16/005/2004, May 18, 2004.

Apple, Betsy, and Veronika Martin. "No Safe Place: Burma's Army and the Rape of Ethnic Women." Washington, DC: Refugees International, 2003.

Ashton, William. "Burma Receives Advances from Its Silent Suitors in Singapore." *Jane's Intelligence Review* 10, no. 3 (1998): 32–34.

Aung Moe Htet, ed. *To Stand and Be Counted: The Suppression of Burma's Members of Parliament*. Bangkok: All Burma Students' Democratic Front (ABSDF) Documentation and Research Centre, 1998.

Aung San Suu Kyi. *Freedom from Fear and Other Writings*. London: Penguin Books, 1991.

——. *The Voice of Hope: Conversations with Alan Clements*. London: Penguin Books, 1997.

Aung Shwe, et al., trans. and eds. *Letters to a Dictator: Correspondence from NLD Chairman Aung Shwe to the SLORC's Senior General Than Shwe*. Bangkok: All Burma Students' Democratic Front (ABSDF) Documentation and Research Centre, 1997.

Aung Zaw. "Operation Delta." *The Irrawaddy* magazine, June 2008.

—————. "Than Shwe's 'The Art of War'." *The Irrawaddy* magazine, March–April 2009.

—————. "Than Shwe: Burma's Strongman?" *The Irrawaddy* magazine, January 2003.

—————. "Than Shwe—Man in the Iron Mask," *The Irrawaddy* magazine, February 2005.

—————. "Tycoon Turf." *The Irrawaddy* magazine, September 2005.

Aye, T., and J. Finch, "Legal Aspects of Hydropower Projects in Myanmar." *International Journal on Hydropower and Dams* 14, no. 1 (2007): 62–70.

Back Pack Health Worker Team. "Chronic Emergency: Health and Human Rights in Eastern Burma." Mae Sot, Thailand, 2006.

Beyrer, C., et. al. "Responding to AIDS, Tuberculosis, Malaria and Emerging Infectious Diseases in Burma: Dilemmas of Policy and Practice." Baltimore: Center for Public Health and Human Rights, Department of Epidemiology, Johns Hopkins Bloomberg School of Public Health, March 2006.

Bird, George W. *Wanderings in Burma*. Bournemouth: F. J. Bright & Son, 1897.

Burma Justice Committee. "International Court Condemns Burma Junta for Its Illegal and 'Grotesque' Record on Detention," press release, March 24, 2009.

Callahan, Mary P. *Making Enemies: War and State Building in Burma*. Ithaca, NY: Cornell University Press, 2003.

Charney, Michael W. *A History of Modern Burma*. Cambridge: Cambridge University Press, 2009.

Chit Hlaing. "A Short Note on My Involvement in the Burma Socialist Programme Party (Unrevised Version)." In "Myanmar Literature Project," Working Paper No. 10:10, ed. Hans-Bernd Zoellner. Druck: Passau University, 2006.

Christensen, Russ, and Sann Kyaw. *The Pa-O: Rebels and Refugees*. Chiang Mai: Silkworm Books, 2006.

Christian Solidarity Worldwide. "Atrocities Continue in Burma as Mutilated Body is Found," press release, February 20, 2006.

—————. "Over 11,000 Displaced Civilians Killed in Latest Burma Army Attacks on Karen," news article, April 26, 2006.

—————. "CSW Visit to the Bangladesh-Burma Border," August 26–31, 2008.

—————. "CSW Visit to the Karen and Mon Peoples on the Thailand-Burma Border," February 2007.

—————. "CSW Visit to the Thai-Burmese Border," April 9–15, 2005.

Committee to Protect Journalists. "10 Worst Countries to be a Blogger." Special Report, April 30, 2009.

—————. "CPJ's 2008 Prison Census: Online and in Jail." Special Report, December 4, 2008.

Dictator of the Month. "Than Shwe: Dictator of the Month," January 2004. http://www.dictatorofthemonth.com/Shwe/Jan2004ShweEN.htm.

Dulyapak Preecharushh. *Naypyidaw: The New Capital of Burma*. Bangkok: White Lotus, 2009.

EarthRights International. "US Court Calls Abuses Committed in Construction of Chevron's Pipeline 'Military Terrorism,'" press release, October 19, 2007.

—————. "The Yadana Pipeline." http:// www.earthrights.org/campaignfeature/yadana_pipeline.html.

Egreteau, Renaud, and Larry Jagan. "Back to the Old Habits: Isolationism or the Self-Preservation of Burma's Military Regime." IRASEC Occasional Paper No.7. Bangkok: Research Institute on Contemporary Southeast Asia, December 2008.

Fink, Christina. *Living Silence: Burma Under Military Rule*. London: Zed Books, 2001.

—————. *Militarization in Burma's Ethnic States: Causes and Consequences*. London: Routledge, 2008.

Foreign Policy and the Fund for Peace. "The Failed States Index: Most Vulnerable Countries 2009." Washington, DC, 2009.

Free Burma Rangers. "A Brutal Reign of Terror—Situation Update: Central Dooplaya District, Karen State, Burma," news report, June 22, 2002.

Genocide Prevention Project. "Mass Atrocity Crimes Watch List 2008–09." http://www.preventorprotect.org/images/documents/gpp_report.pdf.

Gray, Denis D., Associated Press writer, [untitled], February 17, 1994. http:// www.burmalibrary.org/reg.burma/archives/199402/msg00044.html.

Green, Michael, and Derek Mitchell. "Asia's Forgotten Crisis: A New Approach to Burma." *Foreign Affairs* 86, no. 6 (November/December 2007), 147–58.

Heritage Foundation. "2009 Index of Economic Freedom." http:// www.heritage.org/index.

Holland, Heidi. *Dinner with Mugabe: The Untold Story of a Freedom Fighter Who Became a Tyrant*. London: Penguin, 2009.

Houtman, Gustaaf. *Mental Culture in Burmese Crisis Politics: Aung San Suu Kyi and the National League for Democracy*. ILCAA Study of Languages and Cultures of Asia and Africa Monograph Series No. 33. Tokyo: Institute for the

Study of Languages and Cultures of Asia and Africa, Tokyo University of Foreign Studies, 1999.

Human Rights Watch. "Burma: World's Highest Number of Child Soldiers," news release, October 15, 2002.

—————. "'My Gun Was As Tall As Me': Child Soldiers in Burma." New York, Washington, London, and Brussels, 2002.

—————. "Sold To Be Soldiers: The Recruitment and Use of Child Soldiers in Burma." New York, Washington, London, and Brussels, 2007.

International Committee of the Red Cross. "Myanmar: ICRC Denounces Major and Repeated Violations of International Humanitarian Law," news release, June 29, 2007.

International Human Rights Clinic, Harvard Law School. "Crimes in Burma." Cambridge, MA, May 2009.

International Labour Organization. "Forced Labour in Myanmar (Burma): Report of the Commission of Inquiry." Geneva: International Labour Office, 1998.

Irrawaddy, The (magazine). "Thakin Kodaw Hmaing (1876–1974)," March 2000.

Jones, Col. Paul L., as told to Hugh Crumpler. "The Withdrawal from Burma and the Stilwell Walkout." Feature article from *Ex-CBI Roundup* (May 1992). http://cbi-theater-3.home.comcast.net/~cbi-theater-3/stilwellpages/stilwell_walkout.html.

Kachin Environmental Organization. "Damming the Irrawaddy." Chiang Mai, Thailand, 2008.

Karen Human Rights Group. "Chemical Shells at Kaw Moo Rah." A Special Independent Report, KHRG #95-08, February 24, 1995.

—————. "Chemical Shells At Kaw Moo Rah: Supplementary." An Independent Report, KHRG #95-08-A, March 20, 1995.

Kemp, Melody. "Burma Goes Ballistic." Weblog. *Webdiary*, July 2009. http://webdiary.com.au/cms/?q=node/1801.

Khin Ohmar. "Saffron Anniversary." Weblog. *Burma Partnership*, September 22, 2008. http://apppb.blogspot.com/2008/09/burma-update-september-22-2008_2232.html.

Kivimaki, Timo, and Morten Pedersen. "Burma: Mapping the Challenges and Opportunities for Dialogue and Reconciliation." A report by Crisis Management Initiative and Martti Ahtsaari Rapid Reaction Facility, 2008.

Kyaw Hsan. "Stability of the State, Community Peace and Tranquility, and Prevalence of Law and Order Necessary for National Development." Address delivered by Chairman of the Information Committee of the State Peace and Development Council Minister of Information Brig-Gen Kyaw Hsan at the press conference of the Information Committee, Rangoon, November 2, 2006.

Kyaw Yin Hlaing. "Myanmar in 2004: Why Military Rule Continues." In *Southeast Asian Affairs 2005*, ed. Chin Kin Wah and Daljit Singh, 231–56. Singapore: Institute of Southeast Asian Studies, 2005.

——————. "Power and Factional Struggles in Post-Independence Burmese Governments." *Journal of Southeast Asian Studies* 39, no. 1 (2008): 149–77.

Lawrence, Neil. "The Despot and the Diplomat," *The Irrawaddy* magazine, September 2008.

Lee Kuan Yew. *From Third World to First: The Singapore Story: 1965–2000*. New York: HarperCollins, 2000.

Lees, Graham. "Leader's Rumored Sickness Provides Some Small Hope for Burmese Reform." *World Politics Review*, January 23, 2007.

Levin, Burton. "Remembering 1988." *Burma Debate* 5, no. 3 (1998).

Lintner, Bertil. *Aung San Suu Kyi and Burma's Unfinished Resistance*. London: Peacock Press, 1990.

——————. "Burma's Nuclear Temptation." *Yale Global Online*, December 3, 2008.

——————. *Burma in Revolt: Opium and Insurgency Since 1948*. 2nd ed. Chiang Mai: Silkworm Books, 1999.

——————. "Burma's Warrior Kings and the Generation of 8.8.88." *Global Asia* 2, no. 2 (2007): 70–79.

——————. *Great Leader, Dear Leader: Demystifying North Korea under the Kim Clan*. Chiang Mai: Silkworm Books, 2005.

——————. "Myanmar's Chinese Connection." http://www.asiapacificms.com/articles/myanmar_chinese_connection/. This article first appeared in *International Defence Review* 27, no. 11 (1994): 23–36.

——————. *Outrage: Burma's Struggle for Democracy*. Hong Kong: Review Publishing Company, 1989.

——————. *The Rise and Fall of the Communist Party of Burma* (CPB). Ithaca, NY: Southeast Asia Program, Cornell University, 1990.

——————. "The Staying Power of the Burmese Military Regime." Paper presented at a public forum on Burma, Aichi Gakuin University, Nagoya, Japan, March 11–17, 2009.

——————. "Tunnels, Guns and Kimchi: North Korea's Quest for Dollars—Part 1." *Yale Global Online*, June 9, 2009.

Lintner, Bertil, and Michael Black. *Merchants of Madness: The Methamphetamine Explosion in the Golden Triangle*. Chiang Mai: Silkworm Books, 2009.

Lintner, Bertil, and Shawn W. Crispin, "Burma: Dangerous Bedfellows." *Far Eastern Economic Review*, November 20, 2003.

Lloyd Parry, Richard. *In the Time of Madness: Indonesia on the Edge of Chaos*. New York, Grove Press, 2005.

Manzella, Lillian. "Judge Finds Evidence Unocal Used Burmese Military Despite Knowing of Its Abuses," press release by EarthRights International, June 14, 2006.

Maung Aung Myoe. *Building the Tatmadaw: Myanmar Armed Forces Since 1948*. Singapore: Institute of Southeast Asian Studies, 2009.

————. "Building the Tatmadaw: The Organizational Development of the Armed Forces in Myanmar 1948–98." Working Paper No. 327. Canberra: Strategic and Defence Studies Centre, Australian National University, 1998.

————. "A Historical Overview of Political Transition in Myanmar Since 1988." Asia Research Institute Working Paper Series No. 95. Singapore: Asia Research Institute, National University of Singapore, August 2007.

————. "Military Doctrine and Strategy in Myanmar: A Historical Perspective." Working Paper No. 339. Canberra: Strategic and Defence Studies Centre, Australian National University, 1999.

Maung Maung. *The 1988 Uprising in Burma*. Southeast Asia Monograph Series. New Haven, CT: Yale University Southeast Asian Studies, 1999.

McCarthy, Stephen. "Burma and ASEAN: Estranged Bedfellows." *Asian Survey* 48, no. 6 (2008): 911–35.

Ministry of Information. *Chronicle of National Development: Comparison Between Period Preceding 1988 and After* [up to Dec. 31, 2005]. Rangoon: Ministry of Information, 2006.

Minority Rights Group. "Peoples Under Threat 2009." http:// www.minorityrights. org/7927/peoples-under-threat/peoples-under-threat-2009.html.

"Myanmar (Burma): The Biggest Corruption in Burma History: Sr. General Than Shwe's Second Daughter Has Made 200 Million Dollars by Selling Burma's Land to Chinese Tycoons," posted by mm.burma. *Blogger News Network*, March 23, 2007. http:// www.bloggernews.net/1date/2007/03.

National Coalition Government, Union of Burma. Human Rights Documentation Unit. "Bullets in the Alms Bowl: An Analysis of the Brutal SPDC Suppression of the September 2007 Saffron Revolution," March 2008.

——————. "Burma's Aid Woes Underpinned by Military Incompetence," press release, October 3, 2008.

Network for Democracy and Development. "NDD Weekly Inside News Commentary—344." Mae Sot, Thailand, 2008.

——————. "The White Shirts: How the USDA Will Become the New Face of Burma's Dictatorship." Mae Sariang and Mae Sot, Thailand, May 2006.

Pilger, John. "In a Land of Fear," May 4, 1996. http:// www.johnpilger.com/page. asp?partid=280.

Pinheiro, Paulo Sérgio. "Report of the Special Rapporteur on the Situation of Human Rights in Myanmar," delivered to the sixty-first session of the United Nations General Assembly. U.N. Doc. A/61/369 (September 21, 2006).

——————. "Question of the Violation of Human Rights and Fundamental Freedoms in Any Part of the World: Situation of Human Rights in Myanmar. Report submitted by Special Rapporteur, Paulo Sérgio Pinheiro." Presented at the UN Commission on Human Rights, Sixtieth Session. U.N. Doc. E/CN.4/2004/33 (January 5, 2004).

Reporters San Frontières. "Predators of Press Freedom: Than Shwe—Burma." http:// arabia.reporters-sans-frontieres.org/IMG/pdf/Than_Shwe-2.pdf.

——————. "Press Freedom Index, 2009." http:// www.rsf.org/en-classement 1003-2009.html.

Revolutionary Council of the Union of Burma. "The Burmese Way to Socialism," April 28, 1962.

Rogers, Benedict. "Carrying the Cross: The Military Regime's Campaign of Restrictions, Discrimination and Persecution Against Christians in Burma." A report by Christian Solidarity Worldwide, 2007.

——————. A Land Without Evil: Stopping the Genocide of Burma's Karen People. London: Monarch Books, 2004.

Rome Statute of the International Criminal Court. Article 28: Responsibility of Commanders and Other Superiors.

Salai Za Uk Ling, and Salai Bawi Lian Mang. "Religious Persecution: A Campaign of Ethnocide Against Chin Christians in Burma." A report by the Chin Human Rights Organization, February 2004.

Selth, Andrew. Burma's Armed Forces: Power Without Glory. Norwalk, CT: East-Bridge, 2002.

—————. "Burma's Arms Procurement Programme." Working Paper No. 289. Canberra: Strategic and Defence Studies Centre, Australian National University, September 1995.

—————. "Burma's Intelligence Apparatus." Working Paper No. 308 Canberra: Strategic and Defence Studies Centre, Australian National University, June 1997.

—————. "Burma-North Korea: Rumor and Reality." Weblog of the Lowy Institute for International Policy, Sydney. *The Interpreter*, June 29, 2009.

—————. "Burma and Nuclear Proliferation: Policies and Perceptions." Regional Outlook Paper No. 12. Brisbane: Griffith Asia Institute, 2007.

—————. "Burma's 'Saffron Revolution' and the Limits of International Influence." *Australian Journal of International Affairs* 62, no. 3 (2008): 281–97.

—————. "Burma and the Threat of Invasion: Regime Fantasy or Strategic Reality?" Regional Outlook Paper No. 17. Brisbane: Griffith Asia Institute, 2008.

—————. "Burma and Weapons of Mass Destruction." Working Paper No. 334. Canberra: Strategic Defence Studies Centre, Australian National University, 1999.

—————. "Modern Burma Studies: A View From the Edge." Working Paper Series, no. 96. Hong Kong: Southeast Asia Research Centre, City University of Hong Kong, 2007.

—————. "Pariah Partners in Arms." *The Irrawaddy* magazine, March 2004.

—————. *Transforming the Tatmadaw: The Burmese Armed Forces Since 1988.* Canberra: Strategic and Defense Studies Center, 1996.

Shan Women's Action Network. "10,000 Shans Uprooted, 500 Houses Burned in Burmese Regime's Latest Scorched Earth Campaign," press release, August 2009.

—————. "License to Rape: The Burmese Military Regime's Use of Sexual Violence in the Ongoing War in Shan State." Chiang Mai, Thailand, May 2002.

Silverstein, Josef. *Burma: Military Rule and the Politics of Stagnation.* Ithaca: NY: Cornell University Press, 1977.

—————. *Burmese Politics: The Dilemma of National Unity.* New Brunswick, NJ: Rutgers University Press, 1980.

Singapore Ministry of Foreign Affairs. "Letter from Prime Minister Lee Hsien Loong to Senior General Than Shwe, Chairman, State Peace and Development Council, Union of Myanmar," press release, September 29, 2007.

Slim, William. *Defeat Into Victory: Battling Japan in Burma and India 1942–1945.* New York: Cooper Square Press, 2000.

Smith, Martin. *Burma: Insurgency and the Politics of Ethnicity.* London: Zed Books, 1991.

Squassoni, Sharon A. "Nuclear, Biological and Chemical Weapons and Missiles: Status and Trends." CRS Report for Congress No. RL30699, January 14, 2005.

Steinberg, David. *Burma: The State of Myanmar.* Washington, DC: Georgetown University Press, 2001.

Stover, Eric, et al. "The Gathering Storm: Infectious Diseases and Human Rights in Burma." A report by Human Rights Center, University of California, Berkeley and Center for Public Health and Human Rights, Johns Hopkins Bloomberg School of Public Health, July 2007.

Taylor, Robert. *The State of Myanmar.* London: Hurst and Company, 2009.

——————, ed. *Burma: Political Economy under Military Rule.* London: C. Hurst and Co., 2001.

Thailand Burma Border Consortium. "Displaced Villages, 1996–2008." http://www.tbbc.org/idps/map-library/09-03-displaced-high.pdf.

Than Shwe. Address delivered by Commander-in-Chief of Defence Services Senior General Than Shwe at the graduation parade of the 7th Intake of the Defence Services Medical Academy, as documented by the Permanent Mission of the Union of Myanmar to the United Nations and Other International Organizations, Geneva, Switzerland. http://myanmargeneva.org/statement&speech/speech_SGTS/SGTS_%207DSMA.htm.

Thant Myint-U. *The River of Lost Footsteps: A Personal History of Burma.* London: Faber and Faber, 2008.

Thaung Htike. *The American Staff College at Ft. Leavenworth.* Yangon: Bawathetkathi, 1987.

Thu Ye Kaung. "Than Shwe Family Member to USA: Is US Government Welcoming Dictator Than Shwe Family Member in USA?" Weblog. *Jegsburma,* February 23, 2009. http://jegsburma.blogspot.com/2009/02/than-shwe-family-member-in-usa.html.

Tinker, Hugh. *The Union of Burma: A Study of the First Years of Independence.* Oxford: Oxford University Press, 1967.

Transparency International. "Corruption Perceptions Index 2007." http://www.transparency.org/policy_research/surveys_indices/cpi/2007.

Turnell, Sean. "Burma's Insatiable State," *Asian Survey* 48, no. 6 (2008): 958–76.

——————. *Fiery Dragons: Banks, Moneylenders, and Microfinance in Burma.* Hawaii: University of Hawaii Press, 2009.

U Aung Htoo. "The Depayin Massacre: A Crime Against Humanity and Its Effect on National Reconciliation," *Article 2*, vol. 2, no. 6 (2003).

U Ne Oo. "Burma Nuclear Program: The Puzzle on Location." *The Barossa* (South Australia), May 28, 2004.

UNICEF. *The State of the World's Children 2009: Maternal and New Born Health.* New York: United Nations Children's Fund, December 2008.

United States Holocaust Memorial Museum. "Crisis in Darfur (2009 Update)." http://www.ushmm.org/maps/projects/darfur/.

U.S. Congress. *Tom Lantos Block Burmese JADE (Junta's Anti-Democratic Efforts) Act of 2008*, H.R. 3890, 110th Cong., 2nd sess., approved by both the Senate and House, January 3, 2008.

U.S. Congress. House. Committee on International Relations. Subcommittee on International Terrorism, Nonproliferation and Human Rights and Subcommittee on Asia and the Pacific. Statement of Stephen Dun, World Aid. *Human Rights in Burma: Fifteen Years Post-Military Coup.* 108th Cong. 1st sess., October 1–2, 2003.

—————. Committee on International Relations. Subcommittee on International Terrorism, Nonproliferation and Human Rights and Subcommittee on Asia and the Pacific. Statement of Wunna Maung, National League for Democracy. *Human Rights in Burma: Fifteen Years Post-Military Coup.* 108th Cong. 1st sess., October 1–2, 2003.

U.S. Department of Justice. Foreign Agents Registration Unit. Copy of Bain and Associates' filing with the Foreign Agents Registration Unit. http:// www.fara.gov/docs/5205-Exhibit-AB-19970904-EI7AYF03.pdf.

—————. Foreign Agents Registration Unit. Copy of letter from Burmese Ambassador to United States U Thaung to Mr. Joseph E. Clarkson, Chief of Registration Unit, Internal Security Section, Criminal Division, U.S. Department of Justice, April 13, 1992. http:// www.fara.gov/docs/3466-Exhibit-AB-19920401-D0UGTI01.pdf.

—————. Foreign Agents Registration Unit. Copy of DCI Associates' filing with the Foreign Agents Registration Unit. http:// www.fara.gov/docs/5497-Exhibit-AB-20020513-GWTSEN03.pdf.

—————. Foreign Agent Registration Unit. Copy of Jefferson Waterman's filing with the Foreign Agents Registration Unit. http:// www.fara.gov/docs/4990-Exhibit-AB-19970404-EALJCC02.pdf.

————. Foreign Agents Registration Unit. Copy of contract between van Kloberg & Associates, Ltd. and the Government of the Union of Myanmar. http:// www.fara.gov/docs/3466-Exhibit-AB-19911024-DoV4R201.pdf.

————. Foreign Agents Registration Unit. Copy of letter from Lester R. Wolff to U Thaung, Burmese ambassador to the United States, February 1, 1993. http:// www.fara.gov/docs/3690-Exhibit-AB-19930201-DoXY6X01.pdf.

U.S. Department of Labor. Bureau of International Labor Affairs. *2000 Report on Labor Practices in Burma*. Special report prepared at the request of Congress, 2000.

U.S. Department of State. *2009 International Religious Freedom Report*. Report submitted to the Congress in compliance with Section 102(b) of the International Religious Freedom Act (IRFA) of 1998, October 2009.

U.S. Department of Treasury. Office of Foreign Assets Control. "Tay Zaw Financial Network," February 2008. http:// www.treas.gov/offices/enforcement/ofac/ programs/burma/charts/tayza_02062008.pdf.

————. "Treasury Sanctions Additional Financial Operatives of the Burmese Regime," press release, February 25, 2008.

Wakeman, Carolyn, and San San Tin. *No Time for Dreams: Living in Burma Under Military Rule*. Lanham, MD: Rowman & Littlefield Publishers, 2009.

Watson, Roland. "Nuclear Proliferation and Burma: The Hidden Connection." An article posted by Dictator Watch, November 7, 2006. http:// www.dictatorwatch.org/articles/burmanuclear.html.

Webster, Donovan. *The Burma Road: The Epic Story of the China-Burma-India Theater in World War II*. New York: Harper Perennial, 2004.

Win Min. "Looking Inside the Burmese Military." *Asian Survey* 48, no. 6 (2008): 1018–37.

Wintle, Justin. *Perfect Hostage: Aung San Suu Kyi, Burma and the Generals*. London: Arrow Books, 2007.

World Food Programme. "Myanmar." http:// www.wfp.org/countries/myanmar.

World Health Organization. "National Health Accounts: Myanmar," September 13, 2007.

————. *World Health Report 2000: Health Systems: Improving Performance*. Geneva, 2000.

Yawnghwe, Chao-Tzang. "Ne Win's Tatmadaw Dictatorship." Master's thesis, University of British Columbia, April 1990.

Zaw Bo. "A Free People or a Satellite Nation?" Rangoon: Union Solidarity and
    Development Association, 2004.
Zoellner, Hans-Bernd, ed. "Myanmar Literature Project," Working Paper No. 10:10.
    Druck: Department of Southeast Asian Studies, Passau University, 2006.

News Sources

Agence France-Presse (AFP)
Al Jazeera
Asia Times
Asia Week
Associated Press
Atlantic Monthly
Bangkok Post
BBC News
Beijing Today
Boston Globe
Burma Digest
Burma News
Burma Watch, The Nation Weblog
China Review
Daily Telegraph
Democratic Voice of Burma
Financial Times
First Post
Guardian, The
Independent, The
Inner City Press
International Herald Tribune
Irrawaddy, The (online news)
Kachin News Group

Korea Herald
Los Angeles Times
Mizzima News
Myanmar Times
Nation, The (Bangkok)
National, The (Abu Dhabi)
New Internationalist
New Light of Myanmar
New York Times
Newsweek
Progressive, The
Reuters
Straits Times (Singapore)
Sun Daily (Malaysia)
Sunday Times, The
Sydney Morning Herald
Taipei Times
Times, The
Time Magazine
Village Voice
Voice of America
Wall Street Journal
Washington Post
Working People's Daily

INDEX

4th Burma Rifles, 25, 46, 56

88 Generation of Students, 175, 189

Alaungpaya, King, 166, 167

All Burma Monks Alliance, 176

Anawrahta, King, 10, 88, 166, 167

Annan, Kofi, 181

Anti-Fascist People's Freedom League, 20

Aris, Michael, 83, 189

Association of Southeast Asian Nations
(ASEAN), 132, 153–55, 180, 183

Attlee, Clement, 22–23

Aung Gyi, 28, 38, 47, 86

Aung Kyaw Zaw, 66–69

Aung Kyi, 172, 180

Aung Lynn Htut, 29–30, 67–68, 97,
99–100, 108, 112, 160, 206

Aung Phone, 67

Aung San, 17–18, 20–24, 36, 50, 60, 82

Aung San Suu Kyi: 2009 arrest and trial
of, 210–11; ASEAN support of, 154;
assassination attempts of, 87, 107–8
(see also Depayin); Ban Ki-moon's
request to visit, 211–12; election campaigning, 86–88; house arrest, 87–88,
184, 210; and Khin Nyunt, 157, 158–59;

as pro-democracy icon, 82–83; in
talks with Than Shwe regime, 180–81

Aung Saw Oo, 14–15, 34, 48, 59, 64–66, 70

Aung Shwe, 42, 92–94

Aung Thaung, 16, 117, 199–200, 213

Aung Thet Mann, 125, 205

Aung Zaw, 115, 173, 186, 206

Aye Aye Thit Shwe, 116, 207

Aye Aye Yee, 90

Aye Ko, 56, 64, 66, 69, 71, 73, 191

Bain and Associates, 130–31, 133, 149

Ban Ki-moon, 173, 175, 180, 183–84, 211–12

Bayinnaung, King, 166–67

Britain: colonial administration in
Burma, 12, 22; and Second World War,
17, 22

Brown, Gordon, 179

Buddhism: in Burma, 12; origins of, 13;
precepts, 13; used as a political tool,
14, 46, 98, 103–4, 173, 179

Burma: economic policies, 2, 3, 49, 61, 65,
74, 96, 122, 125–26, 156, 192; human
rights record, 2, 52, 98–102, 106–8, 113;
independence struggle, 17, 20, 22–24;
military offensives against ethnic

groups (*see under* ethnic nationalities); name change, xi, 86

Burma Defense Army (BDA), 20, 22

Burma Independence Army (BIA), 17–18, 20, 24

Burma National Army (BNA), 20

Burma Socialist Program Party (BSPP), 47, 60, 66, 84, 85, 208; Central Committee, 70; Third Party Congress, 69; Fourth Party Congress, 66. *See also* National Unity Party

"Burmese Way to Socialism," 41, 46–49, 59, 61, 69

Bush, George W., 120, 135, 179

Canning, Mark, 125, 168, 198, 205, 211

Central School of Political Science, 39, 48

chemical weapons, 140–41

child soldiers, 2, 41–42, 95, 99, 101

Chin, 18, 20, 103, 104

China: arms sales, 138, 139, 206; backing of CPB, 21, 37, 53, 55, 64, 68; "enemy" of Burma, 32–33; and Second World War, 20; veto power in UN Security Council, 139

Chit Hlaing, 38–41, 47–48

Communist Party of Burma (CPB), 21, 25–26, 32–33, 35, 40–41, 52–58, 63–68

Cyclone Nargis, 3, 9, 76, 175, 183–86, 197, 209, 211

DCI Associates, 134–35

Defense Services Academy (DSA), 28–30, 36–37, 41, 50, 65–66, 148

Democratic Karen Buddhist Army (DKBA), 121

Democratic Voice of Burma (DVB), 144–45

Depayin, 106–12, 154–58, 197, 200, 204, 208

drug trafficking, 120–22

Dubai, 6, 128, 179, 206

Dun, Smith, 25, 199

Eastern Command, 64, 67

E Thi, 172

ethnic nationalities, 2, 3, 34, 103–4, 124; ceasefires, 121, 158; and constitution, 182; displacement of, 107, 123; military offensives against, 32–33, 35, 55, 96–98, 101, 103–6, 166, 187, 198 (*see also* Four Cuts campaign); during Second World War, 17–26

forced labor, 75–76, 95, 99, 104–5, 113, 123

Four Cuts campaign, 30, 51–55, 68, 73

Free Burma Rangers, 52, 98, 100

Gambari, Ibrahim, 173, 180–81, 200

Gates, Robert, 184

genocide, 1, 2, 104–5, 214

Goh Chok Tong, 138, 212

Holland, Heidi, 5, 116

Htein Lin, 80

Hussein, Saddam, 128, 155–56

India: arms supplier, 138; colonial government in Burma, 12; cyclone warnings, 3, 183

internally displaced persons, 52, 95

International Committee of the Red Cross (ICRC), 96, 214

International Labour Organization (ILO), 76, 201

Irrawaddy Delta, 9, 17, 23, 25, 77, 183, 185

Irrawaddy Division, 26, 71, 73–76

Irrawaddy magazine, 128, 186

Ismail, Razali, 16, 112, 151–52, 159, 160, 190, 195–96, 204

Israel, 137

Japan: economic sanctions on Burma, 154; invasion of Burma, 17–18, 21; training of BIA, 17, 27

Jefferson Waterman International, 133, 149

Kachin, 18, 20-22, 23, 26, 103, 124

Kachin Independence Organization (KIO), 124

Karen, xi, 18, 21, 22, 103, 186; independent state, 23–24, 35; insurgency, 25–26, 33; military offensives against, 19, 21, 26, 32–33, 35, 95, 97, 100, 105, 140–41, 182; in Second World War, 18–19

Karen National Defense Organization (KNDO), 25–26

Karen National Union (KNU), 32, 58

Ket Sein, 105

Khin Kyi, 83, 86

Khin Maung Nyunt, 28–30, 33, 37, 42

Khin Nyunt, 29, 70, 84–85, 88–91, 97, 112, 134, 151, 152, 156–61, 164, 190–91, 195–97, 207–8

Khin Pyone Shwe, 130–31, 207

Khin Shwe, 131, 203, 206

Kim Jong-il, 3, 143, 151, 155, 156

Kloberg, Edward von, 128–29

Kouchner, Bernard, 184

Kraisak Choonhavan, 190

Kuomintang (KMT), 33, 35

Kyaing Kyaing, 33–35, 118, 166, 171–74, 206

Kyaing Than Shwe, 74

Kyaukse, 10–12, 14–19, 21–22, 26–27, 34, 63, 128, 142, 173–174, 200

Kyaw Tin, 38, 56, 64, 69

Kyaw Win, 17, 72, 143, 213

Kyaw Zaw, 60

Kyi Kyi Shwe, 116, 119, 207

Law, Steven, 120, 125, 203

Lee Kuan Yew, 3, 116, 138, 208

Levin, Burton, 17, 81–82, 84, 91, 93

light infantry battalions, 51, 199

light infantry divisions (LIDs), 31, 36, 51, 53–56, 58, 65–68, 71, 82, 199

Lintner, Bertil, 81, 82, 88, 91, 96, 103, 104, 121, 122, 130, 138, 142, 143, 145, 161, 167, 170, 192

Lo Hsing Han, 120

Mahathir Mohamad, Dr., 153, 154, 175, 195, 205

Maung Aung Myoe, 29, 30, 38, 49, 125, 136, 193

Maung Aye, 29–30, 97, 100, 108, 115, 119, 161, 173, 190–91, 195, 197–98, 207, 213

Maung Bo, 16, 117

Maung Maung, 58, 62, 82, 84–85, 99

"MI" Tin Oo, 60–63, 70, 191

Milosevic, Slobodan, 1, 2, 102

Min Ko Naing, 113, 173

Min Naung, 65, 69

Ministry of Defense, 38, 40, 170

Minzu, 10

Mitchell, Andrew, 189
Mugabe, Robert, 3–5, 116, 150, 155–156
Myanmar. *See* Burma
Myint Aung, 100
Myint Lwin, 65
Myint Swe, 170, 199, 206, 213

National Convention, 93, 121, 155, 158–59,
    164, 182–83, 200–1, 208–9
National League for Democracy (NLD),
    17, 77, 86–88, 92–94, 107–11, 159, 166,
    177, 195, 200–1
National Unity Party (NUP), 85, 88
Nay Lin, 75–76
Nay Shwe Thway Aung, 118–20, 207
Nay Soe Maung, 119
Naypyidaw, 6, 120, 142, 144–45, 163–71,
    197, 203, 205
Ne Win: 1962 military coup, 38, 40–43,
    45–46; deals with drug traffickers, 56;
    demonetization, 79; formation of
    state ideology (*see* Burmese Way to
    Socialism; Revolutionary Council);
    purge of military officers, 60–61, 63,
    65, 69–70; *tatmadaw* reform, 28, 33
New Light of Myanmar, 16, 31, 141, 150, 170,
    201, 214
North Korea: alleged assistance with
    Burma's nuclear research program
    and underground military installa-
    tions, 142–45; arms supplier, 144;
    bombing of S. Korean officials in
    Rangoon, 70
Northern Command, 39, 42, 47, 54
nuclear program, 15, 128, 142–46
Nyein, Ronny, 22, 30, 39, 41, 50, 56, 66, 69

Officer Training School (OTS), 27–33, 37,
    49, 50, 56
Ohn Kyaw Myint, 61–63
Operation King Conqueror, 66
Osborn, David, 62–63

Pa-O, 34–35, 103
Pakistan: arms supplier, 138; nuclear sci-
    entists in Burma, 146
Pakokku, 11, 142, 176, 177
Panglong Agreement, 23–24
Petrie, Charles, 181–82
Pinheiro, Paulo Sérgio, 101, 108, 111, 113,
    134, 182–83
political prisoners, 25, 94, 95, 96, 113, 176,
    210, 211
psychological warfare: Education and
    Psychological Warfare Department, 38,
    39, 46; psy-ops, 39, 41, 42–43, 47, 49, 60,
    84, 90, 151; Psywar Directorate, 38, 39
Pun, Serge, 203, 206
Pyinmana, 20, 26, 27, 144, 163, 164, 168, 171

Rajapaksa, Mahinda, 167
Rangoon Institute of Technology, 17, 79
Rangoon University, 28, 50, 56, 58–59, 80
rape. *See* sexual violence
Revolutionary Council, 31, 46–47, 60, 84,
    203, 208
Rohingya, 104
Russia: arms supplier, 138; nuclear rela-
    tionship with Burma, 15, 142–43

Saffron Revolution, 54, 104, 128, 140,
    176–80, 196
Samak Sundaravej, 14, 184

San Yu, 38, 39, 42, 47, 54, 60, 61, 69, 71

Sao Shwe Thaike, 45

Saw Maung, 83–86, 88–91, 97, 105, 181, 191

Saw Wai, 45

Saya San, 11–12, 194

Seagrim, Hugh, 19

Sein Lwin, 80, 82

Sein Thaung, 30, 32, 56, 57

Selth, Andrew, 7, 137, 145, 146, 165

sexual violence: gang rape of student
    protestors, 80; rape of ethnic minority
    women, 52, 96, 102, 105, 106, 113, 123,
    134; as a weapon of war, 1, 95, 101

Shan, 10, 23, 35, 103; military offensives
    against, 96, 100, 141; resettlement of,
    149

Shwe Mann, 36, 119, 125, 139, 198–99, 205,
    206

Shwedagon Pagoda, 54, 82, 170, 173, 174, 178

Singapore: arms sales, 137–38; Burmese
    companies operating in, 125; real estate
    investment by Burmese, 127–28, 179, 203.
    See also Lee Kuan Yew

Si Thu, 84

Slim, William, 18–21

Smith, Martin, 47, 53, 60, 64, 65, 103

Soe Shin, 213

Southern Command, 52

Southwest Command, 71, 75, 77

State Law and Order Restoration Council
    (SLORC), 84–85, 88, 91, 94, 97, 130, 137,
    140, 190–91, 198, 206, 208

State Peace and Development Council
    (SPDC), 29, 97, 121, 126, 145, 154, 172, 176,
    183, 187, 189, 190–91, 195, 201, 206, 208

Stilwell, Joe, 18, 20, 21

Suharto, General, 72–73, 167, 205, 208

Swan Arr Shin, 176, 200, 203

tatmadaw, xi, 29, 33, 36, 40–42, 52, 84–86, 103,
    160, 166, 190; and Chin Christians, 104;
    and CPB, 52–53, 55, 64, 66–68; military
    training of USDA, 202; and New Win, 33,
    40; offensives against ethnic resistance
    groups, 25, 35, 73, 121, 140–41 (see also
    Four Cuts campaign)

Tay Za, 3, 125, 203–6

Thaksin Shinawatra, 172

Than Sein, 69

Than Shwe: alleged lavish lifestyle, 116,
    119, 121; alleged drug trade complicity,
    120–21; antipathy toward Aung San
    Suu Kyi, 194–196; arms procurement,
    137–39, 144; astrology's influence, 12,
    72, 127, 167, 172–73, 215; birthplace (see
    Kyaukse); instructor in party ideology,
    39, 48; involvement in infrastructure
    projects, 72–73, 77, 92, 124–25, 139, 174;
    military training, 27, 30, 39, 41; preoc-
    cupation with historical kings, 6, 48,
    116, 166, 167, 169, 171; schooling, 17, 27,
    49; suppression of dissent, 2, 148; and
    tatmadaw, 27, 55, 66, 101, 135–37, 148,
    150, 209; use of psy-war tactics, 39–41,
    42, 47, 49, 84, 90, 151

Than Tin, 62

Than Tun, 84

Thandar Shwe, 115–17, 120, 203, 207

Thant Myint-U, 11, 17, 23, 166, 168

Thant Zin Myaing, 36

Thar Yin Myat, 205–6

Thein Naing, 74, 207

Thein Sein, 91, 138, 182, 183, 200

Thirty Comrades, 17, 27, 60

Tin Aye Kyaw, 69

Tin Htoon, 37–38

Tin Oo, 58, 60–62, 86–87, 109, 111

Tin Win Nyo, 69

Tom Lantos Block Burmese JADE Act, 126

torture, 19, 92, 95–97, 102, 106, 123, 156–57, 186, 196, 215

Total S.A., 122

Tun Lin, 69

Tun Yi, 64–66, 68

Turnell, Sean, 122, 126, 127

U Khin Kyaw Han, 12, 15, 107

U Mya Win, 76

Union Solidarity Development Association (USDA), 100, 107–11, 158, 175, 200–3, 208–9, 213

United Nations (UN): genocide, definition of, 105; General Assembly, 106; Human Rights Council, 111; secretary-general (see names of individuals); Security Council, 102–3, 114, 139, 179, 201; special envoys (see names of individuals); special rapporteurs (see names of individuals)

United States: and support of Aung San Suu Kyi, 150; Embassy, 50, 81; lobbyists (see names of individuals and companies); military assistance, 38, 55;

State Department, 2, 30, 96, 132, 133, 134, 150

United Wa State Army (UWSA), 121

Unocal, 122–23, 132–33

U Nu, 24–27, 33, 38, 45, 55, 59, 61, 63

U Thant, 58–59, 212

U Thaung, 15–16, 29, 128–29, 142

U Win Aung, 160

War Office, 41, 54–58, 64–66, 90

White Bridge, 80

Win Myint, 34, 170

Wolff, Lester, 129–30, 133–34

Working People's Daily, 31–32, 35, 38, 39, 42, 51, 53, 55, 74–76, 88

World Food Programme (WFP), 76–77

Wrobleski, Ann, 133–34

Yadana pipeline, 122–23

Ye Myint, 117, 119

Yettaw, John, 210–11

Yokota, Yozo, 113, 158, 160

Zarganar, 210

Zaw Htun, 156

Zaw Min, 100

Zaw Zaw, 119, 203